THEORIES OF INTERGROUP RELATIONS

THEORIES OF INTERGROUP RELATIONS

International Social Psychological Perspectives

DONALD M. TAYLOR
AND
FATHALI M. MOGHADDAM

Second Edition

Westport, Connecticut
London

This book is dedicated to

Richard N. Clarke

whose courage and pursuit of justice
are an inspiration to us both.

Library of Congress Cataloging-in-Publication Data

Taylor, Donald M.
    Theories of intergroup relations : international social
psychological perspectives / Donald M. Taylor and Fathali M.
    Moghaddam.—2nd ed.
        p. cm.
    Includes bibliographical references and index.
    ISBN 0–275–94634–7 (alk. paper).—ISBN 0–275–94635–5 (pbk. :
alk. paper)
    1. Intergroup relations. 2. Social psychology. I. Moghaddam,
Fathali M. II. Title.
    HM291.T36   1994
    302.3—dc20   93–30988

British Library Cataloguing in Publication Data is available.

Library of Congress Catalog Card Number: 93–30988
ISBN: 0–275–94634–7
    0–275–94635–5 (pbk.)

First published in 1994

Praeger Publishers, 88 Post Road West, Westport, CT 06881
An imprint of Greenwood Publishing Group, Inc.

Printed in the United States of America

The paper used in this book complies with the Permanent
Paper Standard issued by the National Information Standards
Organization (Z39.48–1984).

10 9 8 7 6 5 4 3

Contents

Preface to the First Edition

Coauthoring a book that is coherent in style and content represents an exciting challenge. To produce such a book when the overriding aims, themes, and specific content must reflect the views of two authors who have had dramatically different life experiences is an even greater challenge. Either the task of writing is divided, with the risk that the book appears disjointed, or you try to make the book truly a collaborative effort. This is what we set out to do, but because of our very different backgrounds we would not have been surprised if chaos had followed. To our delight, we found almost complete unanimity on important issues. This has given us cause to reflect, and we now realize that while our life experiences seem very different on the surface, they are overshadowed by a much deeper set of shared experiences.

One of us was raised as a "majority" group member in a developed world society, but in a province that has experienced deep cultural and linguistic tension; the other knew firsthand about life in a Third World society. One pursued his interest in intergroup relations in a North American academic context; the other followed precisely the same interest in a European context. The one based in North America has spent considerable time researching and teaching in Europe and in the Third World; the one from the Third World now holds an academic position in North America, after studying intergroup relations in Europe. Both have lived in societies experiencing fundamental conflicts between groups: one in a national context where the separation of regions has been an important issue; the other, in a society experiencing violent revolution.

Thus, the consistencies in the perspective emerging from this volume perhaps arise in part out of these shared life experiences, despite very disparate backgrounds.

Many of the ideas expressed in this volume have evolved over a long time period and have been shaped through the influence of numerous individuals working on both sides of the Atlantic. The authors have had close links with researchers at Bristol University since the 1970s, and are indebted, intellectually and otherwise, to Rupert Brown, Howard Giles, Henri Tajfel, and John Turner. We are profoundly grateful for the opportunity we have had to share our ideas with a number of colleagues and former students, especially Jeannette Bellerose, Mick Billig, Richard Bourhis, Faye Crosby, Lise Dubé, Bob Gardner, Richard Lalonde, Wallace Lambert, David McKirnan, Phillip Smith, Peter Stringer, Patricia Walker, Gillian Watson, and Durhan Wong-Rieger.

We would like to thank Sheila Morrin for the secretarial help she provided during the many revisions that brought the present volume to its final shape.

Finally, we appreciate the support for this project given by George Zimmar from the very beginning.

Preface to the Second Edition

Scott, a robust undergraduate student, upon hearing that his dad and "uncle" Fathali were about to write a second edition of their book on intergroup relations, expressed, no doubt, the sentiments of all students: "I hope you're not going to change three words, call it a new edition, and require all students to buy only the new one!"

Well, Scott, there have been too many exciting advances in the field of intergroup relations for us to make only cosmetic changes. European theories of intergroup relations are taking hold in North America, whole new approaches to enduring social issues such as discrimination have emerged, and topics such as affirmative action, tokenism, and multiculturalism are front and center.

Our own collaboration has been made richer by exciting new personal academic experiences. One of us has been lured to a permanent position at Georgetown University in Washington, D.C., while the older of us has spent much more time conducting field research in native communities in Canada. We have both been stimulated by very different environments, but our intellectual and ideological collaboration has been continuous.

For sharing with us their insights on an ongoing basis, we would like to thank our colleagues Mick Billig, Wally Lambert, John Lydon, Stephen Perrot, Susan Widdicomb, and Stephen Wright and our students Stéphane Perreault, Lana Porter, and Karen Ruggiero. Finally, Michael Koffman, Melinda Morros, and Karen Ruggiero were especially helpful with organizational matters in the preparation of this volume.

1

The Social Psychology of Intergroup Relations

Race riots, religious intolerance, rivalry between the sexes, language groups in confrontation, radical forces clashing with the establishment, civil war, the constant threat of terrorism, bitter labor disputes, and the universal preoccupation with the spread of nuclear weapons and with the environment—these are some of the issues that immediately spring to mind when one considers the social psychology of intergroup relations. The crucial role that these pervasive issues, along with a variety of more local social conflicts, play in our lives is leading the topic of intergroup relations to assume greater importance in social psychology. Unfortunately, to date there has been little or no scholarly work that systematically reviews social psychological theories of intergroup relations.

The present volume is designed as a first step toward filling this gap. Specifically, our aim is to outline a number of major theories, comment upon their key features, and highlight common themes and important differences. In addition, our aim is to present a broad international array of theoretical orientations, with a particular concern for presenting a balance between North American and European perspectives. We are optimistic about the role social psychology can and will play in our understanding of intergroup relations. It is our hope that this volume will help to set the stage for a more concerted effort in the field.

Until recently, intergroup relations had not been given as much attention as it deserved in mainstream social psychology, and there were, at the time of writing the first edition of this volume, very few books that dealt systematically with the topic from a social psychological perspective. The volumes by Billig (1976), LeVine and Campbell (1972), and Kidder and Stewart (1975) came closest, but did not represent up-to-date attempts to review social psychological theories of intergroup relations systematically. In addition, there were very few edited books on the social psychology of intergroup relations (Austin & Worchel, 1979; Gardner & Kalin, 1981; Turner & Giles, 1981). These did not, nor was it their aim to, review major theoretical approaches to intergroup relations.

There have been exciting new developments in the social psychology of intergroup relations since we published the first edition of this volume in 1987. Promising new theories have surfaced, important new research topics have been identified, shifts in research emphasis have subtly emerged, and the influence of cognitive social psychology is apparent. Finally, the number of recently published books (e.g., Abrams & Hogg, 1990; Breakwell, 1992; Brown, 1988; Worchel & Austin, 1986; Zanna & Olson, 1993) is concrete evidence of the accelerated interest in intergroup relations. Our challenge is to incorporate these dramatic new changes in this second edition, and this has required us to make substantive changes while still retaining the overall structure of the original volume.

Thus, in this second edition we address new topics such as affirmative action, tokenism, and multiculturalism. We outline new theoretical perspectives that have arisen from a shift in attention from the perpetrators of discrimination to its victims. We also document how European-based theories of intergroup relations are, for the first time, having a major impact on theory and research in North America. Finally, we underscore how the emphasis on cognitive processes has resulted in a corresponding neglect of emotion; the intergroup conflicts that preoccupy us daily, from violence against women, children, and the elderly to rampant ethnic cleansing, are hardly devoid of emotion.

With so many new developments, then, this second edition, even more than the first, represents our own perspective on the social psychology of intergroup relations. We begin the present volume, as we did the first, with a review of some of the key concepts in the title of this work: "social psychology," "intergroup relations," "theories," and "international perspectives." Having established the context, we alert the reader to certain recurring themes that emerge in one form or another in each of the chapters. Finally, we present a concrete description of the specific chapters and their organization.

SOCIAL PSYCHOLOGY AND INTERGROUP RELATIONS

Social psychology is the study of individual behavior in social contexts. Although the unit of analysis in social psychology is the individual, the context of such behavior can involve, either implicitly or explicitly, both other individuals and social groups. The unique perspective of social psychology in an intergroup context is that the perceptions, motivations, feelings, and overt actions of individuals are studied to identify how they influence, and are affected by, relations between groups.

Within the context of psychology, social psychology is that subdiscipline whose major aim is to bridge the gap between the social and the psychological forces in human behavior. Central to this aim should be the topic of intergroup relations, yet, for some reason, it is not. Most major reviewers of intergroup relations have emphasized the neglect of this topic in social psychology (for instance, Austin & Worchel, 1979; Billig, 1976; Brown, 1988; Worchel & Austin, 1986). Austin and Worchel (1979) have noted that "writings on groups in social psychology are typically one-sided. Texts appear to concentrate uniformly on intragroup processes to the exclusion of intergroup behavior" (p. v). There are currently dozens of introductory texts in social psychology that attempt to cover, in cafeteria fashion, the major topics in the field. An examination of the table of contents of any of these texts will suffice to reinforce the point that intergroup relations is not a central theme. Nor are theories of intergroup relations reviewed in books on theories of social psychology (e.g., Shaw & Costanzo, 1982). Exploring the titles of articles in key social psychological journals leads to the same conclusion: intergroup relations is not a central topic. For example, the *Journal of Personality and Social Psychology* reserves the smallest of its three sections for intergroup relations, and even this small section is shared with interpersonal relations.

Moreover, on those few occasions where groups are mentioned, the meaning, from an intergroup relations perspective, can be misleading. The focus has been almost exclusively on small, closed groups rather than societally based groups that are open and have changing membership (see Lawler, 1985). Thus, the concern is with small work groups or therapeutic groups rather than societally based groups such as social classes, ethnic groups, labor movements, or protest groups. The aspects of small-group life studied tend to concern group productivity, leadership, social influence, and decision making. Finally, the concept of prejudice may surface, suggesting intergroup relations along racial lines. But even here discussion focuses on the individual shortcomings of persons who display inordinate amounts of prejudice, rather than the dynamics of group conflict. The concern is more on what makes a particular individual a bigot or red-neck, as opposed to why an entire society shares prejudicial attitudes (Zanna, 1994). However, as we have noted, one of the exciting recent developments in the field has been an accelerating interest in the social psychology of being a victim of discrimination.

There is no simple explanation for the underdeveloped state of theory and research on the social psychology of intergroup relations; however, we can at least speculate on some of the possible "whys." Steiner (1974) offered one possible explanation. In his view, research topics in a particular discipline are a reflection of the broader concerns of society. Since most social psychological theory and research originates in the United States, an examination of the concerns of that society ought to give us insights into what scientific issues would be salient. Steiner noted that during the 1950s and early 1960s, broadly based intergroup conflicts were not an issue in the United States; hence, there was little scientific interest in the topic. He predicted that the rising social concern for group conflict of the late 1960s and 1970s would be reflected in a renewal of interest in the topic. It is not easy to assess the validity of Steiner's argument, however, since he notes that scientific research usually lags many years behind an initial societal interest in an issue.

A number of writers have taken this "response to societal concerns" explanation one step further, suggesting that it is the "pervasive individualistic ideology" that is characteristic of North American society that allows us to understand why so little attention is paid to group issues (Billig, 1976; Markus & Kitayama, 1991; Moghaddam, Taylor, & Wright, 1993; Moscovici, 1972; Tajfel, 1972b; Taylor & Brown, 1979). They argue that it is the North American belief in the sanctity and importance of the individual—what Sampson (1977) has labeled "self-contained individualism"—that has led to this neglect. The implications of this interpretation are far-reaching. The "response to societal concerns" explanation paves the way for a renewed interest in groups, but the "pervasive individual ideology" explanation leaves little room for the possibility that intergroup processes will become a central concern, at least in North American social psychology.

There is a third possible reason for the neglect of intergroup relations as a topic, one that affects not only social psychology but all of the social sciences. Coser (1956) notes that at one of the first meetings of the American Sociological Society, held in 1907, the major topic was social conflict. By 1930 social conflict was still a central issue at the annual meetings. By 1950, however, Bernard (1950) was prompted to ask, "Where is the modern sociology of conflict?" A partial answer may be found through an examination of the position of the social scientist in society and how that role has changed. Initially the social scientist was an advocate of change; his or her theory and research were not dependent upon funding from the establishment, be it government or industry. The social scientist was a champion of social reform, change, and the associated conflict.

As soon as funding for universities and research emanated from the establishment, interest in social conflict gave way to a focus on social management. Perhaps, then, to a certain extent the piper is calling the tune, and intergroup conflict, because it can be a threatening topic from the point of view of the established order, has become less central. The accuracy of this analysis requires validation, of course, but it must be raised here as one possible explanation for the current status of research into intergroup relations.

Whatever the reasons, social psychology has not kept pace with sociology and political science when it comes to making a concentrated and coordinated research effort to understand relations between societal groups. The result is that the research in social psychology has not been integrated, and the disparate direct and indirect strands of thought have not been systematized so as to provide a solid base from which to build. In this volume we attempt such an undertaking, and the reader will be as surprised as we were at the richness of information that social psychology has to offer when the strands are woven together. Thus, the importance of this volume is underscored by the neglect of intergroup relations as a topic of study in social psychology, and by the richness of the potential contribution of social psychology to understanding individual behavior in an intergroup setting.

A DEFINITION OF INTERGROUP RELATIONS

We have an intuitive grasp of what the topic of intergroup relations entails. Not surprisingly, however, the lack of attention to the field of intergroup relations is matched by an almost total neglect of the task of defining key concepts. At this stage, then, we can offer only preliminary definitions of the terms "relations" and "group," but ones that we hope can orient the reader to the scope of the present volume.

To begin with, we have chosen the title "intergroup relations" rather than "intergroup behavior" or "intergroup conflict." Our reasoning is that the latter two labels are too restricting. "Behavior" denotes the concrete, observable component of intergroup relations but does not include important cognitive processes, such as categorization, stereotyping, attributions, and attitudes, which, although not directly observable, play an important role in understanding relations between groups. To our knowlege, the only authors even to consider the ambiguity in terms such as "intergroup behavior" and "intergroup relations" are Sherif and Sherif (1969). Part of their analysis is consistent with our own. They define intergroup behavior as "the actions of individuals belonging to one group when they interact, collectively or individually, with another group or its members in terms of their group membership" (p. 223). Sherif and Sherif (1969) view the term "intergroup relations" as broader in scope, defining it as "functional relations between two or more groups and their respective members" (p. 223). By functional relations they mean that "the actions by one group and its members have an impact on another group and its members, regardless of whether the two groups are actually engaged in direct give-and-take at the time" (p. 223).

Similarly, we find the term "conflict" to be restricting, but in a different way. Throughout this volume the primary focus will be on conflict between groups. However, while it is conflict that primarily sustains a commitment on the part of social scientists to investigate intergroup and group processes, relations between groups need not always be conflictual. By choosing the term "relations" for the present volume, perhaps we are revealing our optimism, in the sense that at some stage in the future it may be realistic to address the potentially multifaceted nature of relations between groups. In any case, we have chosen the label that seems to offer the fewest predetermined restrictions.

Defining what human interaction qualifies as "intergroup" is more challenging. Once again, our approach is to provide a definition with the fewest possible restrictions. By "intergroup relations" we mean *any aspect of human interaction that involves individuals perceiving themselves as members of a social category, or being perceived by others as belonging to a social category.* A number of points need to be raised about this very broad definition.

First, our definition involves no limitations in terms of the size or type of social category involved. It is true that most often the focus is on large social categories such as race, social class, sex, religion, language, and ethnic background. However, it is our contention that any valid principles about intergroup relations apply to all social categories, regardless of type and size.

Second, our definition does not contain many of the qualifications found in most definitions. For example, we do not insist that in addition to the perception of identity with a social category, there must be shared motivation, goals, or social structure before we define a number of individuals as a group (see Shaw, 1976, for a review). Nor do we require, as do Tajfel and Turner (1979), that individuals share an emotional involvement with the social category or share an evaluation of it before they can be considered part of a group. While all or some of these characteristics may be important, it is nevertheless possible for an individual to be influenced by the mere fact that he or she is identified with a particular social category. Just ask any member of a visible minority group how often he or she has received treatment obviously directed at his or her group identity rather than his or her role position or individual personal characteristics.

Third, we do not require that there be cohesion with a social category, especially as cohesion has been defined traditionally. Group cohesion is usually defined as the sum of the strength of mutual positive attitudes among individual members of a group (Lott & Lott, 1965). We do not consider mutual liking among individuals to be essential for intergroup relations, especially in the context of broad social categories. A person may identify strongly with a group even if he or she does not personally like some or many of its members. Indeed, a person may not even know many of the members of large social categories. Similarly, a person may like several persons as separate individuals, but there may be no sense in which they constitute a category or group.

Finally, our definition does not suggest that only interactions involving large numbers of people qualify as intergroup. For, ultimately, whether an interaction has intergroup implications is psychologically defined (see Turner & Brown, 1981). Take the example of two lovers having dinner by candlelight in a quaint restaurant. By any definition that would be described as an interpersonal interaction in which the focus is on the unique personal characteristics of the particular man and woman. But what if the man makes an inadvertent chauvinistic statement? The woman may feel the need to respond as a representative of all women and may even express opinions that she herself does not endorse but states because she feels the obligation to represent the majority of women at that moment. The man may become defensive and feel the need to defend himself as a man, and if the debate escalates, those in the restaurant may well be treated to a public spectacle. The point here is that just because an interaction involves only two persons, it is not necessarily interpersonal. The psychological meaning of the interaction is what determines whether the relationship is intergroup.

Conversely, the interaction of large numbers of people representing two groups does not necessarily define the behavior as intergroup. A collection of men and women at a social gathering, each making overtures to the other, may be defined by the participants as a series of very interpersonal interactions.

A second example may be useful to indicate even more clearly that the number of people in an interaction is not necessarily a valid criterion for qualifying an interaction as intergroup. Imagine an encounter involving a Hispanic student who speaks in Spanish to an Anglo student he meets on campus. The interaction would appear on the surface to be an encounter between two individuals that is awkward because neither speaks the other's language. However, the Spanish-speaking student may well be making a collective political statement by his refusal to use English. The Anglo student may well be aware that the Hispanic student can speak English—after all, he is studying at an institution where the language of instruction is English. So both parties may recognize that the individual encounter really involves a minority-group statement of public defiance designed to assert pride in group identity and to signal a desire for change in the power relationship between the groups.

Our definition is naturally psychological in its emphasis. The essence is the meaning attached to behavior, not the more concrete observable features of it. In the present context, then, a jealous lover who murders his rival is not engaged in intergroup relations. However, a person who commits murder on behalf of a political group, selecting as the victim some person who is symbolic of the establishment, is very definitely engaging in intergroup relations. Ambiguity arises when the jealous lover happens to be white and his rival black. The meaning for the perpetrator and the victim may have nothing to do with race, but the minute people in the community, reading newspaper accounts of the incident, focus on the racial overtones, intergroup relations are involved.

In summary, for the present volume our concern is with understanding human behavior when it is affected by the perception that category membership is involved. It is hoped that by defining intergroup relations in the broadest terms, we have not made the field even more ambiguous, but have provided a framework for appreciating just how much of human behavior is influenced by the processes of intergroup relations.

WHAT CONSTITUTES A THEORY OF INTERGROUP RELATIONS?

The purpose of this volume is to review major theoretical orientations to intergroup relations. The need for such a review stems from the current state of social psychology as a discipline, and specifically from the psychology of intergroup relations. Walster, Walster, and Berscheid (1978) state the problem succinctly: "Currently, social psychology comprises a myriad of elegant little 'mini-theories'. . . . What we now need is a general theory that integrates the limited mini-theories" (p. 1).

Our belief is that in order for theory and research in intergroup relations to be truly integrated, and our knowledge to become cumulative, it is essential that we review in one volume those theories that qualify as major theoretical orientations. "Major," for the present purposes, refers to those theories that claim to deal with the fundamental issues associated with intergroup relations: how intergroup conflicts arise, what course they take, and how they become resolved. Thus, our focus is on those theories that are broad in scope, theories with enough range that they have the potential to provide some direction for research in the entire field of intergroup relations. Inclusion of a theory is not on the basis of how "good" it is in terms of criteria that are discussed and debated in the philosophy of science (see Kaplan, 1964; Shaw & Costanzo, 1982). Rather, the focus is on theories offering a set of interrelated propositions that deal with a wide range of issues central to intergroup relations.

Fortunately, there are a sufficient number of major theoretical orientations to warrant a careful analysis, but it is not uncommon for researchers working in the context of one orientation to be unfamiliar with the others. The theories represented in the present volume include realistic conflict theory, social identity theory, equity theory, relative deprivation theory, and a five-stage model of intergroup relations.

Each of these theories is broad in scope and attempts to address the pervasive issues in intergroup relations: How do conflicts arise? What course do they take? How are they resolved? However, not all of the theories address the issue of intergroup relations directly. For example, equity theory and relative deprivation theory are more often applied to interpersonal than intergroup relations. Nevertheless, extrapolations are constantly made to relations between social groups, and the obvious relevance of these theories to intergroup relations demands that they be included.

There are a number of social psychological theories, issues, concepts, and processes that are central to intergroup relations, but that are not accorded a chapter on their own. We felt that they could best be appreciated by being treated in a different fashion. For example, it seemed more appropriate to describe resource mobilization theory in the context of the chapter on relative deprivation theory, and to address the promising, but as yet not full-blown, theories of self-categorization and "optimal distinctiveness" in the social identity chapter. Important processes such as stereotyping, attribution, and discrimination are not formal theories in their own right. Rather, they are processes that are so pervasive that they must be integrated into any complete theory of intergroup relations. Finally, topics such as affirmative action, tokenism, and multiculturalism derive their initial importance from important political policies, and as such they need to be treated differently.

THE NEED FOR AN INTERNATIONAL PERSPECTIVE

We have already noted that social scientists studying intergroup relations from one theoretical orientation often are unaware of alternative perspectives. One of the factors contributing to this isolationism is that several of the theories are rooted in North American social psychology, while other influential theories are European-based. The "isolationism" of U.S. psychology has been noted by a number of researchers (such as Berlyne, 1968; Brandt, 1970; Sexton & Misiak, 1984). This isolationist orientation has tended to create a "monocultural" science of psychology in the United States (see Kennedy, Scheirer, & Rogers, 1984). In the field of intergroup relations, there is a tendency for U.S. researchers to neglect work conducted outside North America. A work on social conflict by Pruitt and Rubin (1986), two influential U.S. psychologists, contains minimal references to major European researchers working in the same field. For example, the only work by Tajfel referred to by Pruitt and Rubin is a 1970 article published in *Scientific American*. This gulf between U.S. and European research underscores the importance of our attempts to achieve a more international perspective. As we noted earlier, in the last decade there have been exciting developments in this area. While work needs to be done, for the first time European theory and research are having a noticeable impact on North American thinking.

The need for an international perspective is even more critical in light of our earlier discussion of how "self-contained individualism," as a North American value system, may well have had a profound effect on the limited interest in the social psychology of intergroup relations and the directions it has taken. The European-based theory described in this volume—social identity theory—is far less individualistic in its approach and provides an important contrast with the North American–based theories. By bringing both perspectives together in one volume, we hope to provide at least the beginning of a more international and integrated approach to the study of intergroup relations.

EMERGING THEMES

An overall assessment of the current status of theory and research in intergroup relations can best be attempted after dealing systematically with each of the theories. However, certain themes are so striking that it may be useful to alert the reader to them at the outset.

The first overriding feature to be noted is the reductionist nature of many current theories of intergroup relations. This was hinted at in our earlier discussion of social psychology and has begun to be recognized in the context of intergroup relations (see, for example, Billig, 1976; Sampson, 1981; Tajfel, 1972b, 1979; Taylor & Brown, 1979). At the level of theory and research, the emphasis has been on intra- or interindividual, not intergroup, processes. The result is that individualistically based findings are extrapolated to the group level. While there may be certain valid parallels, it is equally clear that in many instances individual and group processes differ. More important, by not addressing issues in a group context, a number of potentially valuable questions and hypotheses are not even considered.

While the dominant theoretical orientation in intergroup research has involved working from intra- and interpersonal processes to intergroup processes, and from microsocial to macrosocial issues, a few theories have adopted the opposite approach. These theories are characterized by a concern for long-term social changes and large, open groups rather than short-term changes and small, closed groups. They take broad social structural issues as their point of departure, then make assumptions about the role of psychological processes in determining structural changes. In short, their theorizing starts at the macro level and moves to the micro level rather than starting with intra- and interpersonal processes at the micro level and then extrapolating to intergroup processes at the macro level.

A second significant theme is the extent to which the nature of the groups that the theories deal with are open or closed. There is in the field of small-group research a tradition of dealing with closed groups (Ziller, 1965), in which group members are not provided with an "exit" option (A. O. Hirschman, 1970, 1974). This tradition has been influential in inter-group relations as well. The assumption that a group has fixed member-ship, that existing members cannot leave the group and new members cannot be recruited, partly explains why social psychologists have not emphasized the issue of identification with the group: the extent and form that group identity takes is of relatively little significance in groups of fixed membership. However, once we include in our theoretical model groups that have a changing membership, then the issue of identification takes on central importance.

A third persistent dilemma is the relationship of cognitive and emotional states to behavior. One has only to examine the attitude literature to recognize that this is a pervasive issue for much of social psychology (see Wicker, 1969). A negative attitude toward a person or group does not necessarily mean that there will be discriminatory behavior. A person prejudiced against visible minorities may nevertheless serve them in restaurants, respond politely to their questions, or offer jobs to those who are qualified. This same relationship lies at the core of understanding intergroup relations. Many theories in the area of intergroup relations attempt to predict when people will have strong negative feelings. A fundamental recurring problem is understanding when the negative feelings experienced by group members will lead to collective action, individual action, or apparent acceptance of an undesirable situation.

A fourth, related theme is how much of current research on intergroup relations emphasizes cognitive processes. Moreover, when feelings and emotions are included, the experimental, or indeed field, conditions are not such that very strong feelings are provoked. The most striking feature of current intergroup conflicts is their extreme and apparently senseless violence. Capturing the essence of the emotions that must underlie such behavior is the research challenge.

A fifth significant theme concerns the treatment of individual group members by a theory of intergroup relations. That is, are the individual members of a group distinguished on the basis of some characteristic, such as ability, or are they treated as a homogeneous unit? This is particularly important with respect to groups that are "open" and permit social mobility. Will all the members of a group have the same capacity or motivation for attemtping upward social mobility, or will only certain individuals attempt this move?

A sixth theme concerns the extent to which a theory focuses on advantaged or disadvantaged groups, or, more generally, how a theory deals with the notion of power (Ng, 1980, 1982). In most intergroup situations there is a disparity of power between social groups; groups seldom enjoy equal power and status. There seems to be a tendency for theories of intergroup relations not to give equal attention to the perspectives of both advantaged and disadvantaged groups. While some theories adopt the perspective of the advantaged group, others tend to view the situation more from the perspective of the disadvantaged group.

A final theme concerns the relationship among the theories. We will have much to say about this later, but for the moment it is important to point out the extent to which the theories are more complementary than conflictual in terms of the hypotheses they generate. The various theories appear to address issues in parallel rather than making differential predictions about intergroup behavior. We hope that one of the consequences of bringing the theories together in a single volume will be a more discriminating approach to the whole field, with real attempts to understand and predict collective behavior.

ORGANIZATION OF CHAPTERS

Now that we have defined the context and scope of the present volume, it remains to describe the content of the specific chapters more precisely. The theories to be presented in the chapters that follow may not always address the question of relations between groups exclusively or directly, but all do have major insights to offer. What the theories have in common is a concern for the burning issues associated with relations between groups: What are the conditions associated with feelings of collective discontent? What are the social psychological processes that explain the current discontent of blacks in South Africa that was not so apparent a decade ago? Why are women in Western societies expressing collective discontent while those in more traditional and stratified societies seem less vocal? Why do unions seem militant and the unemployed relatively tranquil? This issue of collective discontent is, of course, only one dimension of relations between groups, but it is the issue of greatest concern to lay people and scientists alike.

Beyond this commonality, differences in emphasis will occur. Some theories are especially concerned with how conflicts can be resolved, others focus on how feelings of discontent become translated into action, some focus on relations between groups of equal power, and others are more concerned with unequal power situations. Any complete theory must ultimately deal with all these major issues, and our assessment of the scope of any theory must take this into account.

We begin in chapter 2 with a review of Freud's contribution to the field of intergroup relations. Despite the breadth of his theorizing, his insights in many ways do not qualify as an integrated theory of intergroup relations. However, the scope and depth of his impact provide an important context for reviewing the major theoretical orientations.

Chapter 3 focuses on realistic conflict theory, the one theory in the present volume that has intuitive appeal for economists, sociologists, and political scientists as well as psychologists. In this chapter we include a discussion of "gaming theory" and point to how realistic conflict theory has received renewed impetus from applications to conflict over the environment.

Chapter 4 is devoted to social identity theory, a European-based theory that is beginning to impact intergroup relations research in North America. Self-categorization theory and optimal distinctiveness theory are but two of the recent elaborations of social identity theory that are described.

Equity theory is the focus of chapter 5, and included here is a discussion of recent research in the area of affirmative action. Chapter 6 is concerned with relative deprivation theory and how it has withstood the challenge from resource mobilization theory. The final formal theory, the five-stage model of intergroup relations, is presented in chapter 7. Here we discuss the impact of a research program on tokenism that underscores how subtle yet powerful tokenism is as a form of discrimination.

In chapter 8 stereotypes, attributions, and a newly included topic, discrimination, are discussed. The renewed interest in discrimination arises because of two recent concepts that have proven to be central to the experience of discrimination: attributional ambiguity and the personal/group discrimination discrepancy.

Chapter 9 deals with intergroup contact, which is treated in a separate chapter because contact between groups is a theme that explicitly or implicitly relates to every theory of intergroup relations. Our discussion of contact highlights its role for important social policies of racial and ethnic integration, including desegregation and multiculturalism. Finally, in chapter 10 an attempt is made to consolidate the recurring themes and to speculate about what direction theory and research might take in the near future.

Each major theory is described in a separate chapter, and an attempt is made to maintain a consistent organizational structure within the chapters. However, maintaining consistency of structure is made difficult by a number of factors. First, the theories grow out of very different psychological and social traditions. Hence, definitions and fundamental assumptions differ widely among the theories, as do the approaches to methodology. Second, certain theories address questions of intergroup relations directly, whereas others are more concerned with individuals and impact on our topic only by extension. Finally, certain theories began with a series of propositions that stimulated experimental research designed to test the propositions, whereas in other cases the research preceded—indeed, was the inspiration for—the theory.

However, despite these sometimes profound differences among the theories, a standard format is maintained for all the chapters dealing with major theories. We begin each chapter with an introduction that discusses the fundamental orienting assumptions the theory makes about human behavior, the specific propositions the theory offers for explaining intergroup relations, and the theory's historical underpinnings. In the next section of each chapter, the fundamental propositions of the theory are presented and, where appropriate, prototypical experiments to test the theory are described. The final section involves a critical review of the theory and focuses on its strengths and weaknesses. A conclusion statement rounds off each chapter.

SUGGESTED READINGS

Brown, R. J. (1988). *Group processes: Dynamics within and between groups.* Oxford: Blackwell.

Worchel, S., & Austin, W. G. (Eds.). (1986). *The social psychology of intergroup relations* (2nd ed.). Monterey, Calif.: Brooks/Cole.

2

The Freudian Legacy of Intergroup Research

This chapter is devoted to Freud's influence on both theory and research in the psychology of intergroup relations. His analysis of group processes, insightful as it is, does not constitute a major orientation to intergroup relations. Unlike the major orientations to intergroup relations that will be presented in the following chapters, Freud's model does not deal with relations between groups. Rather, Freud focussed on within-group dynamics to explain relations between groups, and he extrapolated from the level of intra- and interpersonal processes to that of intergroup processes. His analysis was, first and foremost, a psychological theory. Moreover, his model represents an extreme "irrationalist" view of intergroup behavior. Thus, this chapter is presented in recognition of Freud's insights and general influence on our thinking about the psychology of intergroup relations, but is not in the same format as the chapters on the major theories of intergroup relations.

Freud's fundamental influence on scientific research concerning intergroup relations is reflected in such major pioneering studies as *Frustration and Aggression* (Dollard, Doob, Miller, Mowrer, & Sears, 1939) and *The Authoritarian Personality* (Adorno, Frenkel-Brunswik, Levinson, & Sanford, 1950). Many of the most important concepts used in research bearing upon intergroup relations are influenced by Freud. Examples of such concepts are displacement, interference, catharsis, and goal-directed behavior. However, the experimental methods used by the majority of more recent researchers, such as Deutsch (1973), are very different from those employed by Freud.

Freud's ideas of group processes were most clearly elaborated in *Group Psychology and the Analysis of the Ego* (1921). Freud tended to venerate the individual and to be suspicious of the group. In this respect, he can be seen as part of a tradition, particularly strong in the latter part of the nineteenth and early twentieth centuries, that views the collective in a negative light. For example, Sighele (1981) wrote about what he termed the "criminal crowd." Le Bon (1897) and McDougall (1920), both of whom are quoted extensively by Freud throughout his writings on group processes, were also very much part of this "anticollective" tradition.

This "anticollective" theme is also evident in certain areas of more recent social research, such as that concerned with the "risky shift." For example, the apparent tendency for people to take riskier decisions when acting as a group member than when acting as an isolated individual has been interpreted as an example of deindividualization, involving a tendency for the group to release the individual from a sense of responsibility (see Pruitt, 1971). The implicit implication is that collective action involves higher risk and is based upon a less responsible attitude.

FREUD'S MODEL OF GROUP AND INTERGROUP PROCESSES: THREE GUIDING QUESTIONS

Freud's analyses of group processes were guided by three questions: "What . . . is a 'group'? How does it acquire the capacity for exercising such a decisive influence over the mental life of the individual? And what is the nature of the mental change which it forces upon the individual?" (Freud, 1921, p. 72). These questions present the individual as the target of change, in a sense as a victim. The potential influence of the minority party is neglected, and all the focus is placed on majority influence. The nature of this influence is presented as fundamental, the group being assumed to have a decisive effect on the individual. These biases are also inherent in much of the more recent research in minority-majority relations (Moscovici, Mugny, & Van Avermaet, 1985; Papastamou, 1983).

What Is a Group?

Freud limited his analysis to groups with leaders and did not attempt to extend his model to interpret behavior in leaderless groups. He has been criticized on this point (for instance, see Billig, 1976, p. 24), and there are two reasons why such criticisms are to some extent valid. First, there are cultures in which the concept of the group leader, as it is known in most modern societies, does not exist (see Middleton & Tait, 1958). Although fairly exceptional and very limited in numbers, these examples are conceptually very important because they help to focus attention on the potential for the development of leaderless groups. The second shortcoming of Freud's exclusive focus on groups with leaders is that if one is interested in the poor, blacks, or women, for example, these groups do not always have widely endorsed leaders. However, from a Freudian perspective this criticism might be countered by claiming that only in conditions where such groups as blacks do have widely endorsed leaders can they achieve the cohesion and direction necessary for effective group action.

The importance given by Freud to the role of the leader was linked to his views about the social psychological evolution of human societies. He viewed the group as a revival of the primal horde, that is, a collection of individuals ruled despotically by a powerful male. From the beginning, the psychology of the leader was different from that of the followers, particularly in terms of needs and motivations. While the members of a group need to feel that they are equally loved by a leader, the leader need love no one else. This distinction is potentially very important, since it prepares the ground for a structural model of group processes, incorporating elite leaders, who have more power, and followers, who have less power.

Beyond the stress that Freud placed on the role of the leader, through identification, in the formation of a group, his writings entail a number of assumptions about the characteristics of a group. These tend invariably to be negative and in accord with Le Bon's views. Freud saw the group as tending toward extreme behavior; as respecting force and seeing kindness as weakness; as demanding strength and violence of its heroes; as being conservative, traditional, and mistrustful of innovations; as tolerating and being able to abide by contradictory ideas; and as preferring illusions to reality. However, Freud also believed that a group is capable of high intellectual performance, provided it is organized in the correct manner.

From the Freudian perspective, however, the poor, blacks, and women would remain sociological rather than psychological groups until they evolved clearly recognizable leaders through whom they could identify with the group. For example, a number of individuals might meet the criteria for inclusion in the social category "poor" (such as low income level, low education level), but this does not mean that they necessarily feel that "the poor" constitute a distinct group or that they are members of this group. However, if a widely endorsed leader of "the poor" were to emerge, psychological identification with such a group would be more likely, through the links that identification with the leader would bring about between individuals who are potential group members.

The link between the leader and his or her followers is best explained through the concept of identification that has a central role in all of Freudian psychology. Freud sees identification as the earliest form of an emotional tie with an object, which is usually another person. "Identification" refers to a process by which an individual, having developed an emotional tie, behaves as if he or she were the person with whom the tie exists. This behavior may be wholly or partially unconscious.

In the group context, Freud sees identification as forming the essential link between the leader and followers. Identification can arise through the perception of a common quality shared with some other person; the more important the common quality, the more important the tie. A number of individuals have this shared common quality when they introject the same leader within their egos. Thus, Freud defines a primary group as "a number of individuals who have put one and the same object in place of their ego ideal and have subsequently identified themselves with one another in their ego" (Freud, 1921, p. 116).

As an example of how identification can lead to stronger ties between a number of individuals, Freud describes the situation of a "troop" of females or "groupies" who crowd around a singer after his performance. These females could become jealous of one another and try to get near the "loved one" ahead of the others. But since their large numbers do not allow this, they act as a unit and collectively pay homage to the hero. In short, they identify with one another by means of a similar love for the same object. Subsequent research suggests that identification may be such a fundamental process that it can even evolve in relation to an oppressor.

An extreme example of identification with the oppressor is presented in Bettelheim's (1943) research on Jews in Nazi concentrations camps. Year after year of harsh physical conditions and mental torture led some prisoners to surrender mentally. Their efforts to please the guards eventually led them to imitate their oppressors. For example, prisoners showed anti-Semitism (taking on the attitudes of the guards) and wore bits of clothing belonging to guards (symbolic power). It could be argued that the tendency for black children to identify with the white out-group is a less extreme example of the same process (Milner, 1975).

In summary, Freud believed groups with leaders to be the only groups worthy of study. He considered such groups to be composed of individuals who are similar in the sense that they have identified with one another by introjecting the same leader within their egos. Thus, the criterion of similarity plays a key part in Freud's concept of a group. Also, in elaborating the characteristics of a group, he stresses the evolutionary relationship between leaders and followers, and the different psychologies of these two categories of people.

How a Group Influences the Mental Life of the Individual

In explaining how an individual who is part of a group differs from an isolated individual, Freud begins by assuming that subconscious forces become more effective in the behavior of the individual in the group context. The apparently new characteristics that individuals display in the group context are the "manifestations" of the unconscious. In Freud's view, this helps to explain the regression to more primitive states experienced by individuals after they become group members, since all that is "evil" in the human mind is contained in the unconscious "as a predisposition" (1921, p. 74). As evidence that group members revert to primitive states, Freud makes repeated use of descriptions by Le Bon and others depicting human groups as being easily swayed, contradictory, illogical, of low intellectual capacity, and ruled by emotions.

However, the evocation of unconscious forces would not in itself be sufficient to explain the similar and sometimes uniform behavior of group members. Thus, Freud proceeds to elaborate a model of how group members are directed, through suggestion, by the group leader. Just as an analyst can influence a patient through suggestion, so the leader can be viewed as the source for suggestion in a group. Freud went on to draw comparisons between the relationship involving the hypnotist and a patient in psychoanalysis, and the leader and group members. But his model of relations within a group also assumed strong links among the group members themselves, a relationship that can be usefully explained by introducing the concept of libido.

Freud makes the fundamental assumption that love relationships constitute the most important factor binding group members together (1921, p. 91). "Libido" refers to the energy of those instincts that have to do with all that may be comprised under the word "love." Freud does not separate love that involves sexual union from other kinds of love, such as love for one's parents or for one's country. All these tendencies are seen as an expression of the same instinctual emotions.

The idea of libidinal ties among group members, and between the leader and his followers, is elaborated by Freud in his analysis of two important groups: the Catholic church and the army. The most important feature of such groups is the "illusion" that holds them together: "In a Church . . . as well as in an army, however different the two may be in other respects, the same illusion holds good of there being a head—in the Catholic Church Christ, in an army its commander-in-chief—who loves all the individuals in the group with an equal love. Everything depends upon this illusion" (Freud, 1921, pp. 93–94). Freud compares the ties that bind group members to each other and to their leader with the ties that bind the members of a family to each other and to the father.

Christ is described by Freud as being for the group of believers "their substitute father" (1921, p. 94). The Catholic church is like a family, with all its members being brothers. All believers share brotherly love and are bound to each other and to their leader, Christ, through this love.

Thus, in such groups as the Catholic church and the army, each individual is tied by libidinal ties to the leader (Christ, the commander-in-chief) and to the other members of the group. By examining these ties, we can appreciate and explain the lack of freedom experienced by individual group members. These two-way libidinal ties initiate and strengthen feelings of belonging, dependence, and responsibility, which in turn lead to greater conformity and a tendency to obey the leader.

However, the loss of the leader can lead to the disappearance of mental ties between group members. This is because the establishment of bonds among followers is brought about by the establishment of bonds between leader and followers. When the follower-leader bond is eliminated, follower-follower bonds also disappear. It is in such conditions that group panics occur. Freud argues that group panic does not arise from a perception of danger, but is a result of the disappearance of mutual ties between the leader and followers, and consequently among group members (1921, p. 97).

However, in Freud's individual psychology, libidinal ties involve feelings of hostility as well as of love. That is, each intimate emotional relationship between two people that is stable for some time, such as a marriage or friendship, involves a mixture of aversion and love. The concept of psychological ambivalence was central to all of Freud's thinking. For example, its influence can be seen in his analysis of the fusion of love and hate in *The Ego and the Id* (1923), and of the polarity of love and hate in *Beyond the Pleasure Principle* (1920). In *Civilization and Its Discontents*, Freud asserts that love and hate seldom, perhaps never, appear in isolation from each other (1930, p. 119). Freud extended the important concept of psychological ambivalence to the group level and argued that the same ambivalent feelings, involving love and hate, characterize relationships between group members, and particularly between leaders and their followers.

The key difference between psychological ambivalence at the level of the individual and of the group is in terms of the strategies adopted to cope with such mixed feelings. At the individual level, feelings of aversion and hostility tend to be repressed, while at the group level they tend to be redirected toward the out-group. It is in this connection that we can best interpret Freud's claim that it is always possible "to bind together a considerable number of people in love so long as there are other people left over to receive the manifestations of their aggressiveness" (Freud, 1930, p. 114).

When a group is formed, feelings of intolerance and hostility disappear within the group, so that only the "love-related" aspects of libidinal ties tend to remain to influence relations between group members. As long as these libidinal ties remain, feelings of aversion between individuals do not emerge within the group. However, such hostile feelings are redirected toward out-groups. This is an instance of the important process of displacement, of which "displaced aggression" is an often cited case.

We can clarify the meaning of "displaced aggression" at the intergroup level by considering the example of the Catholic church. Its members are bound together by libidinal ties, but "nonbelievers" stand outside this tie. Even a religion that claims to be a religion of love finds it necessary to be hard and unloving toward those who do not belong to the family of believers: "Indeed every religion is in this same way a religion of love for all those whom it embraces; while cruelty and intolerance towards those who do not belong to it are natural to every religion" (Freud, 1921, p. 98). The explanation for such cruelty and hostility toward outsiders is that all the aggressiveness of the believers, the in-group, is displaced outside the group toward nonbelievers, the out-group. If hostile feelings are allowed to grow within the group, the opportunity for developing group cohesion and productivity will be decreased. Consequently, it is important that hostile feelings are redirected outside the group. The selection of particular out-groups as targets of displaced hostility also serves to create a "common threat," and this in turn serves to further strengthen in-group ties.

The decline in religious persecution experienced in modern societies should not, according to Freud, be interpreted as a sign that we have become more tolerant toward nonbelievers. Rather, this greater tolerance is an outcome of weakened religious feelings and the subsequent weakening of libidinal ties that depend upon them. Thus, Freud saw the hostility shown toward out-groups as changing in direct relation to the strength of the libidinal ties within the in-group: the stronger the in-group libidinal ties, the greater the hostility toward out-groups.

In summary, the capacity of a group to exercise a decisive influence over the individual can be explained by referring to "subconscious forces" and "suggestion." That is, subconscious forces become more effective in the group context. Also, the individual becomes more susceptible to suggestion after becoming a group member. However, suggestion is not exercised by the group, but by the group leader. The power of the group leader is acquired through the two-way libidinal ties that bind each group member to the leader and to the other members. Such libidinal ties involve feelings of both hostility and love. Hostile feelings do not emerge within the in-group, but are displaced onto target out-groups. While the group leader has a major influence in directing displaced aggression, the out-groups onto whom this aggression is more likely to be directed are those perceived as being more unlike the in-group. Thus, in Freud's group psychology the criterion of similarity plays a key role in the selection of target out-groups onto whom aggression is displaced, as it does in the development of libidinal ties between group members and the actual formation of an in-group.

The Nature of the Mental Change a Group Forces on an Individual

Three central assumptions underlie Freud's views about the changes that a person undergoes by joining a group. First, it is assumed that a person necessarily undergoes major psychological changes by becoming a group member. Second, it is assumed that such changes generally involve a loss for the individual, particularly in terms of intellectual abilities. Third, the assumption is made that by organizing their group in the necessary way, individual group members can regain what they lost by joining the group. Thus, the more highly evolved and organized groups are assumed to be more similar to individuals in terms of psychological characteristics.

There is a set of consequences of the individual's joining a group to which Freud returns again and again in his writings: "the dwindling of the conscious individual personality, the focusing of thoughts and feelings into a common direction, the predominance of the affective side of the mind and of unconscious psychical states, the tendency to the immediate carrying out of intentions as they emerge" (1921, p. 122). Among these many changes that arise as a result of the individual's joining a group, the two most important are that the individual becomes more susceptible to outside influence and that he or she experiences a loss of intellectual abilities (Freud, 1921, p. 88). However, the individual in a group also has a greater sense of certainty and purpose, and a feeling of power.

Freud argued that what the individual loses by joining a group can be regained if the group achieves the necessary level of organization. In this context, increased organization means greater permanence and continuity in the group, stronger shared goals and value systems guiding the behavior of group members, the presence of ideas guiding the actions of group members, greater specialization and division of labor, and more intense in-group cohesion and rivalry with out-groups. Most important, increased organization means having the ability to act at a higher intellecutal level. Groups that are more highly evolved are also more organized and thus have more of the characteristics of the isolated individual. This is an important point that allows us to better interpret what Freud means when he states that he is concerned only with groups that have leaders and have not been able to organize themselves to such a degree that they take on the characteristics of an individual (1921, p. 116).

Apart from organization, another means through which a group can achieve a better performance is suggestion. According to Freud's model of group processes, probably the most important difference between an isolated individual and a group member is that the latter comes under the influence of a group leader. Freud saw the ties between leaders and followers as having a long history in human evolution, and as forming the basis for the two different psychologies of leaders and followers. Central to this view was the model he had of the family and the development of parent-child relationships, focusing particularly upon the father. This is clearly reflected by the terminology Freud used to discuss the psychologies of leaders and followers:

From the first there were two kinds of psychologies, that of the individual members of the group and that of the father, chief, or leader. The members of the group were subject to ties just as we see them today, but the father of the primal horde was free. His intellectual acts were strong and independent even in isolation, and his will needed no reinforcement from others. Consistency leads us to assume that his ego had few libidinal ties; he loved no one but himself, or other people only in so far as they served his needs. . . . Even today the members of a group stand in need of the illusion that they are equally and justly loved by their leader; but the leader himself need love no one else, he may be of a masterful nature, absolutely narcissistic, self-confident and independent. (1921, pp. 123–24)

To conclude, Freud argued that by joining a group, a person acquires characteristics that are fundamentally different from those of an isolated individual. Such changes tend to involve a loss for the individual in terms of intellectual capacities, but a gain in terms of feelings of power and security. However, through organization, group members can regain the characteristics they possessed as individuals, although major groups such as the church and the army have not yet evolved to such a level. Most important, individuals who are group members differ from isolated individuals in that they are influenced by group leaders, and their freedom is severely restricted by the two-way libidinal ties binding them to the leader and to each other.

THE IMPLICATIONS OF FREUD'S MODEL

Freud's model of group psychology entails at least four major implications for the field of intergroup relations, all of which have to some extent been realized in social research: (1) the assumed basis for intergroup hostility, (2) the model of intergroup relations adopted, (3) the out-group selected as the target of aggression, and (4) subgroups that should be the focus of study within each group.

Freud did not view intergroup conflicts as arising out of conflicts of material interests. At the start of World War I he wrote that nations in conflict put forward their interests in order to justify "satisfying their passions" (1915, p. 288). He explained out-group hostility in terms of psychological ambivalence and displaced aggression. Out-group hostility was seen by Freud as a necessary condition for harmony within the in-group, since if hostile feelings are not displaced onto an out-group, they could turn inward and destroy the in-group.

Second, Freud offered a purely psychological model of intergroup conflicts, as opposed to viewing real conflicts of interests as being the basis of such conflicts. Moreover, his model of intergroup relations is reductionist, in the sense that it tries to extend intra- and interpersonal processes to the intergroup arena. Freud used the same "hydraulic" model that he elaborates at the individual level to interpret intergroup behavior.

Freud's model of intergroup relations is "hydraulic" in the sense that he assumed that the aggressive energies motivating behavior in the group context do not dissipate if they cannot attain their original goal, but surface in the form of displaced aggression toward out-groups. This idea was later taken up by Dollard et al. in their formulation of frustration and aggression theory (1939).

However, Freud proposed that the choice of an out-group toward whom aggression is directed is not random. Rather, the criterion of similarity is assumed to play a central part in this choice. In *Group Psychology*, Freud asserts that the greater the difference between two groups, the greater will be the hostility between them; this explains the strength of such hostilities "as the Gallic people feel for the German, the Aryan feel for the Semite, and the white races for the coloured" (1921, p. 101). More recent research tends to confirm the importance that the criterion of similarity plays in determining intergroup harmony and conflict (see Brown, 1984; Moghaddam & Stringer, 1988).

A fourth important implication of Freud's group psychology for intergroup relations is in terms of the different social strata within each group upon which we should focus in order to better understand intergroup processes. Freud stressed that there are two kinds of psychology, the psychology of the leaders and that of the followers. He generally viewed the followers in negative terms. For example, in *The Future of an Illusion* he postulates a greater degree of ethnocentrism among the masses and refers to them as "lazy and unintelligent" (1927, p. 7). In contrast, Freud regarded leaders as having greater personal abilities, charisma, and strength.

Most important, Freud's analyses lead us to focus upon leaders and to explore intergroup relations primarily by examining the behavior of leaders. Power is monopolized by this elite, who can influence the numerical majority to adopt particular attitudes toward different out-groups. Thus, Freud's model of group processes is in this sense also sociological, since it deals with the power differences between two categories of people: leaders and followers. The different psychologies of these minority and majority groups are viewed as being directly linked to their power differences.

FREUD'S INFLUENCE ON INTERGROUP THEORY AND RESEARCH

Freudian concepts have had a fundamental influence on both theory and research in intergroup relations. As illustrative examples, we shall discuss this influence as it is reflected in two major pioneering studies, *Frustration and Aggression* (Dollard et al., 1939) and *The Authoritarian Personality* (Adorno et al., 1950). These pioneering studies have influenced the way social scientists, particularly psychologists, sociologists, and political scientists, view intergroup conflict. Moreover, they have demonstrated that although Freud's general model of group processes is probably too diffuse to serve as the basis for a social psychology of intergroup relations, certain of his insights can be experimentally tested and used to explain intergroup conflict.

The research traditions established by *Frustration and Aggression* and *The Authoritarian Personality* continued the Freudian bias of reductionism in dealing with intergroup relations. That is, like Freud's model of group processes, they are basically concerned with intra- and interpersonal processes, but they extrapolate from this level to that of intergroup processes. Thus, for example, Dollard et al. (1939) assumed that processes linking frustration and aggression are the same at the interindividual and intergroup levels. This assumption led them to elaborate frustration-aggression theory at the individual level, and then to proceed on that basis to discuss intergroup attitudes and prejudice.

Freud influenced frustration-aggression theory in at least four major ways. First, the fundamental proposition that "aggression is always a consequence of frustration" (Dollard et al., 1939, p. 1) is derived from Freud. In making this assertion, Dollard et al. also conceived of an intervening variable between the frustrating stimulus and the aggressive response. Frustration is viewed as an outcome of a blocking or a prevention of a goal response. A frustrating stimulus produces in the person an instigation to aggress. However, a number of factors can make it difficult or impossible for a person to attack the frustrator, such as the frustrating agent being too powerful. In such circumstances, it is predicted that aggression will be displaced onto an alternative target, a scapegoat. A classic contemporary example of this would be an unemployed man coming home after another fruitless day of searching for a job, and picking on his wife, since the society that will not give him a job seems to powerful to fight. This notion of displaced aggression reflects the second major way in which the frustration-aggression hypothesis has been directly influenced by Freud.

Third, Dollard et al. were influenced by Freud with respect to the characteristics that they believed the scapegoat would have. Following Freud, they identified similarity as the key criterion according to which out-group targets for aggression would be selected: "For the outgroup to be a good scapegoat it must be so far removed from the ingroup by differences in custom or feature that it will not be included effectively within the scope of ingroup taboos on aggression" (Dollard et al., 1939, p. 89). Thus, like Freud, Dollard et al. assert that the more similar the out-group, the less likely it is to be selected as the target of aggression.

The fourth and major way in which frustration-aggression theory has been influenced by Freud is in terms of the hydraulic model assumed by Dollard et al. Following Freud's general model, they assume that the energy motivating human behavior will not "fade away" if it cannot reach its original goal. Rather, this energy will be redirected along alternative channels. Intergroup hostility can arise from this process in the following manner. Frustration leads to an instigation to aggress. However, if the frustrating stimulus cannot be attacked, perhaps because it is too powerful, then the instigation to aggress will not dissipate but will be displaced onto another, possibly weaker, out-group. The occurrence of aggression has a cathartic effect, in that the likelihood of further aggression without fresh instigation decreases. Thus, the instigation to aggress can be decreased only through the expression of aggression.

The influence of Freud is also clearly reflected in more recent applications of frustration-aggression theory to intergroup relations (Berkowitz, 1962; Gurr, 1970; Horowitz, 1973). In particular, the concept of displaced aggression has had an important influence on the way intergroup conflicts have been analyzed. For example, Gurr (1970) has undertaken an extensive interpretation of why rebellions and revolutions occur by relying in fundamental ways on frustration-aggression theory. Central to his thesis on social violence is the notion of displaced aggression. However, the general tendency has been for research on frustration-aggression theory to focus upon behavior at the individual level, the results of these studies being extrapolated to the intergroup level (see Billig, 1976, p. 123).

The Authoritarian Personality, introduced by Adorno et al. (1950), also reflects Freud's influence on the ways in which intergroup behavior has been construed and researched. The events of World War II and the threat of fascism led Adorno et al. to research the "potentially fascistic" individual, "one whose structure is such as to render him particularly susceptible to anti-democratic propaganda" (1950, p. 1). The authors were explicit about the direction their political biases gave the study, as well as about their debt to Freud: "For theory as to the structure of personality we have leaned most heavily upon Freud" (Adorno et al., 1950, p. 5). Although Adorno et al. viewed intergroup attitudes as being determined primarily by personality (intraindividual) variables, their ultimate concern was with the large-scale implications of the potentially fascist personality. As the reader is repeatedly reminded in *The Authoritarian Personality*, the main concern of Adorno et al. was the threat to democratic society posed by the potentially fascist personality types.

Following Freud, Adorno et al. presented an irrationalist account of human behavior. This is clearly reflected in the factors they introduced to account for the potential threat of fascism. They argued that fascism necessarily favors a small group of people and cannot prove that it will serve the best interests of the majority. "It must therefore make its major appeal, not to rational self-interest, but to emotional needs—often to the most primitive and irrational wishes and fears" (Adorno et al., 1950, p. 10). Thus, it is not material benefits and logical arguments that lead a person to support fascism, but primitive and irrational wishes and fears inside the potentially fascistic personality.

Typical authoritarians were presented by Adorno et al. as having suppressed their hostilities toward their parents, projecting this aggression onto "scapegoat outgroups," such as the Jews and blacks. Thus, following Freudian traditions, they placed particular emphasis on the respondents' childhood experiences and relationships with parents. In the case of male participants, the study focused particularly on the respondent's relationship with his father and his history of rebellion against the father, on the assumption that "the pattern developed in relation to the father tends to be transferred to other authorities and thus becomes crucial in forming social and political beliefs in men" (Adorno et al., 1950, p. 315).

In the case of the authoritarian personality type, the repression of aggressive tendencies against parents was seen as part of a general tendency to repress "unacceptable" tendencies and impulses in the self, such as "fear, weakness, passivity, sex impulses" (Adorno et al., 1950, p. 474). This repression leads to the growth of an irrational "shield" comprised of beliefs that protect the authoritarian personality type from the "unacceptable" aspects of reality. Through the mechanism of projection, much of what cannot be accepted as part of one's own ego is externalized, with the result that "it is not oneself but others that are seen as hostile and threatening" (Adorno et al., 1950, p. 474).

Although *The Authoritarian Personality* has been criticized on both methodological and theoretical bases, this ground-breaking study has succeeded in making the topic of authoritarianism an important one in social research. However, some of the more recent empirical studies that have been influenced by *The Authoritarian Personality* do not represent real progress, either methodologically or theoretically (for example, see Forbes, 1985, as reviewed by Taylor & Moghaddam, 1988). The most important recent research that has attempted to build on the pioneering work of Adorno et al. (1950) has been conducted by Bob Altemeyer (1981, 1988).

The research of Adorno et al. (1950) identified nine central traits assumed to be relevant to authoritarianism: submissiveness; conventionalism; aggressiveness; a concern with power and toughness; a reliance on superstitions and stereotypes; a preoccupation with sex; a projection of one's own undesirable traits onto others; a lack of introspection; and destructiveness and cynicism. Starting in the 1960s, Altemeyer (1981) developed and refined a new scale of authoritarianism, and his findings suggest that of the nine traits assumed to be relevant, only submissiveness, conventionalism, and aggressiveness were actually associated (1981, p. 148).

Altemeyer (1988) has used his revised scale, labeled the right-wing authoritarianism (RWA) scale, to identify individuals who are more prone to behave in an authoritarian manner (see also Perrott & Taylor, in press; Zanna, 1994). For example, Altemeyer has found that individuals who scored high on the RWA scale were found to be more likely to support a government crackdown on minority groups. Interestingly, this support does not depend on the nature of the minority group being targeted. Right-wing authoritarians are just as likely to support the government in a crackdown on Communists as they are to support a government crackdown on conservative groups (if conservative groups were to become a target of government restrictions). This is presumably because right-wing authoritarians are submissive to authority, rather than followers of any particular ideology.

Although Altemeyer's (1981, 1988) research has come under attack from some quarters (e.g., Ray, 1985), it represents the most interesting and psychometrically sound work conducted on authoritarianism over the last few decades. Of course, it focuses on the right wing and may reflect a bias among Western social scientists, as was pointed out by critics much earlier (see Christie & Jahoda, 1954), to see a threat from the right rather than the left wing of the political spectrum. Also, Altemeyer (1988) fails to be convincing in his argument that the best explanation of authoritarianism is provided by social learning theory, rather than by instinctual drives, or by the frustration-aggression hypothesis, or by other alternative accounts. Nevertheless, Altemeyer's (1988) work keeps the spotlight on authoritarians, following the tradition set by Adorno et al. (1950), as inspired by Freud. Ironically, Freud was forced to flee his native Austria and spend his final years in exile in England, away from the ultimate authoritarians of his age, the Nazis.

Although the implications of both *Frustration and Aggression* (Dollard et al., 1939) and *The Authoritarian Personality* (Adorno et al., 1950) for intergroup behavior have been criticized (see Billig, 1976; Brown, 1984), they have nevertheless had a fundamental influence on social science models of intergroup relations. Indirectly, this impact has maintained the influence of Freud's group psychology.

CRITICAL REVIEW OF THE FREUDIAN LEGACY

Freud's irrationalist and reductionist account of conflict continues to have a fundamental influence on our views about behavior in the intergroup context, although his model does not constitute a major orientation to intergroup relations. The Freudian legacy is directly reflected by such powerful and highly influential concepts as displaced aggression. This is an example of Freud's ideas that have become influential in the mass media. For example, terrorism has often been interpreted in the media as an example of displaced aggression. From this perspective, a minority group (terrorists) that is too weak to show aggression toward the real object of its hostility (a government) is forced to displace its aggression onto scapegoats (very often the innocent public). The implications are that as terrorists gain access to more powerful weapons, they will probably select more important scapegoats onto whom they can displace their aggression. Of course, such purely psychological interpretations of terrorism do not deal with the political factors leading to minority-group rebellion or the processes of marginalization experienced by political minorities.

An aspect of Freud's model that is promising but has not been followed up in intergroup research is his distinction between the psychology of followers and that of leaders. His different treatment of these two categories could provide a point of departure for a structural model of group and intergroup processes. Also, his emphasis upon the role of leaders in intergroup relations seems to be in harmony with our everyday views about many types of intergroup situations, including those involving international confrontations. The concentration of power in the hands of a top elite and the confrontation of these leaders in international summits would seem to endorse at least some of Freud's emphasis on the role of leaders in intergroup relations.

CONCLUSION

Freud's model of group processes has a number of important implications for intergroup relations, the most critical being that hostility toward out-groups is one inevitable outcome of in-group cohesion. While this is in some ways a pessimistic conclusion, more optimistic possibilities arise when we consider the potentials presented by displacement. Feelings of hostility need not be displaced onto out-groups, but can be channeled along more constructive paths, such as competitive sports. Thus, according to Freud's model, the most promising way to achieve intergroup cooperation lies in creating constructive paths along which displaced aggression can be channeled, rather than changing the material conditions in which social groups exist.

SUGGESTED READINGS

Adorno, T. W., Frenkel-Brunswik, E., Levinson, D. J., & Sanford, R. W. (1950). *The authoritarian personality.* New York: Harper & Row.

Altemeyer, B. (1988). *Enemies of freedom: Understanding right-wing authoritarianism.* San Francisco: Jossey-Bass.

Billig, M. (1976). *Social psychology and intergroup relations.* London: Academic Press.

Dollard, J., Doob, L., Miller, N., Mowrer, O., & Sears, R. (1939). *Frustration and aggression.* New Haven: Yale University Press.

Freud, S. (1921). *Group psychology and the analysis of the ego.* Vol. 18 of J. Strachey (Ed. and Trans.), *The standard edition of the complete psychological works.* London: Hogarth Press.

————. (1930). *Civilization and its discontents.* Vol. 21 of J. Strachey (Ed. and Trans.), *The standard edition of the complete psychological works.* London: Hogarth Press.

3

Realistic Conflict Theory

Realistic conflict theory (RCT) is essentially an economic theory of intergroup behavior that is based upon three central assumptions about human behavior. First, it is assumed that people are selfish and will try to maximize their own rewards. Second, conflict is assumed to be the outcome of incompatible group interests. Third, it is assumed, sometimes explicitly, that the social psychological aspects of intergroup behavior are not determinants of—but, rather, are mainly determined by—the compatibility or incompatibility of group interests. For example, the negative attitudes, stereotypes, and attributions that members of one group have regarding members of an out-group are assumed to stem from the incompatible interests of the two groups involved.

The work of social psychologists guided by RCT is in an important sense devoid of social psychology. Once it is assumed that real conflicts of interests are the cause of intergroup hostility, and intergroup behavior is mainly determined by the compatibility or incompatibility of group goals, then social psychological phenomena assume the role of dependent variables in the intergroup setting. For example, Sherif states that "the bounds for the attitudes of members in different groups towards one another are set by the nature of the functional relations between groups" (1966, p. 63). He proceeds to describe in more detail what these functional relations are:

Groups may be competing to attain some goal or vital prize, in which the success of one group necessarily means the failure of the other. One group may have claims on another group to manage, control, or exploit them, to take over their actual or assumed rights and possessions. On the other hand, groups may have complementary goals, so that each may attain its goal without hindrance from the others or even with their helping hand. (1966, p. 63)

The intellectual roots of this functional approach can be traced directly to the sociologist William Sumner. In his articulation of the concept of ethnocentrism, Sumner wrote:

The insiders in a we-group are in a relation of peace, order, law, government, and industry, to each other. Their relation to all outsiders, or others-groups, is one of war and plunder. . . . Sentiments are produced to correspond. Loyalty to the group, sacrifice for it, hatred and contempt for outsiders, brotherhood within, warlikeness without—all grow together, common products of the same situation. (1906, p. 12)

Thus, according to this functionalist tradition, which Sherif followed, it is competition between groups for scarce resources that leads to perceptual and attitudinal biases against the out-group.

The social psychological aspects of Sherif's research on intergroup behavior concern the development of intergroup processes within the bounds of certain functional relations between groups. This point will be further clarified when we describe his research on intergroup behavior. Sherif has been called "the most important social psychologist in the history of the field" of intergroup research (Triandis, 1979, p. 321), and his experiments on intergroup behavior have become classics. Therefore we describe his work in some detail.

Following our discussion of Sherif's experiments, we focus on gaming research, particularly the work of Morton Deutsch. Most gaming research shares the theoretical and normative underpinnings of RCT. They both adopt the assumption that conflict is bad as their point of departure. Second, in the typical gaming experiment it is assumed that subjects try to maximize their own profits; thus, a selfish model of humankind is adopted. Third, conflict is assumed to arise when subjects try to maximize their own rewards at the expense of others—that is, real conflicts of interests cause conflicts. Fourth, the competing nature of interests is assumed, sometimes explicitly, to be the most important factor determining such social psychological phenomena as attitudes of the parties involved. However, certain scientists in gaming research, such as Deutsch, have explicitly placed greater emphasis on the perceptions and interpretations of the conflicting parties than have the strict functionalists, such as Sherif. Thus, Deutsch states that the objective state of affairs does not "rigidly determine" the presence or absence of conflict (1969b, p. 9), and that the "processes of misperception and biased perception" are among those that can lead to conflict escalation (1973, p. 352).

The strengths and weaknesses of RCT will be discussed in our critical review of the theory. Psychologists guided by RCT have tended to view the resolution of conflict as the most important applied task facing researchers. Deutsch and other would-be "peacemakers" represent the liberal conscience of North America, the "doves" who have urged successive U.S. administrations to settle disagreements with competing powers through negotiations and closer cooperation on joint projects, which they believe could in turn lead to greater international interdependence and mutual trust. In outlining the course of "constructive" and "destructive" conflicts (1973, pp. 351–400), Deutsch clearly is extrapolating from his gaming research to the international scene (see also Deutsch, 1985).

THE PIONEERING WORK OF MUZAFER SHERIF

The details of Sherif's research have been described in a number of publications (Sherif, 1951; Sherif, Harvey, White, Hood, & Sherif, 1961; Sherif & Sherif, 1953; Sherif, White, & Harvey, 1955), but the volume in which the research is most clearly described in its larger social context is *Group Conflict and Cooperation* (Sherif, 1966). Sherif states that "the appropriate frame of reference for staging intergroup behavior is the functional relations between two or more groups, which may be negative or positive" (1966, p. 12). In Sherif's experiments, "functional relations" are equivalent to complementary-noncomplementary group interests. He defines a group as "a social unit that consists of a number of individuals (1) who, at a given time, have role and status relations with one another, stabilized in some degree and (2) who possess a set of values or norms regulating the attitude and behavior of individual members, at least in matters of consequence to them" (1966, p. 12), and intergroup behavior as "relations between two or more groups and their respective members. Whenever individuals belonging to one group interact, collectively or individually, with another group or its members *in terms of their group identification*, we have an instance of intergroup behavior" (1966, p. 12). An important implication of this latter definition is that intergroup behavior need not necessarily involve the physical presence and interaction of entire groups, but can simply mean individuals from two different groups interacting in terms of their respective group identities.

In Sherif's experiments, the material conditions of the experimental context—the tasks and resources given to groups, and particularly the complementary or noncomplementary nature of tasks—were the independent variables, while social psychological phenomena, such as intergroup attitudes and group identification, were the dependent variables. Sherif and his associates carried out three major experiments on intergroup behavior. All of them were conducted in summer camps, and the participants in all three were boys eleven or twelve years old. Only boys who did not have personal ties with each other prior to the experiment, who were healthy and well adjusted, and who were from white, middle-class, Protestant families were included. This selection procedure was designed to decrease the chances of personal acquaintance, abnormal personality tendencies, and pronounced differences in background and physical appearance influencing the results.

The research context was naturalistic, in the sense that the boys believed they were in a normal summer camp situation; they engaged in the kinds of activities boys usually do in such camps. All research staff played the role of camp officials, organizing and officiating events while also acting as participant observers. The groups that Sherif studied had a history from group formation to intergroup conflict, cooperation, and group dissolution; and the time scale of the history was naturalistic, in the sense that the process of group formation and dissolution in such camps is normally completed in a few weeks. There were four experimental stages: (1) spontaneous interpersonal friendship choices, (2) group formation, (3) intergroup conflict, and (4) intergroup cooperation/reduction of intergroup conflict (see figure 3.1).

Spontaneous Interpersonal Friendship Choices

The first two experiments carried out by Sherif and his associates began with this stage, during which the boys were housed together and were free to interact and work with whom they preferred. After relationships had stabilized to some extent, assessments were made of interpersonal attraction among the boys. Next, the boys were divided between two cabins, with about two-thirds of any boy's best friends being placed in the other cabin. By separating the boys from most of those they were spontaneously attracted to, Sherif diminished the possibility that the research results could be explained in terms of interpersonal attraction.

After the formation of the two groups, the boys interacted and carried out tasks almost exclusively with in-group members. The patterns of interpersonal attractions among them changed, so that best friends were now chosen more from the in-groups. Sherif concluded that "friendship choices shift steadily from strictly interpersonal attractions toward ingroup exclusiveness, as a part of group formation and functions" (1966, p. 75).

Figure 3.1
Schematic Representation of Realistic Conflict Theory

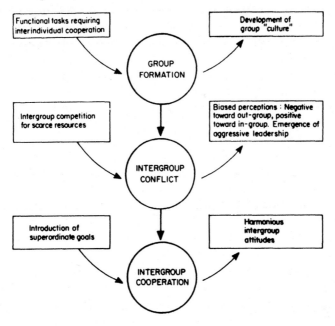

Group Formation

Sherif's third major experiment, known as the "Robber's Cave" study because it was carried out near a famous hideaway reputed to have been used by Jesse James, started with the stage of group formation. The main purpose of this stage was to give the groups a number of tasks, such as cooking, camping, and building, that required the boys in each group to work as a team. In carrying out these group tasks, a status hierarchy and leadership structure emerged within each group, as well as a kind of group identity and subculture involving nicknames for members, group secrets, symbols, names, and preferred ways of doing things.

Intergroup Conflict

The boys did not have contact as groups prior to the stage of intergroup conflict. In the Robber's Cave study, neither group was aware of the presence of the other. As soon as the groups became aware of each other, however, their competitive spirit seemed to be stimulated. That is, upon learning about the presence of an out-group, the boys were extremely eager to take part in intergroup competitions, such as tug-of-war and a treasure hunt. The intergroup rivalry began in a healthy way, but quickly turned harsh and antagonistic. Attitudes toward the out-group generally became negative, while those toward fellow in-group members became more positive. There was also some tendency for leadership to change, so that more "warlike" and aggressive individuals emerged as leaders.

The most interesting psychological findings of Sherif's experiments emerged during this stage, and it is worth deliberating further upon two aspects in particular. First, there was a tendency for subjects to refer to notions of justice and fairness. Second, the boys systematically perceived events in a manner that favored the in-group.

Throughout the stage of intergroup conflict, the boys in Sherif's experiments repeatedly referred to notions of justice. They made claims about their own group playing fair and the other group "playing dirty" and being cheats. When their own group was taken advantage of by a surprise attack or unexpected trick, the other group was described as using unfair, cowardly tactics; but the other group "got what they deserved" when they were attacked without warning or when their schemes were sabotaged. This reminds one of the kinds of manipulations of the meaning of justice that some political parties embark upon, making their interpretations suit their own purposes, depending on whether they are in or out of government, or whether it is their own political record or that of opposition parties that they are talking about (see Brewer, 1979).

The biased perceptions that the boys developed were demonstrated particularly well in a game of "bean toss," in which the aim was to collect as many beans scattered on the ground as possible within a limited time. The boys worked individually, collecting beans in a sack with a restricted opening, so that it was not possible to count the number of beans collected. They then had the task of estimating the number of beans in each sack.

The contents of each sack were briefly exposed to the boys, and each collection of beans purportedly gathered by a different boy was identified solely by the group membership of the collector. In actuality, the same collection of 35 beans was shown each time, this being a number sufficiently large that it could not be counted in the time available. Each boy wrote down his estimate of the number after each exposure. The results showed a consistent tendency to overestimate the number of beans collected by the in-group and to underestimate the number collected by the out-group. This cleverly formulated experiment within an experiment clearly demonstrates the pattern of positive in-group bias that evolves in situations of intergroup conflict.

Intergroup Cooperation

It was in the Robber's Cave experiment that Sherif first operationalized the concept of superordinate goals as a means of transforming hostile intergroup relations into cooperative ones. Superordinate goals are those that have "a compelling appeal for members of each group, but that neither group can achieve without participation of the other" (Sherif, 1966, p. 89). A series of situations was created in which all the boys had to combine resources in order to overcome an obstacle and reach a goal that had common appeal for them. For example, in one situation the boys joined forces and successfully coped with a breakdown of the water supply, and in another they all helped start a truck that was to bring them food. Solving the breakdown of the water supply and starting the truck represented superordinate goals, in the sense that they had a strong appeal for members of both groups, but neither group could achieve them without the participation of the other. In neither case did such mutual cooperation on the task lead to an immediate end to hostilities. However, the series of situations requiring interdependent action did gradually lead to more harmonious relations between the groups.

In evaluating the transformation from conflicting to harmonious intergroup relations that arises between the third and fourth stages, it is important to keep in mind that the groups in this experiment had been brought into existence through their ascribed tasks and made more cohesive through intergroup competition. It seems plausible to argue that once the groups did not have separate tasks, and once the institutionalized competition had been removed, the functional reason for their existence had ceased. Furthermore, the introduction of new tasks that required the formation of a new, larger group for their attainment meant that the functional basis for the evolution of a group combining all the boys was present. It could be plausibly argued, therefore, that the cooperation Sherif achieved in the fourth stage was not between two different groups, but between individuals who had to act as one group in order to complete tasks that required all their combined resources.

The importance of Sherif's research is not in the new or unexpected nature of its results, but in its methodological approach, particularly in its operationalization of the concept of superordinate goals. It is neither new nor unexpected to find that real conflicts of interests lead to intergroup hostilities, or that groups have more harmonious relationships when they have to combine forces to achieve a commonly desired goal. But Sherif's work was innovative in reproducing, under controlled conditions, various processes of group formation, conflict, and cooperation that are normally associated with long-term social change. Also, by demonstrating how the concept of superordinate goals can be effectively operationalized and used to transform groups in conflict into groups in harmony, Sherif fired the imaginations of researchers who came to perceive superordinate goals as a useful instrument for solving intergroup conflicts, from the level of small groups to world powers.

APPLICATION OF THE CONCEPT OF SUPERORDINATE GOALS

Industrial Conflicts

An important domain to which the concept of superordinate goals has been extended is that of industrial conflicts. Examples of such an application are the works of Blake and Mouton (1962) and Blake, Shepard, and Mouton (1964), who report a series of cases where they intervened in the industrial context to solve intergroup labor-management problems. How Blake and his associates applied the Sherifs' ideas in the industrial setting is illustrated by the example of union-management conflict in the Lakeside Company (1964, pp. 123–36). The main practical problem for the researchers was how to influence the perceptions of the conflicting parties so that they would view selected superordinate goals as "the" priority objectives and give less importance to differences of interest. After receiving an invitation from management to intervene in the conflict, Blake and his associates set up training programs to familiarize the participants with social science intergroup concepts, theories, and experiments. At this stage, union representatives viewed the researchers with suspicion and refused to take part in the training programs, claiming they were "just another management manipulation" (1964, p. 125).

Despite this obstacle, the researchers succeeded in motivating the two groups to accept the idea that each of them stood to gain more by cooperating than by fighting. The solution of superordinate goals involved changes in the perceptions of the participants with regard to the importance of various goals, rather than changes in the material conditions that underlay their conflicts of interests—assumed by Sherif to be the real cause of conflict.

International Conflict

The extension of the concept of superordinate goals to the international scene is illustrated by the work of Frank (1967). He proposed that the superpowers should cooperate on a series of programs—for instance, in the areas of environmental and space research—designed to achieve selected superordinate goals. Such activities would, he argued, increase mutual dependence, understanding, and trust, thereby diminishing the risk of another world war. It is this philosophy that underlies the work of the United Nations in its various spheres. For example, through the U.N. Development Program and the almost 40 U.N. executive agencies, such as the U.N. Industrial Development Organization and the International Labour Office, member states cooperate to strengthen the development efforts of Third World countries. The institutional goals of the U.N. executive agencies, which include eradicating illiteracy and overcoming food shortages, could be regarded as superordinate goals. Moreover, there are a number of U.N. bodies, such as the U.N. Peace Corps, and activities, such as the U.N. Conferences on Disarmament, that more directly present world powers with the chance to work toward the assumed superordinate goal of peace. On the one hand, it could be claimed that such activities are effective, since a third world war has been avoided. On the other hand, the criticism remains that the major powers seem to be using the United Nations as just another battleground where they pursue self-serving policies and steamroll opposition motions by using their veto powers.

Desegregated Schools

Elliot Aronson and his colleagues (Aronson, Stephan, Sikes, Blaney, & Snapp, 1978) have made a creative application of the concept of superordinate goals to desegregated schools in the United States. Stimulated by Sherif's pioneering work, Aronson (1984) noted that the key to the superordinate goals associated with intergroup cooperation is mutual interdependence—"a situation wherein individuals need one another and are needed by one another in order to accomplish their goal" (p. 267). Aronson felt that if mutual interdependence could be introduced into a classroom environment to replace the competitive atmosphere between students, a cooperative attitude among students generally and racial groups in particular would develop. To test this notion, the "jigsaw" procedure was introduced: students worked in small groups that were required to perform a task, and each member of the group had information crucial to the group product. Thus, the conditions for mutual interdependence were created.

Repeated applications of the jigsaw procedure in classrooms produce consistent results. The children in these classrooms like each other better, develop a more positive attitude toward school, have a higher self-esteem, and have better exam performances than those in traditional classes. Of special significance is the finding that the increase in liking among the students generally crosses racial and ethnic boundaries. The field of education thus represents another context where the concept of superordinate goals, defined here in terms of mutual interdependence, has an important role to play in fostering intergroup cooperation.

We might wonder why, if the "jigsaw classroom" procedure has so much potential, it has not been used extensively. Surely the current widespread discontent with public education, particularly in North America, would lead authorities to try to widely implement the "jigsaw" procedure. At one level, insufficient funds may prevent such policies. However, the more fundamental reason for not adopting this policy may be the North American ideology of individualism (Sampson, 1977). The "jigsaw" procedure seems to emphasize equality and collective responsibility, rather than competition and individual responsibility. Consequently, in the North American context, the high priority given to individualism and "self-help" may mean that jigsaw-type procedures will not be adopted because they are seen as working against the American interpretation of meritocracy.

In summary, the concept of superordinate goals has had an important impact on the work of research and practicing social scientists. Given Sherif's historical influence in the field of intergroup relations, it is surprising that so little psychological research has been carried out to test the effectiveness of superordinate goals as a means of reducing intergroup conflict in different conditions. Clearly, superordinate goals can be effective in transforming conflict into cooperation, but under what conditions can this transformation be achieved more successfully? Also, are there conditions in which superordinate goals are not useful in achieving intergroup cooperation?

In this connection, an experiment by Deschamps and Brown (1983) produces evidence to suggest that in a condition where groups have comparable motivations in achieving superordinate goals, group distinctiveness would be threatened, and this would lead to greater intergroup differentiation and hostility. Thus, this would seem to demonstrate one condition in which superordinate goals lead to increased rather than decreased intergroup conflict.

A number of other limitations to superordinate goals are also suggested by the research. For example, Diab (1970) attempted to replicate Sherif's findings, but the competing groups Diab created proved to be very unequal. In this situation, the losing group seemed to be completely demoralized, and superordinate goals failed to be effective in bringing about cooperation. In effect, the losing group opted to exit rather than to adopt a superordinate goal and proceed to the cooperation stage of the study.

Related to this is the research of Worchel and his associates, who examined the role of successful outcomes in the effectiveness of superordinate goals (Worchel, Andreoli, & Folger, 1977; Worchel & Norvell, 1980). In Sherif's studies the final phase of intergroup cooperation always ended successfully, and it may have been the success rather than a superordinate goal that resulted in a reduction in hostilities. Research by Worchel and his associates suggests that, indeed, this may be the case under certain conditions. That is, a failure in cooperative tasks can lead to increased hostilities and the out-group being blamed for the groups' failure to reach a superordinate goal.

GAMING RESEARCH, EVOLUTIONARY MODELS, AND RCT

The model of humankind adopted by gaming research is that of a rational, thinking being who is motivated to maximize personal gain. Conflicts are assumed to evolve when incompatible interests are perceived by the parties involved as being more important than compatible interests. Most gaming research follows the tradition of "peace researchers," who assume that the psychologist's task must be to help avoid war, in contrast with the "war gamers," who have adopted the goal of making warfare more efficient (see Billig, 1976, p. 182; Wilson, 1970). Both "war gamers" and "peace researchers" assume that psychologists can help achieve more rational outcomes from intergroup interactions by identifying the pitfalls that lead to irrational decision making.

An essential underlying assumption in gaming research is that extrapolations from the results of experimental studies on interpersonal behavior are valid (see Axelrod, 1984). Indeed, many important research questions being investigated through experimental gaming studies of interpersonal behavior are derived from the context of macro, intergroup, and international relations. This point is well illustrated in the writings of Deutsch (1973, 1985), a leading "peace researcher." With regard to the kinds of concerns that stimulated his initial experimental studies on bargaining, Deutsch states, "Our first bargaining study was concerned with the effect of threat (Deutsch & Krauss 1960, 1962). The study grew out of my concern with some of the psychological assumptions underlying the concept of 'stable deterrence,' a notion that was quite fashionable among political scientists and economists connected with the Defense Department in the late 1950's and early 1960's" (1969a, p. 1083).

The theoretical and experimental approach adopted by gaming research is not, however, always compatible with the kinds of "international" concerns that inspired researchers such as Deutsch. This is not to say that processes leading to intergroup conflict and peace cannot be studied constructively in the experimental laboratory. It is to suggest, however, that to carry out research on interpersonal behavior and then to generalize from its results to the intergroup and international levels is very likely to be misleading.

However, an innovative approach to linking research on individual behavior in the gaming context to intergroup relations has been developed by Axelrod (1984). It focuses upon how individuals pursuing their own interests will act, and what effects this will have on the social system as a whole. In developing "cooperation theory," Axelrod has drawn heavily on concepts from the field of evolutionary biology and has adopted a classical Darwinian approach. He explicitly uses the terminology of evolutionary biology to present his theory of the evolution of cooperative behavior.

Axelrod treats cooperative behavior as an individual trait, like white skin and long legs, that can be passed on to offspring and spread among a population, or become extinct. The point of departure for cooperation theory is that for cooperative behavior to survive and spread, individuals must have a high chance of meeting again, so that they have a real stake in future interactions. This proposition is supported by findings from gaming research (Axelrod, 1984). Also, cooperation cannot gain a foothold if it is carried out by isolated individuals, but it can establish itself if there is a cluster of individuals who base their cooperation on reciprocity and have some interaction with each other. Once established among a social group, cooperation can thrive and protect itself from invasion by less cooperative strategies. This is because of the "survival of the fittest" and the idea that individuals who have cooperative relations with others are more likely to have offspring that survive and thereby continue the cooperative pattern of behavior.

Axelrod's (1984) analysis diminishes the role of planning in the evolution of cooperation. In fact, chapter 5 of his book *The Evolution of Cooperation* is coauthored with Hamilton, a biologist, with the explicit purpose of demonstrating that foresight is not a necessary precondition for the evolution of cooperation. Nevertheless, while foresight is not required, it can assist the spread of cooperation, and Axelrod dedicates chapters 6 and 7 of his book to providing advice on how to improve cooperation.

A number of other researchers coming from a Darwinian tradition have attempted to find links between intergroup behavior among various animals and ecological conditions. Much of this research shares the "realistic" assumption that competition for scarce resources determines the nature of intergroup relations, and some such studies have yielded fascinating results. For example, research in the Shark Bay region of Western Australia has found patterns of alliance formation involving groups of male bottlenose dolphins for the purpose of "herding," and thus having exclusive access to, females (Connor, Smolker, & Richards, 1992). Similarly, intergroup aggression in chimpanzees has been found to mainly involve males competing for access to females, the most important "scarce resource" for reproduction purposes (Manson & Wrangham, 1991). Some researchers have argued that male-male competition for access to females is also the key to understanding intergroup aggression among at least some groups of humans (Chagnon, 1992).

The "realistic," resource-based model of conflict has also been strengthened by the recent "green" movement. Given that human populations continue to rise, and that renewable resources continue to be scarce, there is inevitable competition for such scarce resources. For example, writing in *Scientific American*, Homer-Dixon, Boutwell, and Rathjens (1993) begin their analysis of environmental change and violent conflict with the grim warning that

within the next 50 years, the human population is likely to exceed nine billion. . . . The total area of highly productive agricultural land will drop, as will the extent of forests. . . . Future generations will also experience the ongoing depletion and degradation of aquifers, rivers and other bodies of water, the decline of fisheries, further stratospheric ozone loss and, perhaps, significant climatic change. As such environmental problems become more severe, they may precipitate civil or international strife. (p. 38)

Homer-Dixon et al. (1993) summarize the reports of 30 experts, commissioned to examine specific cases illustrating possible relationships between renewable resources and violent conflict throughout the world. The accumulated evidence clearly suggests that scarcity of renewable resources is already contributing to violent intergroup conflicts in many parts of the world. For example, in Bangladesh there is not enough cropland to adequately feed the current population, but the probability of intergroup conflict will increase even more when the population doubles, as it is predicted to do by around the year 2025.

Thus, gaming research and evolutionary models share the underlying "realistic" assumption that material resources determine intergroup relations. However, researchers influenced by the gaming tradition (e.g., Axelrod, 1984; Deutsch, 1985) move constantly from interindividual behavior in the gaming context to relations between national, religious, and ethnic groups at the international level. Such leaps from individual to group processes are not justified. Also, researchers working in the Darwinian tradition (e.g., Homer-Dixon et al., 1993) have identified broad patterns of behavior that seem to be common to some animals and human societies, and that seem to link intergroup aggression with material conditions, but such research neglects the thorny issue of ideology. Consequently, it fails to inform us about how some groups mobilize, and why some other groups in similar material conditions seem to remain content with their situation as it is.

Characteristics of the Typical Gaming Experiment

A classic experiment in gaming research is the prisoner's dilemma game (PDG) (for reviews, see Rapoport & Chammah, 1965; Nemeth, 1972). It owes its name to an imaginary situation in which two accomplices awaiting trial are faced with a grave dilemma. Each prisoner has the choice of keeping quiet or cooperating with the authorities and informing on the other. If one of them informs and the other keeps quiet, the informer is set free and the other receives a very heavy sentence. If both of them inform, they both receive a severe sentence. If they both keep quiet, however, they both receive a light sentence. The dilemma is intensified by each prisoner's having to make a choice without communicating with the other and, thus, without knowing the choice of the other, so that the choice of strategy always has a hazardous and uncertain outcome. Each prisoner may want to get the best possible deal for himself or herself by informing on the other and getting off free, but neither is certain that the other will not also adopt this strategy and thereby get them both a severe sentence. On the other hand, if a prisoner tries for the next best outcome and keeps quiet, in the hope that his or her accomplice will also keep quiet so they can both get off with a light sentence, his or her plan may backfire, with the accomplice informing and getting him or her a very heavy sentence.

The relationship between the two prisoners is typically represented by a "payoff matrix." We shall discuss the terminology used in connection with these matrices before describing examples of how they are used. The reward structure for players in a game can be either zero-sum or non-zero-sum. In the zero-sum game, each player necessarily wins at the expense of the other, who suffers an equivalent loss. Thus, the joint total change in the fortunes of both players must always be zero. In the non-zero-sum game, there is no direct relationship between the fortunes of the two players; the wins or losses of each depend solely on his or her own choices.

Most games are "mixed-motive" in character, in that the players involved can be motivated to be either competitive or cooperative. Also, most games have a "best rational solution," and all players who follow logical behavior patterns will arrive at the same outcome, known as the "saddle point." The rationale that such logical players follow is based on the "minimax" principle, which involves a minimization of losses and a maximization of rewards.

In the terminology of gaming research, the classic PDG is a mixed-motive, non-zero-sum game with a saddle point. This is because the two players can act either competitively or cooperatively, the sum of their outcomes is not necessarily zero, and there is a "best rational answer"; that is, there exists a strategy for jointly minimizing losses and maximizing rewards, and this is achieved by both players' adopting a cooperative strategy.

Although the general concern of investigators using the PDG has been to identify conditions that lead to mutually cooperative or competitive strategies in interpersonal bargaining, the one dimension this paradigm has generally not included is any kind of bargaining or joint decision making. In the typical experiment, two persons work individually to select one of two strategies, "cooperation" or "competition," that combine to determine the outcome of the game. This outcome consists of rewards that individuals receive, and success is determined by the level of rewards received. Such rewards are usually points, with each point representing a certain amount of money. The main research interest is the repeated plays of the PDG by the same individuals, on the assumption that these repeated plays will tell us something about the development of negotiation behavior. In particular, interest is focused on whether the individuals will act according to their short-term or long-term interests. Since the two participants in a PDG are made aware that they are to take part in repeated plays, they know that any competitive move from one player could lead to retaliation by the other player on subsequent trials. Thus, it is in their long-term interests to cooperate.

A number of variations of the basic PDG design have been formulated, such as the game of "chicken" (Rapoport & Chammah, 1965). This owes its name to a game, one version of which was popularized by the cult hero James Dean, in which two daredevils drive their cars down the middle of the road straight at each other (or toward a cliff), and the first one to turn off is "chicken." If neither turns off, then both are killed. If both turn off at the same time, both share the shame. But if one turns "chicken" and swerves away, and the other drives straight on, then all the glory goes to the latter.

The PDG can be extended to include more than two players, and such *N*-person PDGs (NPDG) have been used specifically to explore "collective action" involving social dilemmas (Kelley & Grzelak, 1972; Liebrand, 1983). Thousands of studies have been conducted in this gaming tradition (Dawes, 1980), and recent trends indicate an interesting link between research in the rational gaming tradition and work in the evolutionary tradition (for example, see the collection of papers in Brown & Smith, 1991). On the one hand, gaming theorists have moved toward a grand theory to explain choice in dilemma situations, and evolutionary theory seems attractive to them. On the other hand, those influenced by the evolutionary tradition have found it useful to move "beyond self-interest" (Mansbridge, 1990) and to consider examples of behavior that seems to be group-serving rather than self-serving in the purely individualistic sense. However, much of gaming research remains uninteresting to social psychologists because it is concerned with "cold" and abstract mathematical models (Brown & Smith, 1991), rather than with "flesh-and-blood" behavior of groups interacting.

The strong appeal that the PDG has had for researchers interested in international peace issues can be explained partly by the analogous dilemmas that seem to confront the players in the PDG context and the world powers in the international arena. Consider the position of competing nations involved in the arms race and fearful of each other. Each is under pressure to increase arms expenditures, and the one that decreases expenditures on arms risks falling under the military domination of the other. Both sides seem to see only two alternatives: increasing arms expenditures or submitting to the power of the other. They seem to see and act only upon the consequences of not increasing arms expenditures.

The policy of increasing arms expenditures means losses for all nations, in the sense that none of them can use these resources for other, more constructive international and domestic purposes. When all parties choose to increase arms expenditures, their payoff is minimal. However, if they cooperate and all decrease arms expenditures, then everyone is relatively better off.

A Sample Experiment

In the typical PDG, subjects are not informed about the kinds of real-life situations that these games are supposed to represent. Would their behavior reflect the norms and values that they consider relevant to such real-life situations if the representative nature of the experimental situations was explained to them? This question has been investigated by Eiser and Bhavnani (1974).

Eiser and Bhavnani tested the hypothesis that it should be possible to influence subjects' behavior in the PDG by altering how they perceive the requirements of the task. This was achieved by telling subjects beforehand the general context in which their behavior would supposedly be interpreted. For example, in one condition subjects were told that "such studies have frequently been used in the past to simulate international negotiations—cooperation and conflict—such as might occur between two nation states" (Eiser & Bhavnani, 1974, p. 95). There were four conditions. The control condition was run according to standard PDG procedures, without any reference to a general context. Subjects in the second, third, and fourth conditions were told that their behavior was supposed to be interpreted in the context of international negotiations, or economic bargaining, or interpersonal interactions, respectively.

The 80 subjects, 40 male and 40 female, were tested in groups of even numbers. The significance of the even numbers is that each subject was separated from the others, but told that he or she had been paired with an unidentified other. The subjects then went through 10 trials of the standard PDG, with the rewards allocated as shown in figure 3.2.

Figure 3.2
The PDG Reward Matrix Used by Eiser and Bhavnani

SUBJECT (2)

		Red	Black
SUBJECT (1)	Red	3,3	4,0
	Black	0,4	1,1

Subjects indicated their strategy choices by pressing either red or black counters on the same trial; then they would both receive three points or one point each, respectively. If, however, S2 pressed red and S1 pressed black, S2 would receive no points and S1 four points.

Results showed significant differences between responses across conditions, with cooperative responses being highest in the "interpersonal interaction" and "international negotiations" conditions. There were no significant differences between the responses by sex. It seems that cooperation between subjects was highest in those conditions where feelings about fair play and justice had a greater chance of being evoked, rather than in the economic bargaining or control conditions where competitive feelings were more likely to be brought to the forefront. The findings of this experiment suggest that how subjects interpret the context of the PDG can significantly influence the way they act in this experimental setting. Therefore, it is important to pay attention to Eiser and Bhavnani's suggestion that "extrapolations from the results of PDG experiments to particular kinds of real-life situations must depend for their validity at least partly on whether the subjects themselves interpret that game as symbolic of the situations in question" (1974, p. 97).

Gaming Research and Power

Although gaming research has generally focused on the interactions of parties that have equal power, there are a number of important exceptions to this general trend. For example, variations of the Deutsch and Krauss "trucking game" (1960, 1962) have been used to allow for some manipulation of power as an independent variable. This game typically involves two subjects, who are required to imagine that each is in charge of a different trucking company. They will receive a fixed sum for each trip they make to carry merchandise from point A to point B, minus their operating costs. These operating costs are calculated at a fixed rate per unit time. For example, they could receive 100 points for each trip made, minus 1 point in operating costs for each second they are on the road. Therefore, if they complete a trip in 30 seconds, they will receive 70 points. In addition to a long route, the players have the option of taking a short route.

It would obviously be more profitable for both players to take the short route, since the time each trip takes—and hence operating costs—would then be decreased. However, the short route has only one lane, and the players have to come to an agreement about taking turns using it. By placing a gate on this short route and giving one of the players control over it, the experimenter can make one player more powerful than the other. In such situations, the player in control of the gate bargains from a position of strength, since he or she can prevent the other player from using the short route. In this condition, the player with more power has been found to do better. However, a less obvious finding is that both players in this condition did less well than their counterparts in conditions where the players had equal power (see Deutsch, 1985, pp. 124–29). One interpretation of this finding is that in situations where there is a dominant power who can use threat, both parties have to dedicate some of their resources (such as time) to dealing with destructive conflict (Deutsch, 1973). As a consequence, they have less resources to invest in achieving constructive tasks—in this case, transporting merchandise from point A to point B.

Negotiation and Third-Party Intervention

The gaming tradition has also influenced research in negotiation and mediation, or third-party intervention. This area of research is becoming increasingly important, particularly in the growth of an applied social psychology (see Bercovitch, 1984; Fisher, 1983; Kressel & Pruitt, 1985; Zartman & Berman, 1982). There are at least six areas in which knowledge from mediation research has been applied: (1) industrial mediation, such as areas involving labor and management; (2) community mediation, such as areas involving racial groups; (3) family and divorce mediation; (4) public resource and environmental mediation, involving ecological issues; (5) judicial mediation; and (6) mediation at the international level, involving disputes between nation-states. Although the most spectacular and perhaps most important area of mediation is at the international level (see Rubin, 1981; Zartman & Touval, 1985), the most empirically sound data produced by research on negotiation and mediation seem to derive from the gaming tradition. We shall briefly discuss representative examples.

An important factor in bargaining situations is the medium of communication. For example, it is more difficult to communicate subtle attitudes and moods by telephone than by meeting face-to-face. This is often recognized when we postpone discussing delicate matters until we have the opportunity to talk with the person(s) involved face-to-face. Also, the degree of formality of a context influences how free we feel to express ourselves in an unreserved manner. A series of experiments by Morley and Stephenson (1969, 1970a, 1970b) investigated the influence of the medium of communication and the formality of a situation on negotiation outcomes. In these experiments the two negotiating sides always had unequal cases, so that one side was always negotiating from a position of relative strength. A 2×2 experimental design was created in which the medium of communication (face-to-face versus telephone) and degree of formality (interruption permitted in procedure versus interruption forbidden) were manipulated. The expectation was that the face-to-face and less formal conditions, by allowing more interpersonal communicating between the parties, would tend to decrease the chances of victory for the party with the stronger case. This expectation was confirmed. That is, the more opportunity there was for the personal characteristics of the negotiators to enter the situation, the less outcomes depended upon the actual strength of the bargaining case of each side.

Consistent with this finding, Stephenson and Kniveton (1978) demonstrated that a seating position that facilitated interpersonal nonverbal communication decreased the chances of a party with the stronger case exploiting its advantage. At one level these findings might seem trivial, since surely negotiations on such important matters as arms control should not be influenced by such "unimportant" factors as the seating positions of the negotiating sides. However, we need only recall the long and heated debates that the United States and the Vietcong had about the shape of the negotiating table for the Vietnam peace settlement to remind ourselves that negotiators themselves do in fact often give high priority to such apparently trivial issues as seating arrangements

Gaming Experiments and Intergroup Behavior

When evaluating gaming experiments, which invariably involve two-person interactions, we should keep in mind that these situations are also supposed to represent instances of intergroup and even international interactions, since both individuals and groups are assumed to behave in similar ways under similar conditions: "I am asserting that nations as well as individuals acquire information, make decisions, and take actions, and that they will act in similar ways under similar conditions" (Deutsch, 1969a, p. 1091). Although there has been much criticism of this kind of extrapolation from the level of interpersonal to that of intergroup processes (for instance, see Tajfel, 1972b), there have been few attempts to investigate the effect of increasing the numbers of participants in the basic two-person experimental game, so that it becomes intergroup rather than interpersonal. A study that did focus on this issue was conducted by Stephenson and Brotherton (1975); it involved negotiations between two mining supervisors on one side of an issue that concerned their work role and two persons on the opposing side. Whereas in the situation involving only two persons a compromise position would be reached, with each participant willing to move closer to the position of the other, interactions involving groups of two persons led to outright victory for one of the groups. Also, the nature of the debates was influenced by increased size. There was less tendency to avoid argument and conflicting views, and more effort to achieve a clear decision on the issue.

Stephenson and Brotherton's (1975) findings suggest that, under certain conditions, people tend to be more competitive in the intergroup than in the interindividual context. This finding is in agreement with those of a number of other experiments using the PDG paradigm that have been carried out to compare intergroup and intragroup game playing (for instance, Wilson & Kayatani, 1968; Wilson & Wong, 1968). In these experiments, two teams of two subjects each play against each other in the PDG for rewards; then the two members of each team play a similar game to settle how their winnings will be divided. Thus, each intergroup trial is followed by an intragroup trial. By comparing the responses of subjects when they play as part of a team, in an intergroup situation, with their responses when they play alone against a single other, differences between cooperative and competitive behavior in the intergroup and intragroup context are assessed. Results suggest that people are more competitive in the intergroup context.

CRITICAL REVIEW OF RCT

RCT has a number of important strengths that ensure it a central place in the field of intergroup relations. First, RCT is group oriented and has led to research that deals with genuine group interactions and intergroup processes. The classic example of this is Sherif's (1966) series of experiments, whose importance is derived mainly from their truly intergroup nature. Second, RCT makes logical sense and conforms to our everyday understanding about why there might be conflict between groups. That is, it makes intuitive sense that groups with real conflicts of material interests should experience greater potential conflict than groups whose material interests do not conflict.

However, RCT and the research it has stimulated tend also to have a number of weaknesses that should be mentioned. These weaknesses concern (1) the definition of conflict; (2) the assumption that all conflict is bad; (3) the treatment of minority groups; (4) the subjects typically used in research stimulated by RCT; (5) the lack of concern for open groups; (6) the neglect of power as an issue; and (7) the emphasis upon psychological solutions to problems arising out of material conflicts of interest. We shall briefly review each of these weaknesses in turn.

First, the area of conflict research is plagued with the problem of defining conflict. At one extreme, "realistic conflict" has meant competition for points between subjects who have just been introduced to each other and are taking part in brief experimental games, while at the other extreme, it has meant a life-and-death struggle between nations, with the possibility of atomic war as the outcome. Clearly, when interpretations of conflict and its mode of operationalization in research are so varied, and particularly when the consequences of conflict are so different—from losing points in a game to suffering an atomic war—extrapolations from one level of analysis to another should be undertaken with great caution.

Second, there has been a tendency in RCT to assume that all conflict is necessarily wrong and must be avoided. This generalization has been accompanied by a tendency to extrapolate from conflict at the interpersonal level to conflict at the intergroup and international levels. In the editorial in the first issue of the *Journal of Conflict Resolution*, in which much of the gaming research is published, the editors say:

It [conflict] occurs in many different situations: among members of a family, between labour and management, between political parties, and even within a single mind, as well as among nations. Many of the patterns and processes which characterize conflict in one area also characterize it in others. . . . Price wars and domestic quarrels have much the pattern of an arms race. Frustration breeds aggression both in the individual and in the state. (*Journal of Conflict Resolution*, 1957, *1*[1], p. 2)

Very little experimental research has been carried out to test the assumption that "the patterns and processes which characterize conflict in one area also characterize it in others." The meager evidence that exists (for example, Stephenson & Brotherton, 1975) suggests that it is an invalid assumption, at least in certain conditions.

While the "peacekeeping" concern to which RCT has led should be applauded, the use of terms such as "war" and "peace" in connection with interpersonal behavior and groups, such as labor and management in industry, can be justly criticized. The subtitle of the *Journal of Conflict Resolution* is *A Quarterly for Research Related to War and Peace*, and the journal was launched in 1957 with the words "By far the most important practical problem facing the human race today is that of international relations—more specifically, the prevention of global war" (*Journal of Conflict Resolution*, 1975, *1*[1], p. 1). In this first issue we find an article by Schelling (1957) titled "Bargaining, Communication, and Limited War," and one by Douglas (1957) titled "The Peaceful Settlement of Individual and Intergroup Disputes." In both cases, the implication is that just as peace must be preferred to war at the global level, so harmony must be preferred to conflict at the interpersonal and intergroup level.

However, under certain conditions conflict can have constructive and positive consequences. This is particularly true from the perspective of disadvantaged groups. For example, a disadvantaged group experiencing prejudice and exploitation at the hands of an advantaged group might have no choice but to resort to conflict in order to achieve greater equality. To label such conflict "harmful" and to show a bias for peace and harmony in such a situation might strengthen the position of the advantaged group and thus allow the exploitation to continue.

Since war is "wrong" and since humans are rational, thinking beings, it follows that war comes about as a result of judgmental errors. Thus Deutsch talks about the United States "blundering" into the "atrocities and stupidities of the war in Vietnam" (1969a, p. 1087), and about the vicious circle of inaccurate perceptions and misunderstandings that leads to increased destructive conflict (1973). Since human behavior is determined by the world people perceive (Deutsch, 1962, p. 101), and since inaccurate perceptions lead to hostility and conflict, the psychologist, as peacemaker, has the task of helping to achieve accurate perceptions and rational thinking. Such accurate, rational thinking would lead humans to give less importance to differences of interest and goals that can be achieved independently, and more priority to superordinate goals.

It is in this connection that the normative and theoretical underpinnings linking the work of Sherif and others (such as Blake et al., 1964) with gaming research become clear. In both instances, the best solution that subjects can achieve—from the perspective of the experimenters—is to perceive that they are better off cooperating than fighting, and to work toward superordinate goals. In the typical gaming research experiment, only when both subjects act cooperatively do they achieve maximum joint rewards. Thus, this fits Sherif's definition of superordinate goals. If one subject acts cooperatively and the other competitively, then the cooperative subject is "exploited" and will probably try to retaliate by a competitive move on the next trial. This vicious circle could lead to the destructive conflict Deutsch describes (1973), with negative outcomes for both parties.

A third criticism is that the truly psychological implications of RCT remain unexplored, particularly as they relate to minority groups. Given the presence of real differences of group interests, what are the factors that lead minority groups to perceive themselves as groups with distinct and different interests in some conditions, and not in others? It seems to be the case that in some situations minority groups do perceive themselves to have distinct and different interests, yet their relationship with the majority group remains one of cooperation rather than conflict—despite the absence of perceived superordinate goals. What are the psychological factors influencing this situation? In some conditions, minorities enter into conflict with majorities that are far more powerful and cannot possibly be defeated—what is their rationale and how do they perceive success? These are examples of questions that reflect the psychological implications of RCT, but remain unexplored partly because of the normative approach that makes the assumption that conflict is bad and aims to resolve conflict, while neglecting the real conflicts of interest that are assumed to be the cause of conflict.

While the idea that war is bad and should be avoided is endorsed by most researchers, the notion that all conflict is bad does not receive universal approval (see Plon, 1974); nor should it, when we consider the often conflicting interests of minority and majority groups. The present socioeconomic structure in both developed and developing societies is such that the allocation of resources among various groups is unequal. Minority groups attempting to improve their position in terms of power, wealth, status, and the like are generally opposed by majority groups, who in turn are attempting to maintain or improve their advantaged position. In this situation, the avoidance of conflict means support for the status quo, and thus the maintenance of majority-group superiority. The tendency for researchers to regard intergroup conflict as necessarily wrong and something that should be avoided has, therefore, led to support for majority-group interests—although this support is not always explicit or even intended.

Social psychologists have tended to study intergroup processes, such as those concerning conformity and social influence, from the perspective of the majority. Moscovici (1976, 1980), whose research represents an important exception to this trend, clarifies this issue and points researchers in a new direction.

The psychology of social influence has, until now, been based on a psychology of conformity. . . . It has been fashioned and considered from the point of view of the majority, authority, and social control. The time is ripe for a new orientation; an orientation towards a psychology of social influence which will also be a psychology of innovation . . . a psychology which will be thought out and fashioned from the point of view of the minority, the deviant, and of social change. (Moscovici, 1976, p. 2)

However, in practice this "new orientation" has had negligible influence on research. The small upsurge of interest in minority-group strategies (see Mugny, 1984) that came about during the late 1960s and 1970s was probably influenced by the outcome of American involvement in Vietnam. The determined policy of North Vietnam in its long war against the French and then the United States, which resulted in the final withdrawal of the United States from South Vietnam, dramatically illustrated what a minority could achieve in the face of a relatively powerful majority group.

A fourth point is that the subjects in gaming experiments are typically undergraduate students, while the persons who participate in the vicious circle of threat and counterthreat at the international level are national leaders. Deutsch's tendency to extrapolate from the results of gaming experiments to the context of international relations can be criticized on the grounds of sampling procedures: the populations from which subjects are selected are very different from the populations to which the experimental results are applied. In order to achieve results that can be used to interpret the actions taken by key decision makers, subjects should be selected from the population of key decision makers. This criticism applies less to Sherif, who has been far more careful in interpreting and going beyond his experimental results. However, in assessing Sherif's intergroup research, we should keep in mind that he used schoolboys aged 11–12 as subjects. This population is probably exceptional in its inclinations toward intergroup competitiveness, since a major part of school and social life for this age group of boys in North America consists of teamwork and team competitions.

A fifth critical point is that Sherif's findings would probably have proved even more insightful if the groups involved had been open, rather than closed, so that members had an exit option. This would have increased the parallel with real-life situations, where one of the options open to people is to drop out and actively rebel against the system and its competitive "games." As we noted in chapter 1, the tendency has been for researchers to neglect the exit option and to include only closed groups in their experimental studies.

A sixth criticism is that the almost exclusive concern of researchers with groups of equal power has been accompanied by a neglect of power as a subject for social psychological study (for a review of some exceptions, see Ng, 1980, 1982). However, although differences of intergroup power have received negligible research attention, power differences between group members are, at least implicitly, central to the research. Much gaming research, particularly that concerned with bargaining behavior, attempts to illuminate the processes involved when group leaders, such as heads of governments and representatives of labor and management, meet to negotiate their differences in a realistic conflict situation. These leaders have the power to take decisions on behalf of their group members; also, their status and influence tend to be higher than those of other group members.

Finally, while offering a materialistic account of why conflicts arise, RCT has led to research that offers psychological solutions for resolving conflict. Although real conflicts of interest are assumed to be the cause of conflict, the resolution of conflict is seen to come about best by changes in the perceptions of the conflicting parties, so that they view superordinate goals to be their priority. Thus, the conflicts of interest that led to the conflict in the first place need not be removed in order for peaceful relations to be achieved, but they must be superseded by superordinate goals.

CONCLUSION

RCT has probably influenced social psychological research on intergroup behavior more than any other theory. This influence is constructive in that it has led social psychologists, who tend to ignore the larger social context of the individual's behavior, to focus attention on real conflicts of interest as "the" source of conflict. The concern to prevent global war, which inspired much of both fieldwork and experimental gaming research guided by RCT, is to be applauded. The resolution of international conflict is undoubtedly an important applied task for social psychologists. But putting an end to exploitation is arguably an even more important task, especially if we adopt the premise that conflict arises out of real conflicts of interest. Disadvantaged, exploited groups have real conflicts of interest with advantaged, exploiting groups, and thus there is a great need to carry out more research from their perspectives rather than the perspectives of the majority.

SUGGESTED READINGS

Axelrod, R. (1984). *The evolution of cooperation.* New York: Basic Books.
Blake, R. R., Shepard, H. A., & Mouton, J. S. (1964). *Managing intergroup conflict in industry.* Houston: Gulf.
Deutsch, M. (1973). *The resolution of conflict.* New Haven: Yale University Press.
Sherif, M. (1966). *Group conflict and cooperation: Their social psychology.* London: Routledge & Kegan Paul.

4

Social Identity Theory

Social identity theory, formalized by Tajfel and Turner (1979, 1986), has been the most important impetus for social psychological research on intergroup relations since the late 1970s (Messick & Mackie, 1989). This theory attempts to explain relations between groups from a group perspective. This characteristic sets it apart from a number of other major social psychological theories, particularly equity theory (chapter 5) and relative deprivation theory (chapter 6), that have been applied to explain intergroup relations but were not originally developed for this purpose. Even though social identity theory is nonreductionist, it is ultimately a psychological theory, since its focus is on the process of identity.

The theory assumes that individuals are motivated to achieve a positive "social identity," defined as "that part of an individual's self-concept which derives from his knowledge of his membership in a social group (or groups) together with the value and emotional significance attached to that membership" (Tajfel, 1978a, p. 63). This desire will prompt individuals to make social comparisons between the in-group and out-groups, with the ultimate aim to achieve both a *positive* and *distinct* position for the in-group. Thus, the explanation provided by social identity theory rests on psychological processes, such as identification, social comparison, and psychological distinctiveness.

In recent years social identity theory has been elaborated, and a number of new theoretical formulations have emerged. J. C. Turner (1990) proposes that there are now two social identity theories, "the original intergroup theory, which is an analysis of intergroup conflict and social change and focuses on individuals' need to maintain and enhance the positively valued distinctiveness of their ingroups compared to outgroups to achieve a positive social identity . . . and the more recent self-categorization theory . . . which represents a general theory of group processes based on the idea that shared social identity depersonalizes individual self-perception and action" (pp. x–xi). However, in addition to self-categorization theory (Turner, Hogg, Oakes, Reicher, & Wetherell, 1987), a number of other theoretical developments arising out of the social identity "tradition" established by Tajfel (1982b) are worth noting. Examples of such theoretical developments are models of self-regulation in the group (Abrams, 1990), optimal distinctiveness theory (Brewer, 1991), and the construct of ethnolinguistic vitality (Giles, Bourhis, & Taylor, 1977; Giles & Johnson, 1987). Social identity theory has also strongly influenced recent theoretical developments focusing on minority influence (Moscovici, 1985; Mugny & Pérez, 1991) and minority (versus majority) discrimination (Sachdev & Bourhis, 1984, 1985, 1987, 1990). The wide-ranging influence of the "Bristol school" that evolved out of the ideas and larger-than-life personality of the late Henri Tajfel is also evident in the work of other researchers studying identity (e.g., Breakwell, 1986, 1992), as well as in the recent "norm violation" model of intergroup relations (DeRidder & Tripathi, 1992). It is useful to review the evolution of social identity theory through considering its context.

THE CONTEXT OF SOCIAL IDENTITY THEORY

Henri Tajfel chose to throw his hospitable, European, pluralistic energies into stimulating a "European" social psychology. I think he was particularly eager to set up a base that would be distinctive to the reigning American social psychology. Bruner (1981, p. xiii)

The central proposition of social identity theory, that people desire to belong to groups that enjoy distinct and positive identities, can be used to understand how social psychology in Europe developed and why it developed the way it did (Moghaddam, 1987, 1990). Appreciating the development of social psychology in Europe is important here, for it provides insights into certain concepts that are central to social identity theory. The relationship between European and American social psychology remains an example of minority-majority relations, with European researchers having far less influence than researchers in the United States in terms of what constitutes "mainstream" social psychology. Indeed, in the global context "mainstream" is almost synonymous with U.S. social psychology as conducted in the United States.

For example, even the chapter on intergroup relations in the *Handbook of Social Psychology* (Stephen, 1985) pays little attention to European research, and particularly to Tajfel's work. This is surprising, because research on intergroup relations is more extensive and advanced in Europe compared to the United States. Stephen (1985) makes reference to Tajfel's (1970) paper in *Scientific American* and to his early ideas on a "generic norm" of in-group favoritism, but formulations of social identity theory already available at that time (e.g., Tajfel & Turner, 1979) are ignored. The reductionist treatment of intergroup relations provided in the *Handbook* (Stephen, 1985) stands in sharp contrast to the more progressive European writings on this issue (Abrams & Hogg, 1990; Billig, 1976; Hogg & Abrams, 1988; Tajfel, 1978b, 1982b, 1984; Turner & Giles, 1981). Clearly, American social psychologists seldom look beyond their own borders (Cole, 1984; Lewicki, 1982).

European social psychology has aimed to define itself as a discipline distinct from the social psychology of North America and more reflective of European social concerns and intellectual traditions. The movement took shape in the late 1960s, and its first practical outcomes were the establishment of the European Association of Experimental Social Psychology (1969), the *European Journal of Social Psychology* (1971), and the European Monographs in Social Psychology (1971). The key figure, of course, was Henri Tajfel. However, we should also record the contributions of a number of other European social psychologists to the development of social identity theory. For example, Doise (1978), from the University of Geneva, contributed in important ways to the early development of the theory. Tajfel edited a two-volume appraisal of progress in European social psychology (1984) before his death and in this way recorded the advances made in European social psychology as a distinct discipline (for a review of the history of European social psychology, see Jaspers, 1986).

Among the important European intellectual traditions that influenced the development of European social psychology and, subsequently, social identity theory were the concern for evaluating phenomena within the wider social context in which they occur, and the tendency to view society as forces in conflict rather than in cohesion. The first of these led to the attempt to "make social psychology truly social," while the latter led to a move away from what has been described as the social psychology of the "nice person" (Moscovici, 1972, p. 18) to a social psychology of competing individuals and groups struggling to enhance their own position in the context of changing social conditions.

It is not coincidental that the movement toward a European social psychology took shape in the late 1960s, at a time when radical political forces were so influential. The year 1968 has been compared with 1848, when revolutionary fervor swept through Europe and the established order in many countries was seriously challenged through ideological and violent means. When the plenary conference of the European Association of Experimental Social Psychology was held at the University of Louvain in Belgium in the spring of 1969, the concern many participants showed for seeking new paths of research and theorizing was, as Tajfel noted (1972a, p. 2), probably influenced by the recent student revolution. Just as students in many countries, particularly France, embarked upon pitched battles with an establishment they saw as corrupt and exploitative, so they challenged their teachers and demanded that science, particularly social science, be explicit in its ideology and "relevant" to the major problems of the day, such as social inequality and exploitation.

As Moscovici, another key figure in the development of European social psychology, explained:

Our disciplines do not appear to the younger generation as disinterested and objective as we claim them to be. They have taken it upon themselves to remind us of the ideological implications of what we do and its role in the preservation of the established order, as well as the absence of social criticism in our work. They blame us for finding refuge in methodology under the pretext that using adequate methods is equivalent to scientific investigation. We assert that our interest is in the problems of society. They answer that we calmly ignore social inequalities, political violence, wars, underdevelopment or racial conflict. As far as they are concerned, we are safely ensconced in the "establishment." (1972, p. 21)

In responding to this challenge, European social psychologists were motivated to evolve a distinct identity for themselves vis-à-vis North American social psychology, which had the image of being "establishment" oriented and biased toward the status quo.

The two most important features of North American social psychology against which the new European social psychology "rebelled" were the tendency to adopt reductionist explanations and the adoption of models that describe people as rational and living in cohesion. The concern for studying phenomena within the context in which they exist and providing explanations that incorporate the qualities of both the part and the whole can be traced directly to Hegel. Although some North American researchers have been influenced by this approach (see Caplan and Nelson, 1973; Ittelson, 1973; Ittelson, Proshansky, Rivlin, & Winkel, 1974, for example), North American social psychology has tended to be unaffected by it in practice.

European social psychologists aimed to achieve a distinctly different approach by focusing on the individual within the context of broad social change, so that the "social" aspects of social psychology would be given relatively greater importance, and both the part (individual) and the whole (society) could be incorporated into the model developed. Thus, Tajfel stated: "Ideally, the central issue of social psychology should be the study of psychological processes accompanying, determining, and determined by social change" (1972a, p. 4). This incorporation of wider social processes also involved an emphasis on intergroup behavior, not through reductionist approaches that focus on intra- and interpersonal behavior, but through models that deal with intergroup processes as such. The mood of Western societies in the late 1960s and the sometimes intense intergroup clashes taking place within them is undoubtedly part of the reason for the emergence of this new approach.

The widespread radical movements of the late 1960s presented social psychologists with a view that showed humankind as being neither cohesive, peaceful, nor rational, and could not be adequately explained by the model of humankind offered by major North American social psychological theories. European social psychologists increasingly felt the need to develop concepts that more accurately reflected the discord and conflict present in society. Writing about this period, Moscovici said:

I encountered . . . difficulties with some of the maxims implicit in a good deal of current research: "we like those who support us"; "the leader is a person who understands the needs of the members of his group"; "we help those who help us"; "understanding the point of view of another person promotes cooperation." This "social psychology of the nice person" was to me then—as it still is today—offensive in many ways; it had little relevance to what I knew or had experienced. Its implicit moral stand reminded me of another maxim (which is perhaps not as controversial as it appears): "it is better to be healthy and rich than to be ill and poor." I know from my own social experiences that we seek out those who differ from us and that we can identify with them; that we can love someone who is contemptuous of us; that leaders may impose themselves on others through violence and through following unremittingly their own ideas—and that often, in doing this, they are not only admired but also loved; and that, after all, is it not an opponent who often comes to know us best? (1972, pp. 18–19)

In expressing these views, Moscovici seems to have been reflecting a general concern among a group of very influential European social psychologists for a move toward a model of humankind that is more reflective of the harsher realities of life, and that is also concerned with change and conflict at the intergroup level.

In contrast with the focus on individual mobility entailed in North American social psychology, the movement toward a European social psychology has placed relatively greater emphasis on social change involving groups struggling to enhance their position vis-à-vis other groups. This change of emphasis has been made partly on ideological grounds, since it is the North American capitalist ideology that has been viewed as being at least partly responsible for the preoccupation of social psychology with competition and conflict at the level of the individual, and a neglect of competition and conflict at the level of groups, such as ethnic groups and social classes.

Our outline of social identity theory in this chapter begins not with the central concepts but, rather, with the experiments from which the theory grew. Tajfel's early research on the categorization of nonsocial stimuli and the work at Bristol on social categorization are described in some detail. This is followed by a discussion of four concepts that are central to social identity theory: social categorization, social identity, social comparison, and psychological group distinctiveness. We have chosen this particular sequence because this is precisely how events evolved: a striking set of findings from a series of experiments led to the formulation of a broadly based theory of intergroup relations.

The scope of social identity theory is quite extensive in comparison with other social psychological theories of intergroup behavior. The theory attempts to deal with the whole range of responses that disadvantaged group members might make in trying to improve their individual and group positions.

We begin our description of social identity theory by tracing its empirical underpinnings, especially the classic minimal group experiments. In the next section we outline the major theoretical constructs that define the theory.

AN OUTLINE OF SOCIAL IDENTITY THEORY

Tajfel's Early Work on Categorization

Much of Tajfel's early work was on the cognitive basis of categorization, using nonsocial stimuli. His most lasting contribution to social psychology may be his elaboration of certain continuities, from the nonsocial to the social setting, of a number of consequences of categorization. In explaining the nature of these continuities, it is useful first to clarify the functions of categorization, then to proceed to explain in some detail an example of the experiments Tajfel carried out on the categorization of nonsocial stimuli. We conclude this section by clarifying how the experiments using nonsocial stimuli are linked to the later work on social categorization and intergroup behavior carried out by Tajfel, Turner, and others at Bristol.

The Categorization of Nonsocial Stimuli. The categorization process has the function of organizing in fundamental ways the information we acquire from the environment. People actively select information from the environment and simplify the task of processing it by ignoring certain dissimilarities and giving priority to, or exaggerating, certain similarities between objects. This process orients and assists our actions. For example, if we are camping and we need a hammer with which to knock tent pegs into the ground, we might start searching for any hard object, such as a piece of wood or a stone, to serve our purpose. During our search we may ignore many dissimilarities that objects may have, such as what they are made of or their shape, and concentrate on those qualities that would make them equivalent to one another for the purpose of hammering a tent peg. That is, there are certain features that objects should have in order to fit into our category of "objects that can serve the purposes of a hammer." By ignoring those characteristics that are irrelevant to it, we are speeding up our search enormously. This process leads to our simplifying the environment, a simplification that is essential if we are to be able to process effectively, and act upon, the potentially endless amount of information available to us. While there are contradictory accounts of how information is processed (compare Bruner, Goodnow, and Austin, 1956, with Neisser, 1967, for example), the highly important role that categorization plays in this process is generally agreed upon.

Through a series of experiments (Tajfel, 1957, 1959; Tajfel & Wilkes, 1963), Tajfel developed the idea that the categorization of nonsocial stimuli leads to perceived uniformity within individual categories and distinctiveness between them. In one experiment (Tajfel & Wilkes, 1963), the stimuli used were a series of eight lines that differed in length by a constant ratio. Subjects were asked to estimate the length of each line in turn. There were three experimental conditions. For subjects in condition 1, the four shorter lines were labeled A, and the four longer lines were labeled B. For subjects in condition 2, the lines were randomly assigned to A and B. In condition 3, the lines were presented without labels.

The series of eight lines was presented to subjects a number of times in successive random orders. Subjects in condition 1, therefore, became increasingly familiar with the relationship between labels and lengths of lines. Results showed that they exaggerated the differences in lengths between categories A and B considerably more than those in the two control groups. Also, as the subjects in condition 1 became more familiar with the relationship between the lengths of lines and labels (A and B), they further exaggerated the differences between the categories. There was also a tendency for subjects in condition 1 to judge the lines within each category to be more similar to one another than did the subjects in the other two conditions.

The Categorization of Social Stimuli. There seem to be certain outcomes of the categorization process that are present both when the stimuli categorized are social and when they are nonsocial. These "continuities" link Tajfel's earlier work on the categorization of nonsocial stimuli and his later work on social categorization and intergroup behavior. Categorizing people does, however, have some unique properties.

In categorization experiments using nonsocial stimuli, subjects do not necessarily relate to the categories through reference to a system of norms and values. For example, in the Tajfel and Wilkes (1963) experiment, the eight lines did not have social significance for the subjects, and subjects did not act upon any system of social norms and values when estimating their lengths. However, if the stimuli used in a categorization experiment were social, then the subjects would be linked to them through values and norms. For example, if subjects were given the task of grouping various other people into different categories, then the choices they made might depend on the values they ascribed to these various others. A subject who was racially prejudiced probably would not place whites in the same group as blacks because of the different values he or she ascribed to blacks and whites.

Another factor that intervenes when subjects are asked to categorize people is that they sometimes identify with certain of the people they are categorizing, and their own statuses thus become affected by the choices they make. For example, if we take the case of the racially prejudiced white person, when grouping black and white others, such a person would identify with the white group, and any racial mixing that took place would, from that person's perspective, negatively affect his or her status. Such a person would try to make sure not to mistakenly place any blacks in the white group, with which he or she identifies. This concern with racial purity has been evident in various societies, the classic examples being Nazi Germany and, until recently, South Africa. Pettigrew, Allport, and Barnett (1958) used an innovative experimental method to demonstrate this type of behavior in the context of South Africa.

Pettigrew et al. (1958) presented pairs of photographs of faces and asked subjects to identify the race of each. The subjects were Afrikaners, English-speaking whites, Coloreds, Indians, and Africans. Through using the perceptual phenomenon of binocular rivalry, which was caused in this case by showing a picture of a different face to each eye, considerable uncertainty was introduced into the task of recognizing the race or ethnic group of each face. The Afrikaner subjects (the dominant group in South Africa, who assume themselves to be racially superior) showed much greater caution in placing faces in the European category and a greater tendency to place faces in the "extreme" group of African rather than the "neutral" group of Colored or Indian. It seems that, rather than risking one of the non-Europeans slipping through and endangering the purity of their own white group, the Afrikaners preferred to adopt a strategy of overexclusion from the European group and overinclusion in the African group. They were, it seems, acting to achieve as clear-cut a distinction as possible between their own group, which they assumed to be high-status, and low-status others. They achieved this distinction by using the extreme category of African more often, so that the categories that fall between African and European (Coloreds and Indians) became less populated.

The experiment by Pettigrew et al. (1958) demonstrates in a rather dramatic manner two points we wish to clarify at this stage: first, when people are grouping other people, values and norms influence their choices, and second, when the person making choices is identified with one of the groups, his or her own status is affected by the outcomes of the groupings. When this identification takes place, there seems to be a tendency to try to achieve intergroup distinctiveness.

The prejudiced behavior of subjects in the study conducted by Pettigrew et al. (1958) took place in a context rich with social norms and values. But what would be the minimum conditions required for subjects to show a desire for intergroup differentiation? For example, if the subjects did not know the identity of others they were categorizing, but only that some of these others belong to the same group as themselves, and some belong to different groups, how would they react? Would this be a sufficient basis for subjects to identify with their own group and try to differentiate between it and the other groups? As we saw from our discussion of realistic conflict theory in chapter 3, the usual conditions for intergroup conflict include two groups that are clearly categorized according to some important value dimensions and that have a history of competition and confrontation over some important resources. What if these conditions were only minimally met? Following Tajfel and Wilkes's (1963) experiment that used eight lines as stimuli and found that labeling the four shorter lines A and the four longer ones B leads to intercategory differentiation and perceived intracategory uniformity, would the mere fact that unidentified others are labeled A and B, and the subject is in B (for example), lead to the subject's differentiating between the two categories? These are the kinds of questions that led to the now-classic minimal group experiments.

The minimal group experiments on social categorization and intergroup behavior carried out by Tajfel and his associates during the late 1960s and 1970s are simple in design, but complex in the method they adopt for identifying and measuring intergroup bias. We describe the minimal group paradigm, and for a detailed description of the complex matrices that are used as dependent measures in this paradigm, the reader is referred to Bourhis, Sachdev, and Gagnon, 1994. The minimal group experiments were designed to isolate social categorization as an independent variable and measure its influence, if any, on intergroup behavior. There are two distinct parts to the minimal group experiment: during the first part, social categorization takes place on a trivial criterion and unidentified others are placed in either the same category as the subject or in a different one; in the second part, subjects allocate rewards to these others, some of whom are in the same category as themselves.

Tajfel and his associates set out to define an intergroup situation where two social categories are created but where none of the other conditions usually associated with intergroup conflict are present. Thus, unlike earlier research demonstrating that arbitrary categorization can lead to intergroup bias (Rabbie & Horwitz, 1969), and that even groups in "noncompetitive" situations might show in-group favoritism (Ferguson & Kelley, 1964; Sherif, 1966), the groups used by Tajfel and his associates were designed to be truly "minimal." That is, for example, none of the conditions associated with realistic conflict as discussed in chapter 3 should be operating. The criteria they set included the following: there should be no face-to-face interaction between respondents; group membership should be anonymous; the criteria for social categorization should not be linked with rewards to be allocated between groups; the rewards should not have any utilitarian value for the person making them; respondents should have available a variety of both fair and discriminatory options for allocating rewards; and the rewards should be meaningful to respondents.

The First Minimal Group Experiment. The subjects in the first minimal group experiment (Tajfel, 1970; Tajfel, Flament, Billig, & Bundy, 1971) were 64 British schoolboys, aged 14–15. The experiment was in two main parts.

The experiment began with subjects doing a dot-estimation task. They were then assigned to one of two conditions, with different instructions. In the neutral condition, subjects were told that findings show that in dot-estimation tasks some people tend to consistently overestimate the number of dots, while others tend to consistently underestimate the number, but that these tendencies are unrelated to accuracy. In the value condition, subjects were told that some people are consistently more, and some less, accurate at dot-estimation. It was hypothesized that greater in-group favoritism would occur in the value than in the neutral condition.

In part 2, subjects were told that the experimenter wished to take advantage of their presence to conduct an investigation involving a completely different kind of judgment task. For the purpose of convenience, they would be divided into groups on the basis of their performance at dot-estimation. In fact, however, the division of subjects into groups was done on a random basis. Subjects were told their group membership privately and were not aware of the group membership of others. Next, subjects in the neutral condition were told that they would be assigned to a group on the basis of whether they underestimated or overestimated the number of dots. Those in the value condition were told that groups would be formed on the basis of dot-estimation accuracy. The more accurate would be in one group and the less accurate in another.

The second judgment task required subjects to allocate rewards to in-group and out-group members. This amounted to allocating rewards and penalties, in real money, to others who were identified only by code numbers. Subjects were taken to separate cubicles, informed privately of their own group identity, then instructed on the format for making allocations.

The most important aspects of the allocations made by subjects in this first experiment were the following:

1. On no occasion would subjects be rewarding or penalizing themselves; their choices determined only the outcomes of others.

2. They would know only the group identity, and not the personal identity, of the individuals they were rewarding.

3. The amount of money each person received would depend on how much others had rewarded him or her.

4. Everyone was guaranteed a standard sum of money for taking part in the experiment.

5. There were three types of allocation decisions: (a) subjects were allocating for two members of the in-group other than themselves; (b) subjects were allocating for two members of the out-group; (c) subjects were allocating for a member of the in-group, other than themselves, and a member of the out-group.

The results of this experiment demonstrated that when subjects were faced with a choice between an in-group member and an out-group member, they favored the in-group at the expense of the out-group. The nature of this discrimination did not differ significantly between the two (value and neutral) conditions. On the choices where subjects were giving rewards to two out-group members or two in-group members, they showed no bias and instead tended to allocate rewards equally. On the basis of the discrimination showed by the subjects, which favored the in-group and was biased against the out-group, Tajfel and his associates concluded that group formation and discriminatory intergroup behavior had developed as a result of social categorization per se, without the presence of any of the normal conditions associated with intergroup bias.

Extensions of the Basic Minimal Group Findings. By the mid-1970s considerable evidence had been gathered to support the proposition that social categorization per se, as far as it could be isolated experimentally, can, under certain conditions, be a sufficient basis for intergroup discrimination (for example, Allen & Wilder, 1975; Billig, 1973; Billig & Tajfel, 1973; Doise, Csepeli, Dann, Gouge, Larsen, & Ostell, 1972; Tajfel, 1974a; Tajfel et al., 1972; J. C. Turner, 1975). In explaining these findings, Tajfel and his associates emphasize social categorization and social comparison processes as the psychological processes "intrinsic to or stimulated merely by ingroup-outgroup divisions which tend to create discriminatory social relations" (J. C. Turner, 1981, p. 77). However, among the features of the minimal group paradigm that we need to examine more closely are the relative importance of self versus group interests and the importance of the "trivial" basis for social categorization.

An important question that arises with respect to the minimal group paradigm is to what extent subjects in experiments are showing bias toward self-interest rather than group interest. This issue was not tested by

Tajfel et al. (1971) because subjects were placed in a position where they could reward only the in-group or the out-group directly; there was no opportunity to reward the self directly. However, a number of studies were later carried out to test the relative importance of self versus group interests in the minimal group context (J. C. Turner 1975, 1978a; Turner, Brown, & Tajfel, 1979).

In the first experiment (J. C. Turner 1975, 1978a), subjects first indicated their degree of liking for a set of pictures. Similarity between subjects was defined in terms of these aesthetic preferences. In the second part of the experiment, subjects awarded money to others. There were three conditions. In condition 1, the control condition, there was no explicit mention of groups by the experimenter. Subjects would allocate rewards to themselves and similar/dissimilar others (similarity was on the basis of picture preferences). Each person was to receive all the money allocated to himself or herself. In condition 2, subjects were ostensibly categorized on the basis of similarity (on picture preferences). They made choices for themselves and others, the others being in-group and out-group members. Each person was to receive all the money awarded to himself or herself. In condition 3, subjects were ostensibly categorized into two groups on the basis of similarity (on picture preferences). However, they were told they would receive an equal share of the money their in-group received.

Thus, in condition 1 there was no categorization; in condition 2 there was categorization, but the individual could reward himself or herself directly; in condition 3 there was categorization, but the individual could not reward himself or herself directly (only the in-group could be rewarded). The results demonstrated that whenever possible, subjects were biased toward themselves. Only in the third condition, where self-interest was directly linked to that of the group, was there in-group favoritism. The predictions of how subjects would like others, if their identities were revealed, also showed that there was in-group favoritism only in condition 3.

The same trend of bias toward the self, rather than the in-group, was found by J. C. Turner in a second experiment (1975, 1978a). However, this bias was modified when subjects first allocated money to in-group and out-group members, and afterward had the chance to allocate rewards to themselves directly. It seems that when subjects had the chance to act in terms of group membership, they developed some level of loyalty to the in-group; this meant that they were prepared to make sacrifices and modify their bias toward the self in order to reward the whole group. However, their basic self-bias persisted.

On the same theme, Turner et al. (1979) tested the hypothesis that subjects would be willing, to some degree, to sacrifice group and personal monetary profit in order to achieve positive group distinctiveness. Results reveal that some degree of sacrifice was made in the predicted manner, but that the trend of bias toward the self found by Turner (J. C. 1975, 1978a) still existed.

These findings are of fundamental importance, since they seem to indicate that subjects have a preference for improving the position of the self, although the strength of this bias can be modified when group loyalty develops. This kind of behavior seems to be present in real work settings when individual workers agree to place the interests of an entire labor union ahead of their individual interests and move toward better working conditions through collective action. That is, instead of aiming for rewards that might benefit them more individually, workers are influenced by group loyalty and agree to make their individual demands subservient to collective needs.

Exploring Sociostructural Factors through the Minimal Group Paradigm

The hallmark of European social psychology, and social identity theory in particular, has been the attempt to achieve a truly *social* psychology. The writings of Tajfel and other European researchers (see the representative chapters in Tajfel, 1984) make clear that a concern for sociostructural factors, such as group power and status, is part of what they believe constitutes a social explanation, as opposed to simply a psychological or "reductionist" explanation, of social behavior. The motivation to incorporate sociostructural factors such as power has led social identity theory to be primarily concerned with groups of unequal power. It is rather ironic, then, that the initial minimal group studies that led to the theory involved groups of equal power.

The first attempts to build upon social identity theory by developing the role of sociostructural factors appeared in the "ethnolinguistic vitality" construct of Giles, Bourhis, and Taylor (1977). Giles et al. (1977) defined vitality as "that which makes a group likely to behave as a distinctive and active collective entity in intergroup situations" (p. 308). They proposed that vitality is shaped by three sociostructural factors: demography, institutional support/control, and status. However, these theoretical formulations were not at that time tested through the minimal group paradigm. A series of studies by Ng (1980, 1982) on groups with unequal power demonstrated that groups with greater power tend to discriminate more than those with equal or less power, but these studies did not meet the criteria of the minimal group paradigm.

A series of experiments by Bourhis and Sachdev (Bourhis, 1992; Sachdev & Bourhis, 1984, 1985, 1987, 1991), however, have used the minimal group paradigm to examine the role of sociostructural factors in intergroup relations. In these studies, group power was defined as the degree of control a group has over its own fate and that of out-groups, with "fate" operationalized as the amount of resources a group is allocated. Extremes of power were created by establishing conditions in which the power of the in-group and the out-group could range from 0 percent control (no power) to 100 percent (absolute power), with 30 percent (low power) and 70 percent (high power) lying between these two extremes.

Sachdev and Bourhis (1984, 1985) confirmed Ng's (1982) finding that members of dominant groups discriminate more than do members of "subordinate" groups. However, they also found that discrimination by "high power" groups was more extreme than that by "absolute power" groups. The "absolute power" groups were more discriminating than "no power" and "low power" groups, and at least as discriminating as the "equal power" groups. The "absolute power" groups seemed to be more secure in their positive and distinct social identity, and thus more willing to allow out-groups to "bask in the glow" of their positive identity. An example of this "benevolent paternalism" in real life might be the upper-class members of the white Anglo-Saxon Protestant (WASP) majority in North America who show liberal attitudes toward ethnic minorities, whereas lower-class WASPs tend to be relatively less tolerant of ethnic minorities (Lambert & Taylor, 1986, 1990).

In a second series of experiments, Bourhis and Sachdev (Bourhis, 1992; Sachdev & Bourhis, 1987, 1991) used the minimal group paradigm to explore the relationship between gender and power, both in stable and unstable intergroup contexts. The most important finding was that it is the position of individuals in the power structure, rather than their "dispositional characteristics" as males and females (as suggested by J. A. Williams, 1984), that determines intergroup discrimination. The importance of sociostructural factors is also underlined by the finding that subordinate and powerless groups will discriminate against dominant groups in unstable intergroup contexts. In earlier studies (e.g., Sachdev & Bourhis, 1984), powerless groups did not discriminate, because the intergroup context was stable and powerless groups had nothing to gain by discriminating. Bourhis and Sachdev experimentally demonstrated that instability in the social structure brings the possibility of change and the betterment of minority conditions, and it is in such conditions that minorities are more likely to discriminate and perhaps mobilize.

The "Trivial" Basis of Social Categorization in the Minimal Group Paradigm

An important aim of Tajfel and his associates was to minimize the importance of the criteria used as the basis for social categorization in the minimal group paradigm. Criteria typically used as a basis for social categorization have been performance on a dot-estimation task (Tajfel, 1970) and aesthetic preferences (J. C. Turner, 1975). These have been referred to by Tajfel as being "unimportant" (Tajfel, 1978d, p. 439) and "trivial" (Tajfel, 1978c, p. 77), and similar descriptions have been used by J. C. Turner (1981, p. 75). However, it needs to be appreciated that in this context terms such as "trivial" and "unimportant" are not correct in a literal sense. In terms of the influence that they have on intergroup behavior, such criteria cannot be said to be "trivial" or "unimportant," since they are sufficient to evoke strong and consistent ingroup bias. Indeed, there is evidence to suggest that the effect of such criteria can be as powerful as "important" criteria in the context of the minimal group paradigm (Moghaddam & Stringer, 1986).

Moghaddam and Stringer (1986) tested the hypothesis that there would be no difference between the influences of two criteria of different real-world importance when each is used independently as the only criterion for social categorization in the same minimal group setting. In condition 1, social categorization was on the basis of a dot-estimation task, a "minimal" criterion. In condition 2, social categorization was on the basis of the participants' schoolhouse system, a highly important criterion from the perspective of participants. Results showed that while participants in both conditions were biased toward the in-group, supporting the findings of Tajfel et al. (1971), there was no significant difference between the levels of bias shown across conditions. The profound impact of social categorization is underlined by the findings.

This finding is in line with evidence from field studies that suggests that individuals will ascribe importance to what may be in most contexts a "trivial" phenomenon and exaggerate certain characteristics of their in-group or of relevant out-groups in order to achieve a clearer and more meaningful basis upon which to differentiate between themselves and others. From anthropological studies it is apparent that the boundaries of ethnic groups are sometimes objectively blurred, but subjectively perceived as distinct and prominent, in order to preserve and legitimize a certain status hierarchy. For example, Maquet (1961) reports that in Ruanda, the height differences between two major groups, the Tutsi and the Hutu, were emphasized and exaggerated. This exaggeration helped to achieve intergroup differentiation and also had certain value connotations. The Tutsi were the dominant group, and their exaggerated height superiority played an important part in defining and maintaining their higher social status. LeVine and Campbell (1972, pp. 81–113) provide a useful review of anthropological evidence on ethnic boundaries that reveals how in many cases the boundaries between ethnic groups can be seen as arbitrary and trivial when viewed objectively, but are ascribed importance in order to play a crucial role in interethnic differentiation.

There are also many examples from modern industrial settings where a criterion for social categorization might seem trivial from the perspective of outsiders, but assumes great importance from the perspective of group members. For example, soccer might be viewed as being "just a game," and the fact that Pat and Mick support different soccer teams might not be of great significance in the work setting. However, when they enter the soccer stadium to support their rival teams, the previously "trivial" basis for social categorization can suddenly become highly important—as demonstrated by the tragic deaths of British and Italian soccer fans at Brussels, in June 1985.

FOUR CENTRAL CONCEPTS IN SOCIAL IDENTITY THEORY

Oh, if I had done nothing simply from laziness! Heavens, how I should have respected myself, then. I should have respected myself because I should at least have been capable of being lazy; there would have been one quality, as it were, positive in me. . . . Question: What is he? Answer: A sluggard; how pleasant it would have been to hear that of oneself! It would mean that I was positively defined . . . I should then be a member of the best club by right, and should find my occupation in continually respecting myself.

Feodor Dostoevsky (1821–81)
Notes from the Underground

The first series of results from experiments using the minimal group paradigm were interpreted by Tajfel and his associates, using the concept of "generic norm" (see Billig, 1972; Tajfel et al., 1971). This proposed the presence of a social norm of in-group favoritism that subjects perceived to be relevant to the minimal group situation. However, an explanation based on the concept of generic norm was of little value once the behavior under question became other than simple in-group favoritism. Thus, the need for an explanatory model that could account for more complex behavior patterns in the minimal group and other contexts led to the evolution of social identity theory.

Four major concepts developed out of the minimal group experiments: (1) social categorization, the segmentation of the world so as to impose an order on the environment and provide a locus of identification for the self; (2) social identity, that part of the individual's self-concept that derives from knowledge of his or her membership in a social group, together with the value and emotional significance attached to that membership; (3) social comparison, the process through which characteristics of the in-group are compared to those of the out-group; and (4) psychological group distinctiveness, assumed to be the state desired by individuals in which the in-group has an identity that is perceived by the group members as being both distinct and positive vis-à-vis relevant comparison groups. In briefly elaborating upon the intellectual roots of these concepts, we shall argue that psychological group distinctiveness is the most innovative and probably the most important contribution made by social identity theory to social psychology. Since we have already discussed social categorization at some length in the context of the minimal group experiments, we shall not elaborate further on that concept at this stage.

Social Identity

In social identity theory, the knowledge that one belongs to certain groups and the value attached to group membership, in positive and negative terms, represent the individual's social identity. The two essential features of the concept are that group membership is viewed from the subjective perception of the individual, and that the value-laden nature of group membership is highlighted and given importance.

The idea that groups have social values and that one acquires certain values through group membership has influenced research in social psychology since its early days. This is demonstrated, for example, by the early studies reporting the phenomenon of black children devaluing their own group and preferring the white out-group (Lasker, 1929), a phenomenon later described as "misidentification." By describing this behavior as "misidentification" (see Milner, 1975), researchers are suggesting that subjects are defining their group membership in a way that does not correspond to the material realities of the group situation, with the aim of being part of the high-status out-group. These processes—the subjective structuring of the social environment and the need to belong

MISIDENTIFICATION

to a positively valued group—are also incorporated in social identity theory.

In postulating that humankind has a need to achieve a positive social identity, Tajfel and his colleagues were working according to a long-accepted idea that people desire to be positively evaluated (Goffman, 1963). This desire seems to be responsible for the preference people have been shown to have for favorable rather than accurate evaluations of themselves (Eiser & Smith, 1972). People's attitude seems to be "Don't tell me the truth about how I am doing, just tell me how well I am doing." It is interesting that much of the critical debate about the "cooperative subject" and "experimenter bias" in the psychology experiment has centered on the assumption that subjects wish to be favorably evaluated by the experimenter (A. G. Miller, 1972). Critics of the experimental approach have argued that subjects look for cues in the experimental situation that will tell them what the experimenter expects them to do, then comply with these expectations because they want to be favorably evaluated.

Thus, the basic proposition that individuals are motivated to achieve a positive social identity is supported by evidence from a wide range of studies. Social identity theory has extended this idea to the intergroup level, in order to propose that individuals are motivated to belong to positively evaluated groups. This extension opens the way to explorations of possible behavioral strategies that might be adopted when an individual perceives his or her social identity as inadequate.

Social Comparison

The only "reality" tests that matter with regard to group characteristics are tests of social reality. The characteristics of one's group as a whole (such as its status, its richness or poverty, its skin color, or its ability to reach its aims) achieve most of their significance in relation to perceived differences from other groups and the value connotation of these differences. (Tajfel, 1978a, p. 66)

While the desire for a positive social identity is viewed by social identity theory as the psychological "motor" behind the individual's actions in the intergroup context, the social comparison process is seen as the means through which the individual obtains an assessment of his or her group's social position and status. The role of social comparison as an explanatory concept in social psychology has gained considerable importance since Festinger (1954) introduced his theory of social comparison. Festinger concerned himself only with comparisons of opinions and abilities on which, it was hypothesized, people need to evaluate themselves. The motivation for such evaluations, he argued, was the need to reduce uncertainty and achieve accuracy in self-evaluation.

However, there is an impressive body of evidence to suggest that social comparisons involve much more than opinions and abilities (see Manis, 1972, for example). Festinger's assumption that social comparison is a less preferred means of self-evaluation than "objective" comparison and is used only when objective comparison is not available is negated by evidence (R. L. Miller, 1977). In line with these more recent findings, Tajfel and his associates have assumed a far more extensive range of application for social comparison processes than did Festinger. More specifically, they have assumed that it is through the social comparison process that individuals achieve an understanding of the relative status and value of their own group and, thus, the status and value they acquire through membership in their group. Consequently, Tajfel and his associates have proposed that social comparisons at the intergroup level play an important role in shaping the actions of individuals.

Psychological Group Distinctiveness

As an alternative to the "nice person" model of humankind, European social psychologists could rely upon an intellectual tradition, influenced by Marx and Freud, that presents a model of self-centered, irrational humankind struggling to improve their position in a conflict-based society. Such human beings would show an almost neurotic concern with their own identity, and one of their key traits would be an idiosyncratic view that shows the self in a positive light. The participation of such persons in intergroup life would be characterized by competition rather than cooperation, and by a strong desire to achieve distinctiveness, to stand apart from other groups, rather than to converge and become more similar. In social identity theory it is postulated that group members will desire to achieve an identity for their group that is both distinct from, and positive in comparison with, other groups.

The idea of a need for distinctiveness had already been elaborated in biological and socioeconomic analyses; what social identity theory introduced is the idea of a need for psychological distinctiveness. The concepts "diversification of life-style," "vacant spaces," and "competition," stemming from the work of Darwin and adapted to interpret social life by Durkheim (1960), among others, are part of a general theoretical orientation that shows the processes of competition and innovation leading to greater diversification of life-styles and to the creation or discovery of new "vacant spaces." The influence of this theoretical orientation can be seen in present-day social research (see Lemain and Kastersztein, 1971–72). For example, it influenced Mulkay and Turner's (1971) outline of the relationship among overproduction, scarce resources, and innovation in three different social settings: the saints in North African Islam, French painting in the nineteenth century, and the twentieth-century scientific community. The work of Lorenz (1966), which explores the role of aggression in achieving space allocation, is influenced by the same principles.

Ecologists and ethologists, among others, have focused upon the use of material resources, so that the vacant spaces with which they are concerned are principally food and territorial space. However, in social psychology a tendency has developed, fully crystallized in social identity theory, to extend the same principle to include the use of social identity and the need for groups to find (or create) vacant (distinct) identities for themselves to occupy. While basic biological needs are seen as a drive behind animals' moving to find the vacant spaces that make food and territory available to them, psychological motives are postulated by social identity theory to be the drive behind attempts by groups to find identities that show them in a distinct and positive light.

Through its interpretation of distinctiveness, social identity theory leads to the hypothesis that similarity can lead to discrimination rather than attraction (Brown, 1984). This hypothesis is contrary to a wide range of theories that assume a relationship between similarity and attraction, including Freudian theory and frustration-aggression theory (see chapter 2), belief congruence theory (Rokeach, 1960), balance theory (Heider, 1958), social comparison theory (Festinger, 1954), reinforcement theory (Byrne, 1971), and exchange theory (Homans, 1961). Interestingly, social identity theory was not supported by Allen and Wilder (1975), who found that out-group similarity does not influence intergroup bias in the minimal group context. However, Allen and Wilder (1975) failed to check the salience of the similarity criteria used for social categorization from the perspective of respondents. When these precautions were incorporated in the experimental design, Moghaddam and Stringer (1988) found support for social identity theory by demonstrating that out-group similarity can lead to greater, rather than less, discrimination.

SCOPE OF SOCIAL IDENTITY THEORY

Social identity theory is fairly extensive in scope, compared with other social psychological theories of intergroup behavior (see figure 4.1). Specifically, the theory attempts to provide answers to the following

Figure 4.1
Schematic Representation of Social Identity Theory

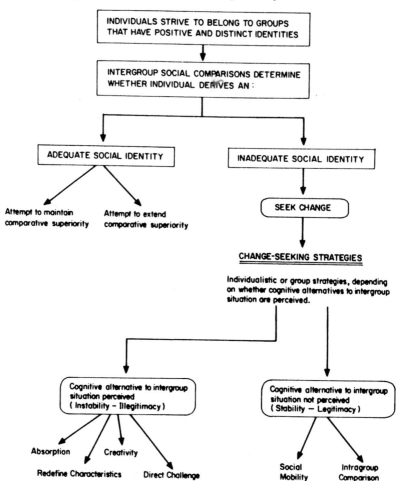

questions, some of which have already been addressed in terms of the four key concepts:

1. Why individuals desire to be members of high-status groups.
2. Why individuals desire to belong to groups that have distinct identities.
3. In what conditions group members will act as a group in order to try to change situations with which they are dissatisfied.
4. What strategies group members will adopt in order to improve their group position.

5. In what conditions and through which strategies group members will act individually in order to try to improve their own (individual) position rather than adopt group strategies to try to improve the position of the whole group.

The theory begins with the four basic concepts we have already described. Categorization is conceived of as a basic cognitive tool that allows individuals to structure the social environment and define their place in it. The knowledge that he or she belongs to certain groups and the value attached to group membership, in positive and negative terms, represent the individual's social identity. This component (social identity) forms an important part of the self-concept.

It is hypothesized that individuals wish to belong to groups that compare favorably with, and are distinct from, other groups and that lead to positive evaluations for themselves. Through intergroup comparisons, individuals will come to view their own group as psychologically distinct, and, in relation to relevant comparison groups, they will try to make the in-group more favorable. The attempt to achieve a comparatively superior position for the in-group, on the basis of valued dimensions, is the key factor leading to discriminatory intergroup behavior.

The dynamic nature of this theory becomes apparent when it deals with situations involving potential social change. Change will be desired by individuals whose group membership provides them with inadequate social identity; "inadequate" in this context refers to either a negative social identity or a social identity that is not as positive as one with which the individual is satisfied. Clearly, members of disadvantaged or minority groups will fall into this category. Members of the dominant group will want to maintain or extend their comparatively superior position. Members of the disadvantaged group will wish to achieve some change in the intergroup situation, so that their social identity can be comparatively improved. These contradictory aims result in competition and conflict, with a move by one group being met by reactions from the other group. Since only through social comparison is social identity meaningful, it is the relative position of groups that is important. Therefore, competition and conflict are seen as an essential aspect of the intergroup situation.

THE IMPORTANCE OF COGNITIVE ALTERNATIVES

An inadequate social identity is not by itself enough to motivate a group to change its position. The presence of perceived cognitive alternatives to the existing intergroup situation is required in order that a strategy for achieving social change be embarked upon. Unless members of disadvantaged groups are aware of cognitive alternatives, they will not attempt to act upon their dissatisfactions and change their intergroup situation. For example, during the late 1960s and early 1970s, a number of Third World countries saw the possibility of changing their power relations with the West by using oil as an economic weapon. Once the idea became recognized by other Third World countries, they attempted as a group to organize and to challenge the Western powers, partly by implementing the 1973 oil embargo. Whether such cognitive alternatives are perceived depends upon two factors: the extent to which individuals believe the present intergroup situation can be changed and their position in the hierarchy can be altered (stability-instability), and the extent to which the present intergroup situation and hierarchy are seen as just and fair (legitimacy-illegitimacy).

When a group with an inadequate social identity does perceive cognitive alternatives to the present intergroup situation, any one or a combination of four different strategies for achieving intergroup change may be adopted. First, a group may attempt to be absorbed into the dominant group. This strategy requires fundamental cultural and psychological change to become successful. For example, an immigrant arriving in North America might try to "lose" completely his or her original national/cultural identity and become "an American." A second strategy might be to redefine the previously negatively evaluated characteristic of the group, so that it is now positively evaluated (for instance, "Black is beautiful"). A third strategy involves the creation and adoption of new dimensions for intergroup comparison and evaluation—dimensions that have not previously been used and on the basis of which the group has a greater chance of defining itself more positively. For example, the "native peoples" of Canada might refer to their ancient traditions and cultures, in comparison with which the history of the "new Canada" might seem unimpressive. The fourth strategy involves direct competition with the dominant group. That is, a negatively evaluated group might directly challenge the position of the relatively positively evaluated group or dominant group in the status hierarchy. This strategy is most likely to lead to direct conflicts and clashes. All four strategies, adopted by a group with inadequate social identity, will lead to dominant-group members reacting and adopting strategies to maintain or increase their dominance.

When members of disadvantaged groups do not perceive cognitive alternatives to the present intergroup positions, they will do nothing to change their group situation, but may well adopt individualistic strategies to improve their individual positions. An individual may, as one strategy, attempt to exit from the disadvantaged group and join a more positively evaluated group. This is the strategy of social mobility, but it is available only when the group is an open one and exit is available as an option (cf. A. O. Hirschman, 1970). If exit is not possible because, for example, the individual cannot change his or her skin color or sex, the individual may choose the strategy of comparing himself or herself with others within his or her own group (see Smith, 1985, p. 171). This form of interpersonal intragroup comparison is less likely to lead to unfavorable evaluation of the individual.

SOCIAL MOBILITY AND SOCIAL CHANGE

This account of intergroup behavior places considerable importance on whether the individual perceives social mobility or social change as possible. Social mobility consists of a "subjective structuring of a social system" (however small or large the system may be) in which the basic assumption is that the system is flexible and permeable, that it permits a fairly free movement of the individual particles of which it consists (Tajfel, 1974b, p. 5). Social change is, at the other extreme,

the subjective modes of structuring the social system in which the individual lives. It refers basically to his belief that he is enclosed within the walls of the social group of which he is a member; that he cannot move out of his own into another group in order to improve or change his position or his conditions of life; and that therefore the only way for him to change these conditions (or for that matter, to resist the change of these conditions if he is satisfied with them) is together with his group as a whole, as a member of it rather than someone who leaves it. (Tajfel, 1974b, pp. 5–6)

Earlier in this chapter, we referred to the ideological reasons for an attempt to develop a European social psychology that places greater emphasis upon intergroup behavior and large-scale social change. The incorporation of the concept of social change reflects this European approach. Social change necessarily involves intergroup confrontation, since one group's efforts to improve its position vis-à-vis the dominant group will be met by a reaction from those attempting to maintain or improve their own relatively favorable position. Social mobility, by contrast, does not threaten the relative position of groups.

STUDIES THAT HAVE TESTED SPECIFIC HYPOTHESES

The development of social identity theory took place after the basic minimal group paradigm had been tried out—indeed, the theory was developed partly to explain the findings of experiments using the minimal group paradigm. After the formal elaboration of the theory, a number of studies were carried out to test specific hypotheses derived from it. However, some research findings seriously challenge a number of the basic propositions of social identity theory. We shall discuss two such examples. First, we discuss the findings of a study by Brown, Wade, Mathews, Condor, and Williams (1983) that tested the hypothesis, central to social identity theory, that there should be a positive association between the degree of group identification and the extent of positive intergroup differentiation.

According to social identity theory, the stronger the identification of the individual with the group, the more he or she will attempt to achieve intergroup differentiation. Brown et al. (1983) tested this prediction in three different settings: a bakery, a department store, and a paper mill. The subjects' strength of identification with the in-group was measured, and their attitudes toward other groups in the organization were assessed. On the basis of these attitudinal measurements, indexes of intergroup differentiation were computed and correlated with measures of group identification. Results showed that in different groups within each organization, very different relationships between identification and differentiation emerged, ranging from significantly negative (contradicting the prediction of social identity theory) to significantly positive (as predicted by social identity theory). The overall relationship between strength of identification and intergroup differentiation was only weakly positive. Clearly, a very central assumption entailed in social identity theory is challenged by these findings.

However, not all researchers have interpreted the propositions of social identity theory to mean that strength of identity should necessarily correlate with intergroup differentiation. For example, Smith (1985) has argued that the theory deals mainly with salience and security of social identity in intergroup relations, and he presents a case for viewing salience, security, and strength as distinct constructs. From this perspective, the findings of Brown et al. (1983) do not necessarily contradict the propositions of social identity theory.

Social identity theory proposes that whether disadvantaged group members attempt to adopt group or individualistic strategies to improve their position will depend on the presence, or absence, of cognitive alternatives. When cognitive alternatives do not exist, no possible change in the status quo is conceived. In such situations, members of disadvantaged groups are said to have secure identities (Tajfel, 1978b). The presence of cognitive alternatives depends on two factors: perceived legitimacy/illegitimacy and stability/instability. A number of experimental studies have attempted to vary levels of perceived legitimacy and stability in order to test the effects of these variables on intergroup behavior (Caddick, 1981; Commins & Lockwood, 1979a, 1979b; Turner & Brown, 1978). This relationship has also been investigated by field studies (Brown & Williams, 1983; Skevington, 1980). The findings of the experimental and field studies have not, however, been in agreement. There is evidence from the experimental studies that perceived illegitimacy of the status relationship of two groups leads to intergroup discrimination. However, this finding is not supported by evidence from field research (see Brown & Williams, 1983, for example). Also, increased perceived instability does not seem by itself to lead to greater intergroup discrimination (see, for example, Turner & Brown, 1978). This evidence seriously challenges important predictions in social identity theory.

CRITICAL REVIEW OF SOCIAL IDENTITY THEORY

Surely a theory should be evaluated not only on the basis of how valid its predictions prove to be, but also on the criterion of how effective it is in stimulating fruitful research. Social identity theory should probably be judged as being more successful on the second criterion, since it has inspired an impressive amount of important research since the mid-1970s (see Tajfel, 1978b, 1982a, 1982b, for reviews), but certain of its major predictions have been seriously challenged by research findings. Having been significantly affected by the movement to develop a distinctly European social psychology, the influence of social identity theory has tended to remain confined to Europe, although it began to make some headway in North America by the end of the 1970s (see Austin & Worchel 1979).

Among the positive attributes of this theory, there are two that are noteworthy. First, social identity theory is relatively extensive in scope, dealing with a wide range of individual and collective responses that disadvantaged group members might make to the position of their group vis-à-vis more advantaged groups (the social mobility–social change continuum). Second, social identity theory has once again placed "identity" as a, if not the, central issue of research on intergroup behavior.

By incorporating the concept of social change, social identity theory has highlighted the important role social psychologists could have in explaining the behavior of the individual in the grand arena of the social order. In particular, the concepts of legitimacy/illegitimacy and stability/instability link the perceptions people have of the social order and what they are likely to do in the face of these perceived social realities. This link is very important, but almost completely neglected by social psychologists. It bridges the gap between the sociopolitical order and the actions of individuals. For example, if I see the present social order as legitimate and stable, then I am very unlikely to try to change it through intergroup confrontation or any other means. On the other hand, I might very well try to improve my individual position by working toward such things as a better job and a bigger house, and thus effectively work to strengthen the present social order.

An important issue referred to in passing by social identity theory is where the individual gets his or her perceptions of legitimacy and stability. Social identity theory makes passing reference to ideology to answer this question, the idea being that the dominant ideology will influence the perceptions that people have in terms of legitimacy and stability. The strength of social identity theory is that it leads us at least to raise such issues, although to date it does not provide satisfactory answers to them.

Apart from the fact that some of its major assumptions seem to be challenged by research evidence, social identity theory has a number of other limitations that we should address. First, it fails to specify the priorities individuals will have in deciding what to do in the intergroup context. To clarify this point, it is useful to refer to the flowchart of the major behavior paths predicted by the theory (figure 4.1). A number of particular strategies are set out, but at each stage there is no indication of whether the individual will show a priority for one strategy or another. For example, we reviewed experimental evidence (J. C. Turner, 1975, 1978a; Turner et al., 1979) suggesting that when subjects are given a chance to reward the self directly in the intergroup setting, they will show bias toward the self, although this bias will be modified if they first make allocations to other in-group and out-group members. Given this finding, and given the individualistic, competitive nature of modern societies, particularly Western capitalist societies, we could argue that individuals will always show a priority for adopting individualistic rather than group strategies for improving their position. This could be the case regardless of whether cognitive alternatives exist. However, social identity theory does not incorporate such a leaning toward this perhaps more realistic individual mobility strategy.

To give another example of the need to specify priorities with respect to the strategies, if an individual is part of a group wanting to adopt group strategies to achieve social change, what he or she will do will depend largely on what his or her priorities are with respect to the strategies available for action (such as absorption, redefining characteristics, creativity, direct challenge). It is not enough simply to specify the strategies available and, in some cases, to go further and specify the prerequisites for being able to adopt such strategies; it is also necesary to specify how motivated people are to adopt each strategy relative to other available strategies. The priorities of individuals in the intergroup context need to be clarified.

The theory would be strengthened if it were extended to deal with another important kind of social mobility: that on a purely psychological level. According to social identity theory, when an individual does not perceive cognitive alternatives to the existing intergroup situation and has an inadequate social identity, the individual may attempt to change his or her individual situation through social mobility. That is, he or she will be motivated to move out of his or her disadvantaged in-group and attempt to gain entry to a higher-status group. If successful, the individual would acquire a more adequate social identity. The theory predicts that if exit from the group is not possible, then intragroup social comparisons will take place, so that the individual can try to achieve adequate social identity through this means. However, in many cases, minority-group members may not be able to actually leave the in-group, but they may do so on a purely psychological level. The "misidentification" of black children with the white out-group is a classic example of this kind of exit (see Milner, 1975).

Social identity theory can be criticized for being tautological in its use of the concept of salience. Indeed, Abrams (1992) views this as the "foremost" theoretical problem in the theory: "When social identity is salient individuals are said to act as group members (and should they fail to, the explanation is that social identity is not salient *enough*)" (p. 61).

Another aspect of the theory that seems tautological is its conceptualization of the link between self-esteem and discrimination (Abrams & Hogg, 1988). Social identity theory conceptualizes self-esteem as both a motive for, and a consequence of, in-group favoritism. In experimental terms, self-esteem could act as both an independent and a dependent variable in tests of social identity theory. Some experimental evidence does suggest that intergroup discrimination influences self-esteem (e.g., Lemyre & Smith, 1985), but, in a critical assessment of the literature, Hogg and Abrams (1990) concluded that the research evidence is contradictory. Hogg and Sunderland (1991) attempted to experimentally clear up the controversy and showed that depressed self-esteem motivates discrimination, whereas successful discrimination does not elevate self-esteem. However, neither social identity theory nor the studies it has generated have given adequate attention to different self-enhancement strategies used by people with high and low self-esteem (Brown, Collins, & Schmidt, 1988).

The charge has also been made that social identity theory treats individuals as "cognitive automatons" (Abrams, 1989) whose behavior is entirely regulated by their perceptions of the social world. Related to this is the criticism that although Tajfel incorporated emotions in the definition of social identity, referring to the "emotional significance attached to . . . membership" (1978a, p. 63), the role of emotions is entirely neglected in the theory. In this and other respects, the theory can be criticized for being too cognitive and simplistic. For example, social comparison processes and discrimination are not treated in their full subtlety and complexity.

Differences in identity sources for males and females are also neglected in social identity theory (Skevington & Baker, 1989). In defense of social identity theory, however, we should point out that males and females are but one example, albeit perhaps the most important example, of majority and minority groups, respectively. Thus, the theory does include males and females as examples of majority and minority groups, but it does not consider relations between the sexes to be any different in principle than any other intergroup relationship. Some theorists have attempted to progress beyond such generalizations, arguing that male social identity is "agentic," derived through competition, while female social identity is more "communal," derived through personal attachments and intimacy (Williams & Giles, 1978; J. A. Williams, 1984).

A further shortcoming of social identity theory is that it treats social categorization as an "all-or-none" phenomenon that is static, rather than as a dynamic process. Research in the "account-gathering" or "narrative" tradition has highlighted the processes of category construction and deconstruction (D. Edwards, 1991). Much of this research focuses on conversations in the everyday lives of people in "natural" settings, revealing how categories are created, maintained, and revised through people's talk (for example, see Widdicomb & Wooffitt's [1990] analysis of talk among "punks" and their category membership). Interestingly, Billig, who as Tajfel's student was one of the initiators of the minimal group paradigm (Tajfel et al., 1971; Billig, 1972, 1973), is spearheading research that highlights category construction in everyday language (Billig, 1987, 1991, 1992).

Similarly, social identity theory can be criticized for representing the strategies of social mobility and social change in simplistic terms. The theory presents these individualistic and collective strategies as alternative routes, where the adoption of one route excludes the possibility of the other. But field research among minorities suggests that a person might attempt to simultaneously move up the status hierarchy individually and as a group member (Moghaddam, 1992).

A number of further criticisms focus on the research methods, principally the minimal group paradigm used to test social identity theory. First, the minimal group paradigm provides for a clear demonstration of discrimination, but not of distinctiveness. Second, the paradigm does not shed light on intragroup processes, such as within-group minimization of differences, as outlined by social identity theory. Third, social identity is a construct that has not been studied directly (for an important exception, see the work of Brown, 1988). Fourth, the paradigm presents respondents with the opportunity to "rate" both the in-group and the out-group on the same scale. However, there is evidence that when given the opportunity, respondents will rate both in-group and out-group positively on different scales (Mummendey & Schreiber, 1983; Mummendey & Simon, 1989).

Despite these shortcomings, we believe that social identity theory has been much more constructive than is implied by commentaries from some researchers (e.g., Schiffman & Wicklund, 1992). Social identity theory remains the most influential social psychological model for intergroup research. An indication of the success of the theory is that it has influenced a diverse array of theoretical developments in recent years, and the most important of these deserve to be described.

ASSESSING THEORETICAL DEVELOPMENTS INFLUENCED BY SOCIAL IDENTITY THEORY

Self-Categorization Theory

It is appropriate to begin this review by considering self-categorization theory, because it has been developed by a research team led by J. C. Turner (Turner, 1985; Turner et al., 1987), Tajfel's onetime student and later collaborator. Self-categorization theory is broader in scope than social identity theory. More importantly, self-categorization theory is first and foremost a cognitive theory of individual behavior within group contexts. The focus of the theory is on the change that takes place from personal to social level of identity, through the evocation of different self-categorizations in various contexts. The theory proposes that group behavior involves a change "in the level of abstraction of self-categorization in the direction that represents a depersonalization of self-perception, a shift toward the perception of self as an interchangeable exemplar of some social category and away from the perception of self as a unique person defined by individual differences from others" (Turner et al., 1987, pp. 50–51).

However, for Turner et al. (1987), depersonalization can be a gain rather than a loss in identity, because it can be a mechanism through which individuals may act in terms of the historically acquired characteristics of their group.

The emphasis on psychological processes, particularly social comparison, and the attempt to develop quantifiable concepts, particularly the meta-contrast ratio, do give self-categorization theory the look of a formal psychological theory, and even seem promising in experimental contexts (e.g., Hogg, Turner, & Davidson, 1990). However, a major shortcoming of self-categorization as an intergroup theory is that it seems to neglect sociostructural factors and to be devoid of the "passion" involved in real-life conflicts. In short, this theory presents humans in the image of thinking machines. While social identity theory has been criticized for neglecting the issue of affect, self-categorization theory can be faulted for giving little attention to both motivational and affective issues.

Other Recent Theoretical Developments

Among other theoretical developments influenced by social identity theory, there are few fully developed models of intergroup relations. For example, research on minority-group influence is leading to a model that encompasses only some aspects of minority-majority relations (Moscovici, 1985; Mugny & Pérez, 1991), as is work on self-regulation in the group (Abrams, 1990). The construct of ethnolinguistic vitality (Giles et al., 1977; Giles & Johnson, 1987) is still far from being a complete model of intergroup relations. Although language can contribute to the demarcation of group boundaries and the development of group identity, many groups exist without a common language. In short, language is a contributor to, but not a prerequisite for, intergroup behavior. Consequently, any theory of intergroup relations that focuses on language will necessarily be restricted to a small number of cases, which may not even be the more important cases (see the debate between J. Edwards, 1985, 1992, and Sachdev & Bourhis, 1990, in press, on the issue of language and group identity).

The "norm violation" model (DeRidder & Tripathi, 1992) is related to recent work by "discursive" and "narrative" psychologists (see Bruner, 1986; Harré, 1993; Moghaddam & Harré, 1992), who attempt to explain social behavior through normative models. Interestingly, Wetherell's (1982) research had previously suggested that the findings of the minimal group paradigm do not exclude a normative explanation, and Jost and Azzi (1992) have provided further experimental support for a normative explanation. A strength of DeRidder and Tripathi's (1992) model is that it is supported by well-documented field research in diverse cultural contexts. For example, in an analysis of Hindu-Muslim relations in India, an account is given of how conflict arises through a "norm violation," represented by the introduction of a pig (supposedly by Hindus) to a Muslim prayer gathering. In such intergroup conflicts, norm violations presumably can pose a threat to positive and distinct social identities.

As is the case for most normative models, however, the "norm violation" model lacks predictive power. DeRidder and Tripathi (1992) need to further elaborate this model in order to clarify the specific outcomes of norm violations in different conditions. For example, we could presumably identify cases where the introduction of a pig to a Muslim prayer meeting might not lead to intergroup conflict.

Brewer's (1991) optimal distinctiveness theory is the most promising extension of the social identity model to date. Brewer's theory is particularly interesting since she is an American social psychologist, and her theory illustrates how a European theory is beginning to have an influence on social psychology in the United States. Brewer proposes that individuals are motivated to achieve an equilibrium between opposing needs for assimilation and differentiation. The feeling that one is too individuated increases vulnerability to isolation and stigmatization, thus activating the need for collective identity. The other extreme of feeling totally deindividuated, on the other hand, means that a person is too indistinctive, and this intensifies the need for individual identity. Thus, individuals are motivated to belong to groups that "optimize" the needs for assimilation and differentiation.

Brewer's research shows the influence of the "Bristol school" in several ways. For example, following social identity theory, Brewer's model adopts a group-centered definition of social identity, but keeps separate the issues of the distinctiveness and the evaluative aspects of group membership. Brewer is also influenced by the minimal group paradigm in the design of experiments to test her theory.

One of the most promising aspects of Brewer's theory is the place it gives to cultural factors, while one of its disadvantages is the use it makes of terms that imply a mechanistic conception of social behavior (e.g., "drives"). The opposing "drives" for assimilation and differentiation are assumed to be influenced by cultural norms, among other factors. Thus, the model has the capacity to accommodate cross-cultural findings pointing to cultural variations in the optimal level of category distinctiveness or inclusiveness. However, although Brewer (1991) may be correct in stating that "there is a limit to the cultural shaping of fundamental human needs," (p. 478), this begs the question of whether such "fundamental needs," if they exist at all, include the needs of assimilation and differentiation.

In conclusion, a number of promising recent theoretical developments have been strongly influenced by social identity theory. A challenge for those adopting a social identity approach is to explore intergroup relations through a focus on subjective identifications, but at the same time to give adequate attention to the role of material factors in their models. Such an approach would guard against radical idealism. Brewer (1991) may be correct in claiming that "people die for the sake of group distinctions" (p. 475), but in many cases the ultimate basis of group distinctions may be material rather than purely psychological.

CONCLUSION

Social identity theory focuses on social psychological processes to explain intergroup behavior, defining the group in terms of the person's perceptions of group membership. It is a theory dealing with extensive ranges of behavior, from social mobility to social change. In all these features, it is fairly distinctive as a social psychological theory of intergroup behavior. However, partly because this theory evolved as part of a European social psychology, its influence in North America has remained relatively limited. The dynamism of this theory and its truly psychological nature, together with the impressive body of research it is stimulating, will ensure that its influence will spread to North America.

SUGGESTED READINGS

Abrams, D., & Hogg, M. A. (Eds.). (1990). *Social identity theory: Constructive and critical advances*. London: Harvester Wheatsheaf.
Hogg, M. A., & Abrams, D. (1988). *Social identification: A social psychology of intergroup relations and group processes*. London: Routledge.
Tajfel, H. (Ed.). (1982). *Social identity and intergroup relations*. Cambridge: Cambridge University Press.
Tajfel, H., & Turner, J. C. (1979). An integrative theory of intergroup conflict. In W. G. Austin and S. Worchel (Eds.), *The social psychology of intergroup relations* (pp. 33–47). Monterey, Calif.: Brooks/Cole.

5

Equity Theory: Reconciling Affirmative Action

In this chapter we will be focusing on equity theory, the most prominent of a number of theories that deal with justice in human relationships. Why a chapter on justice when the theme of the present volume is intergroup relations? Whenever minority or disadvantaged groups in a society take action, there is a persistent theme in the accompanying rhetoric. Phrases such as "our fundamental rights have been violated," "the treatment we receive is unfair," and "we have legitimate claims" are typical. In short, justice seems to be central to conflict, and for this reason theories whose main focus is justice in interpersonal relationships can have important implications for intergroup relations.

Justice can be viewed as a socially defined standard for the evaluation of resource distribution in human relationships. Research in social justice is currently dominated by equity theory, although significant contributions have also been made by Lerner's (1977) "just world" theory, and Deutsch (1975, 1985), Leventhal (1979), Sampson (1975), and Austin (1979) have elaborated a number of fundamental concepts in the area of justice.

Essentially, equity theory deals with two questions: (1) What do people think is fair and equitable? and (2) How do they respond when they are getting far more or far less from their relationships than they deserve? How do they react when they see their fellows reaping undeserved benefits—or enduring undeserved suffering? (Walster, Walster, and Berscheid, 1978, p. vii).

It is this second question that most explicitly links equity theory to issues in intergroup relations, such as the preconditions for conflict, the form conflict might take, and how conflicts are resolved. It is equity theory's focus on the evaluation of fairness, and responses to it, that make it a potentially heuristic theory in the present context.

There are additional features of equity theory that make it a potentially valuable source of insights into social behavior generally and intergroup relations in particular. First, there is an elegant simplicity and parsimony to its fundamental propositions that provide a focus and coherence to hypotheses that emerge from it. Second, the theory is comprehensive, claiming at least to provide the beginnings for a badly needed general theory of social behavior. Finally, the theory makes certain nonobvious predictions that offer new insights into social behavior. These aspects of the theory provide some indication of why it has assumed such an important position in current social psychology generally.

An important comprehensive review of equity theory is provided by Walster and her associates (Walster et al., 1978). Current notions of equity lean heavily on earlier formulations as far back as Aristotle, and more recently include Homans (1961), Blau (1964), and the extensive work of Adams (1965). Central to the theory is its focus on relations among people rather than on the individual in isolation. However, the theory is essentially individualistic in the sense that it tends to focus on individuals interacting with other individuals. In describing the theory, it will constantly be necessary to extrapolate to the group level, and such inferences are problematic at best.

The chapter is divided into five main sections. In the first section, an outline of equity theory is presented. It becomes clear from this outline that equity theory presents a model of the individual as a rational being who computes the inputs and outcomes for the self and others, then compares the derived ratios, to arrive at a notion of justice. The conditions leading to such rational behavior can be fairly readily simulated in controlled, laboratory conditions. In such controlled conditions, inputs and outcomes can be accurately varied and estimated, and the hypotheses derived from equity theory can be tested relatively accurately. The task of defining equity theory concepts, such as "inputs" and "outcomes," is far more difficult, however, in the context of the real world.

Equity theory has a number of interesting implications with respect to the behavior of advantaged and disadvantaged groups, and we describe the most important of these in the second and third sections, respectively. By definition, advantaged and disadvantaged groups have conflicting interests, since the former will have to lose their advantaged position if the latter are to achieve equality. However, many disadvantaged groups seem to perceive their position vis-à-vis the advantaged group as just. Equity theory provides an explanation for this rather curious attitude, using psychological processes as the basis for its explanation. Furthermore, equity theory can be used to explain differences in the strategies used by advantaged and disadvantaged groups, and to account for how both of these different strategies can help strengthen the position of the advantaged group(s).

In the fourth section we focus on affirmative action as a controversial political policy designed to deal with societal discrimination. Our focus will be on how to reconcile affirmative action with equity theory.

Equity has a number of fundamental limitations as a theory of intergroup behavior, and we discuss the most important of these in our critical analysis of the theory. Equity theory presents a model of the individual as a rational being in a marketplace context: a being who works through estimates of inputs and outcomes in order to calculate ratios and then to compare his or her ratio with that of others in order to arrive at a notion of justice. This approach reflects North American cultural values, particularly with respect to the emphasis that the model places upon individuals rather than groups. The North American culture, which gives priority to self-help and individual responsibility, leads to justice being seen more in terms of the individual than of the group.

This approach is based on the assumption that it is the qualities of the individual, such as courage, hard work, and intelligence, that will determine an individual's progress. Group membership, be it male or female, black or white, rich or poor, is judged to be a secondary factor, except in a case like affirmative action, where it may be a primary factor. Inputs and outcomes, together with justice and injustice, are therefore discussed in terms of the individual. In extending equity theory to the intergroup context, we find that the theory, in its present form, does not adequately account for a number of important types of behavior.

AN OUTLINE OF EQUITY THEORY

Simply stated, equity theory proposes that people strive for justice in their relationships and feel distressed when they perceive an injustice (see figure 5.1). People define justice on the basis of an analysis of the inputs and outcomes for those involved in a relationship. Inputs are contributions that persons (or groups) make in the form of attributes, abilities, or efforts, and outcomes are rewards (or punishments) that may be tangible (such as pay, services) or intangible (such as status, liking). Justice exists when the

Figure 5.1
Schematic Representation of Equity Theory

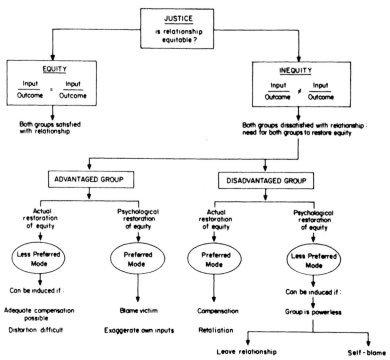

ratio of inputs to outcomes for one person (or group) is equal to the input/outcome ratio of the other. This ratio is calculated through the following formula:

$$\frac{\text{Inputs by person (group) X}}{\text{Outcomes for person (group) X}} = \frac{\text{Inputs by person (group) Y}}{\text{Outcomes for person (group) Y}}$$

Crucial to the idea of equity theory is that for justice to exist, the outcomes for those in a relationship need not be equal; rather, it is the *ratio* of outcomes to inputs that must be equal. Some concrete examples may help our understanding of this most fundamental proposition of equity theory. Because the emphasis is on ratio rather than on outcome, it is possible to have a perfectly equitable relationship in which, for example, a man treats a supposedly intimate relationship very casually while the woman invests her life in it. What makes it a just, and therefore satisfactory, relationship from an equity theory perspective is that the man in our example puts little into the relationship but gets little out of it. The woman, by contrast, may put much more in, but as long as she gets proportionally more out of the relationship, justice will be perceived to prevail. Similarly, the fact that there are substantial pay differences between laborers and professionals does not necessarily lead to a perception of injustice. As long as those in professional occupations are judged to be making proportionally more inputs (such as education, responsibility) than laborers, the situation is judged to be fair.

Having established the basic concept of ratios involving inputs and outcomes, it is necessary to be a little more precise in our formula for equity. We began with the basic formula $Ox/Ix = Oy/Iy$ because it most clearly emphasized the ratio concept that is basic to equity. However, as Walster, Berscheid, and Walster (1973) point out, the formula does not consider inputs that may be negative. Take the case of two persons (X and Y) in a relationship such that the inputs and outcomes are as follows: input x = 5, outcome x = –10, input y = –5, outcome y = 10. Using the basic equity formula, the relationship would appear to be equitable, since the resulting ratio is (–2) in both cases. But intuitively this makes little sense: Person X contributes positive inputs to the relationship but receives negative outcomes, whereas person Y receives positive outcomes even though his or her inputs were negative.

Walster et al. (1973) address this problem by proposing a formula that maintains the fundamental conceptual definition of equity but permits negative inputs and outcomes:

$$\frac{Ox - Ix}{/Ix/} = \frac{Oy - Iy}{/Iy/}$$

In this formula /Ix/ and /Iy/ denote the absolute value of inputs for x and inputs for y. If the numbers used in the earlier example are applied to the present formula, the results now make intuitive sense. The result for person X is (–3), whereas for person Y it is (+3), showing clearly that person Y is getting undeserved rewards from the relationship with X. In fact, the formula has been refined even further (see Walster et al., 1978), but the essential rationale remains unchanged.

However, although equity theory assumes that people move forward along rational paths to arrive at a definition of justice, it does not assume that the notion of justice achieved necessarily corresponds with objective reality. It is subjective perceptions, influenced by emotional needs as well as irrational judgments of justice, that form the basis of social action; and such subjective perceptions can, and often do, deviate from objective reality. For example, in the case of the laborer who compares the ratio of his or her own outcomes and inputs with that of the lawyer, it is how the laborer subjectively estimates the four main variables—(1) own inputs, (2) own outcomes, (3) the lawyer's inputs, and (4) the lawyer's outcomes—that is important and influences the laborer's behavior, not necessarily the objective status of these four variables. The laborer might imagine that his or her inputs in terms of training are equal to those of the lawyer when, in fact, they may be far less; or the laborer may assume that the outcomes received in terms of "enjoyment from life" are far more than what the lawyer gets when, in fact, they are far less. This emphasis on subjective perceptions and social comparison processes, through which ratios of outcomes and inputs are compared, makes equity theory very much a psychological theory of social behavior.

When an analysis of inputs and outcomes leads to the perception that equity is not attained, psychological discomfort is felt by the person making the analysis. The person experiencing the discomfort of inequity may be either or both of the individuals in a relationship—or, indeed, an outside observer of a relationship—and the key is the individual's subjective analysis of the ratio of inputs and outcomes. This discomfort is felt as psychological stress or tension that is highly unpleasant. As a response to the discomfort generated by the perception of inequity, the person takes steps to restore equity to the relationship, thereby removing the psychological distress. A person experiencing the distress of inequity can restore equity in one of two ways: (1) the actual restoration of equity, whereby the inputs or outcomes of one or both parties in the relationship are changed so that the ratios are made equal, or (2) the psychological restoration of equity, whereby the reality of the inputs and outcomes is cognitively distorted so that the ratios are made equal. For either the actual or the psychological restoration, there are four basic elements in the equity equation that can be changed: the inputs or outcomes of one person in the relationship, or the inputs and outcomes of the "other" (or any combination of these).

Thus, in a case where women in the face of inequity on the job attempt the actual restoration of equity, there are four basic elements that can be adjusted to produce equity: women can be paid more, men can be paid less, women can be asked to make less work input, or men can be required to put in more work. Alternatively, using a psychological restoration strategy, equity can be restored by coming to believe that women do work less, and so forth for each of the inputs and outcomes. Even where women have apparently identical inputs—as when they hold the same jobs as men—psychological restoration can be achieved by believing, for example, that women are not as dedicated to the job.

Equity theory has a number of important political implications, which we can highlight by elaborating upon this example. Because a person experiencing the distress of inequity can restore equity either actually or psychologically, the question arises as to why some disadvantaged groups, such as women, seem willing to use the second strategy and cognitively distort the reality of the inputs and outcomes, so that the ratios for them and the dominant group (men) would come out equal. Obviously, such cognitive distortion is materially harmful to the disadvantaged group. If women who are doing the same job as men accept the idea that they are putting less into it, when in fact they are putting in just as much, or even more, then they are more likely to accept less material rewards than they deserve. Among the political implications of this process are that advantaged groups, in this case men, might try to create conditions in which the disadvantaged group, women, will attempt to restore equity through psychological rather than actual means. The claim by some women's liberation advocates that men's control of the educational and mass communications systems has given them power to manipulate women and make many of them feel content with their disadvantaged position can be usefully seen in this light.

At first glance it would seem that equity theory makes a fundamental assumption about humankind that is at odds with most current psychological thought. That is, most psychological theories assume that individuals are self-interested or, in equity terms, will try to maximize their outcomes. Equity theory seems to imply that people are not motivated by self-interest but, rather, by fairness. However, Walster et al. (1978) and, in a clearer manner, Lerner (1977) claim that theories of justice do not in fact challenge the assumption of self-interest. Rather, equity theorists argue that people need an agreed-upon set of norms for exchange precisely so they can maximize their own rewards. That is, individuals need a shared understanding of contingencies in their universe so they can direct their behavior toward maximizing their own outcomes.

An elegant example of this is provided by Sampson's (1976) reference to Hardin's (1968) "tragedy of the commons." The "common" is traditionally open pasture land where all villagers can freely allow their animals to graze. The system works to perfection until one individual decides to add one animal to the herd, thereby increasing his or her personal gain. The addition of one animal by itself is harmless, but when all villagers attempt personal gain by increasing their herds, everybody loses. The common is now so overgrazed that no herd can survive. Thus, the individual maximization of outcomes requires a shared set of social norms, and hence some form of equity. This argument would therefore suggest that equity theory fits easily into most modern conceptions of the nature of humankind.

However, it is instructive that the "common" example represents a case where people have similar, rather than conflicting, interests. The common can be used by all villagers, and everyone has equal rights of use. The rational approach to using such a facility would be through a shared set of social norms allowing maximum use of the facility by each individual while preserving it. However, in most, or perhaps all, societies there are real differences of ownership level, as well as conflicts of interests, between individuals and groups, and the status quo tends to favor the relatively advantaged. Equity theory suggests that both the advantaged and the disadvantaged groups seek to maximize their own outcomes, and what they need for this is a shared understanding of contingencies in their universe. It may be, however, that at times the disadvantaged group will not act according to this rational model of humankind, but will reject the established social norms and seek fundamental social change.

Nowhere is the paradox involving the collective and individual maximization of rewards described by the "common" fable more striking than in the environmental issue. Nation-states compete with one another in order to gain maximum rewards at the expense of the other. However, it could be that an individual nation ultimately gains little or nothing by sacrificing the environment for immediate economic gain. The strongest and weakest economic competitors are capable of destroying the environment for the entire planet, and so without norms of justice the biggest "common" of all, the planet, may be lost to everyone.

Finally, it is important to point out that equity theory involves an integration, first made by Adams (1965), of two important traditions in social psychology: behavioristic notions of social exchange (Thibaut & Kelley, 1959) coupled with a motivation for cognitive balance (Heider, 1946; Festinger, 1957). Consistent with a behaviorist perspective, relationships are viewed in terms of exchange in which the relationship is maintained by the capacity of each participant to provide reinforcement for the other. Further, the focus on apparently calculable inputs and outcomes is consistent with the mechanistic view of human behavior often associated with behaviorist thinking.

The idea that inequity is associated with psychological distress grows directly out of principles such as cognitive dissonance. Festinger (1957) conceived of dissonance as psychological distress that resulted from an incompatibility of cognitions, attitudes, or behaviors *within* the individual.

With equity the distress still lies within the person but arises out of dissonance in resource distribution *between* people. The fact that equity theory is rooted in principles that have already enjoyed a lengthy tradition in psychology no doubt partly explains its pervasive influence in mainstream social psychology.

Having presented equity theory in summary form, we are now ready to formulate some of the interesting hypotheses that bear directly on intergroup relations. From equity theory it can be hypothesized that a group that receives less than it feels it deserves will experience distress—hardly a novel prediction. Of greater interest is the prediction that an overbenefited group will feel psychological distress and be motivated to restore equity. A number of experiments lend credence to this hypothesis (such as Adams & Rosenbaum, 1962). Prototypic of such experiments is one by Austin and Walster (1974). Their experiment addressed two important hypotheses relevant to the present context. First, it was hypothesized that persons who are given an equitable reward will be less distressed than persons who receive an inequitable reward (that is, persons who are either underrewarded or overrewarded). A second interesting hypothesis was that when persons are treated inequitably, they will experience less distress if they expected overreward or underreward than if they did not.

The results confirmed both hypotheses, and it is important to appreciate the implications of the findings for intergroup relations. First, it seems that advantaged groups may well feel distress and hence be motivated to make a fairer distribution of resources among societal groups. Second, but more disconcerting, it would seem that disadvantaged groups who expect to be treated inequitably accept such treatment to a greater extent than those who do not expect it.

With these suggestive findings as an example of the potentially interesting hypotheses that arise from equity theory, we can turn our attention to a more careful analysis of the implications of the theory for advantaged and disadvantaged groups.

ADVANTAGED GROUPS

In extrapolating and generalizing the findings obtained in the experiment of Austin and Walster (1974) to real intergroup situations, it is tempting to be optimistic about the ultimate resolution of situations where advantaged groups exploit those who are disadvantaged. This optimism becomes tempered when we examine equity theory's predictions about how an over- or underbenefited person will restore equity. Faced with inequity, people can actually or psychologically restore equity. These two strategies have very different practical outcomes.

Psychological Restoration of Equity

Naturally, advantaged groups, motivated out of self-interest, will be more likely to use a psychological strategy, avoiding the necessity of actually having to compensate the disadvantaged group, and perhaps of compromising their advantaged position in the process. Thus, advantaged groups are more likely to cognitively distort relative inputs and outcomes in order to restore equity. Of particular interest for intergroup relations is the tendency to distort the disadvantaged group's inputs or, in Lerner's (1971) terms, derogate or blame the victim. If the advantaged group can convince itself that disadvantaged group members' inputs (such as intelligence, willingness to work) are proportionally lower than their own, then relatively fewer outcomes can be justified and distress alleviated. Ryan (1976) discusses this process eloquently in the context of racism. He describes two forms of blaming the victim:

The old-fashioned conservative could hold firmly to the belief that the oppressed and the victimized were born that way—"that way" being defective or inadequate in character or ability. The new ideology attributes defect and inadequacy to the malignant nature of poverty, injustice, slum life and racial difficulties. But the stigma, the defect, the fatal difference—though derived in the past from environmental forces—is still located within the victim, inside his skin. (p. 7)

From an equity perspective, then, Ryan's analysis involves advantaged group members' psychologically restoring equity by devaluing the inputs of disadvantaged group members. Also, whether disadvantaged group members are born with less input potential or have less input potential because of environmental circumstances, the results are the same.

Actual Restoration of Equity

Advantaged individuals or groups may experience distress, but as we have seen, they can conveniently use psychological rather than actual means of restoring equity. Does this mean that advantaged groups will never truly compensate victims and restore actual equity? Certain hypotheses arising out of equity theory indirectly suggest that there are conditions that at least raise the probability of an actual, as opposed to a psychological, restoration strategy. There is some evidence that exploiters will resist either inadequate or excessive compensation and favor adequate compensation (see Berscheid & Walster, 1967). Specifically, if advantaged groups can be led to see a mechanism for actual compensation that is adequate, this raises the likelihood of such a strategy being adopted. Walster et al. (1978) point out in speculative fashion the subtle implications in an intergroup relations context:

If we generalize shamelessly from the preceding findings, we might speculate that a more effective strategy for the blacks might have been to minimize their description of their suffering, and to make it clear that if available compensations were extended it would completely eliminate the debt owed to them. While this is not true, it may have been a profitable strategy, since it would have insured that the blacks would have at least received minimal compensation. (p. 38)

Beyond this, equity theorists propose that the less exploiters have to distort reality, the more successful are psychological restoration techniques. Indeed, Rosenberg and Abelson (1960) have shown that individuals prefer to distort reality as little as possible. Thus, the exploiter may well be pressured into actual compensation for the disadvantaged if confronted with objective and visible information about inputs and outcomes that leaves little room for cognitive distortion.

A further proposition bears directly on the likelihood of psychological restoration techniques being used by exploiters. The hypothesis is that anticipation of future interaction with another inhibits the use of distortion (see Pannen, 1976). The idea is that continued interaction raises the probability of the exploiter having continually to confront himself or herself with distortions, whereas with no anticipated contact the exploiter will not have to face the results of inequity. The message is clear for disadvantaged minorities: Do not separate socially and thereby allow exploiters conveniently to avoid confronting inequity. Instead, constantly, through interaction, make inequalities salient and psychological distortions unacceptable. In this manner, the chances for actual restoration are heightened.

In summary, equity theory offers the novel proposition that over-benefited participants in a relationship feel psychological stress and the need to restore equity. While cognitive distortion offers exploiters a way out, there would seem to be conditions that at least heighten the probability of there being an actual redistribution of resources. If there is any validity to this proposition, mobilization of disadvantaged groups against injustice may indeed reap important rewards.

DISADVANTAGED GROUPS

Actual Restoration of Equity

The choice between actual and psychological strategies for restoring equity that affect advantaged groups has profound implications for disadvantaged groups. Just as members of the advantaged group prefer psychological restoration techniques, so members of disadvantaged groups naturally prefer the restoration of actual equity. Moreover, within the context of actual restoration, compensation would be preferred to retaliation. That is, equity theory leads us to conclude that victims or disadvantaged groups would prefer that their own outcomes be increased (compensation) rather than those of the exploiter or advantaged group being decreased (retaliation).

However, once again this "rational" approach to conflict solving predicts behavior patterns that only a "rational" person would follow. There are many instances (such as race riots, through which material destruction takes place) where the victims or disadvantaged group members are out to avenge what they see as wrongdoings and unjust behavior, and they seek to do this by harming the advantaged group rather than by getting compensation for themselves. Such destructive, "irrational" behavior, which seeks to harm the advantaged group rather than to compensate the disadvantaged group, is difficult to explain through equity theory or extrapolations from it. Even more difficult to explain is the propensity for rioters to vent their destruction on members of their own group.

The use of violence, or the threat of violence, by a disadvantaged group in order actually to restore equity has important implications for intergroup relations. Donnerstein, Donnerstein, Simon, and Ditrichs (1972) conducted a particularly interesting experiment using white subjects who feared retaliation for injustice by blacks. The researchers were interested in the level of shocks white subjects would deliver to black subjects when the experiment was designed so that the black subject did not know who was delivering the shock as opposed to when the white subject was known to the black target. Second, in one condition the white knew the black would have a chance to retaliate, whereas in the other condition it was clear that no retaliation was possible. The results showed clearly that whites gave higher levels of shocks to blacks when the white subjects were anonymous and when there was no fear of retaliation from the black subject. Anonymity or retaliation made no difference when white subjects shocked fellow white targets. Of course, for ethical reasons, although subjects believed they were shocking a target person, no shocks were actually delivered.

The social implications of these findings are far-reaching. As Donnerstein et al. (1972) conclude, "The variables of nonanonymity and expected retaliation might act to promote racial equality by minimizing aggressive behavior by white persons initially and/or by arresting justification techniques after aggressive action has terminated" (p. 244).

Psychological Restoration of Equity

Despite the possibility for retaliation, disadvantaged groups face a particular problem with actual restoration techniques, in that both compensation and retaliation presuppose the power and capability to bring about equity. Being disadvantaged, the group by definition lacks the fundamental resources needed to bring about actual equity. Thus, often the only option for disadvantaged group members is to restore psychological equity, which really means coming to believe that their disadvantaged position is deserved. If disadvantaged group members can downgrade their own inputs or exaggerate those of the advantaged group, then differential outcomes are justified. Although such a view does not serve the interests of the disadvantaged group, there are two powerful forces that enhance the probability of its adoption. First, the disadvantaged group needs to restore equity in the face of the lack of power to actually redistribute inputs and outcomes. Second, the advantaged group has a vested interest in propagating this victim-blame perspective.

These two powerful forces combine to explain an important puzzle: How is it that disadvantaged groups often do not immediately and directly take collective action aimed at obtaining a more favorable distribution of society's resources? From an equity perspective, such inaction is understandable, and it is even possible to understand how such a group might come to believe that its disadvantaged position is right and just.

A final strategy open to those who suffer from inequitable treatment is to escape the distress of inequity by leaving the relationship. This exit option has not received much attention in the equity literature but is one that may be central to relations between groups. A cursory glance at the number of separatist movements, be they political or psychological, is striking. In Canada, Quebec separation is the most salient, although strains of western separation also linger. A similar theme emerges to a greater or lesser extent among the Basques of Spain, the Welsh and Scots of Great Britain, native peoples in North America, and some militant feminists who advocate a world without men.

The exit option has received little research attention from social psychologists. An interesting exception is a study by Valenzi and Andrews (1971), who conducted a realistic field study in which clerks were hired for a six-week period at the same hourly rate. When the clerks returned for work on the second day, a new pay structure, designed by the experimenters to produce inequity, was introduced. Among the findings reported is that while none of the overpaid and equitably paid clerks left, 27 percent of the underpaid clerks left the job. Such data are important because in most laboratory investigations, subjects will usually continue for the sake of the experiment despite inequitable treatment. A further example of psychological separation comes from an experiment by Schmitt and Marwell (1972). They gave workers a choice that put them in a dilemma: They could work in a group and be paid inequitably or work alone and be paid equitably but much less than they would have received in the group. Despite the obvious economic loss, many opted to work by themselves for equitable pay, thereby psychologically removing themselves from the distress generated by the group relationship.

Presumably, although direct evidence is lacking, disadvantaged persons or groups opt for separation when they have no realistic hope of restoring equity—often, we might suppose, because of a lack of power to induce a fairer distribution by the advantaged group. Leaving the relationship or separating may well provide groups with the opportunity to strengthen their resources and to strategically reenter the relationship only when they feel they are in a position to demand and receive actual equity.

This brief description of advantaged and disadvantaged group strategies for maintaining and restoring equity permits some appreciation of how equity theory provides possible insights into certain persistent puzzles in the area of intergroup relations: the mechanisms by which advantaged groups maintain their power, and how they can at times be induced to instigate a fairer redistribution of rewards, are explained; and how disadvantaged groups come at least to tolerate their situation can be appreciated. We now turn our attention to those conditions specified by equity theory whereby disadvantaged groups may take dramatic action, and what form that action might take.

When the Best of Intentions Backfire

Members of the advantaged establishment, especially those in political office, often express frustration at the current social unrest that is typical of North American society and of many others. The frustration is expressed in the form of "The more we do to make the distribution of resources more equitable for disadvantaged groups, the more discontent they express and the more militant they become." This unexpected reaction may deter any charitable desires that advantaged groups may have and thereby create a vicious circle. Some interesting extrapolations from equity theory have led to thought-provoking experiments in this context. One in particular was conducted by deCarufel and Schopler (1979). As part of a larger experiment, they had subjects in a simulated industrial setting perform a clerical task. Subjects believed that their pay was being determined by a student who was chosen to be the allocator. After the first series of work sessions (part 1), the allocator created inequity by keeping more than half of the money he had been given to divide with the worker-subject. After a break the allocator made a decision about a new pay structure (part 2). In the "constant" condition the worker was again treated with inequity; in the "equity" condition the money was divided equally; and in the "overcompensation" condition the allocator gave the worker more than half the money.

The finding of particular interest here is how those in the equity and overcompensation conditions reacted. We might expect that those in the overcompensation condition would be more satisfied (the subject received 14 cents or 15 cents; the allocator kept 10 cents or 9 cents) than those in the equity condition (the subject received 12 cents; the allocator kept 12 cents). Surprisingly, the findings were opposite to this prediction; satisfaction was lower in the overcompensation than in the equity condition.

How might this be explained? The authors speculate that the allocator may have been the instigator of dissatisfaction in the worker by his or her zeal to overcompensate. That is, perhaps the allocator, through a distribution of overcompensation, was unknowingly communicating a message. In the equity condition the message would be "There should be fairness from now on [referring to the allocations for part 2], and I have accomplished that by dividing the money equally." In the overcompensation condition the allocator may well have been communicating to the subject "You deserve not only equal pay in part 2 but compensation for part 1 of the experiment." This would trigger an expectation of compensation on the part of the subject that was not met. The pay differential favored the subject, but was not enough totally to make up for the inquity of part 1. Hence, a degree of dissatisfaction resulted.

The implications for intergroup relations are significant. Advantaged groups that initiate social programs may well be triggering rising expectations in disadvantaged groups. These expectations may be of the form "We not only want what is equitable now, but what will make up for the past."

RECONCILING AFFIRMATIVE ACTION AND EQUITY THEORY

Over the past two decades affirmative-action programs have been widely introduced across North America. Such programs represent a sociopolitical response to problems arising from perceived injustices against disadvantaged groups. In particular, affirmative action is a response to the perception that certain categories of people, namely, women and visible minorities, are discriminated against in a manner that is inconsistent with the "meritocracy" ideology of justice that is fundamental to Western democracy (for review, see Crosby & Blanchard, 1989; Jones, 1991).

The need for affirmative action arises because of perceived violations to "equity," yet affirmative-action programs are themselves highly controversial because they too are perceived by some to violate the principles of equity (e.g., Glazer, 1988). The American ideal is predicated on the assumption that the unit of attribution for equity considerations is the individual. It is assumed that the individual gets what he or she deserves in terms of economic, political, and social status rewards (outcomes) on the basis of individual accomplishment (inputs). Affirmative-action programs challenge this ideology by explicitly giving recognition to group characteristics such as gender and ethnic/racial heritage as legitimate inputs for the acquisition of economic and political rewards (see Gordon, 1981).

Perhaps it is this fundamental ideological shift that helps explain people's reactions to affirmative action. Not only is there the expected opposition from advantaged group members due to self-interest, but also some opposition among disadvantaged groups who presumably have the most to gain (Dovidio, Mann, & Gaertner, 1989; Nacoste, 1989; Tougas & Veilleux, 1988; Veilleux & Tougas, 1989). Indeed, Taylor and Dubé (1986) found that people reacted negatively to judgments based on social, as opposed to individual, aspects of their identity, irrespective of the valence or justification for such judgments. Thus, Taylor and Dubé (1986) suggest that affirmative-action programs that, by definition, emphasize group identity may evoke negative reactions from the very people they are intended to benefit.

A major challenge to analyzing the social psychological processes associated with affirmative action is the number of specific political programs and definitions that are labeled "affirmative action." Despite a lack of consensus as to conceptual definition, there are certain useful distinctions that can be made. The most basic distinction is between forms of "soft" and "hard" affirmative-action programs. For example, Tougas and Veilleux (1988) and Veilleux and Tougas (1989) differentiate between programs that aim to remove barriers to equal opportunity for women (soft) and those that give preferential treatment to women (hard). Similarly, Young (1986) differentiates between nondiscrimination strategies in which decisions are based on individual merit (soft) versus restitutional and reverse discrimination strategies that give preferential treatment to disadvantaged group members (hard). This distinction between "soft" and hard" affirmative-action programs is a fundamental one because both are labeled affirmative action, yet "soft" programs explicitly endorse the principles of individually based equity, whereas "hard" programs involve an ideological shift to a group-based concept.

The fact that the distinction between "soft" and "hard" programs is associated with two opposing ideologies may explain the reactions of disadvantaged groups to affirmative-action programs. Consistently, for example (see Tougas & Veilleux, 1988; Veilleux & Tougas, 1989), women support "soft" forms of affirmative action but are reluctant to endorse "hard" forms. Research in our own laboratory supports this conclusion (Porter, Taylor, & Koffman, 1993). Indeed, in one study, Matheson, Echenberg, Taylor, Rivers, and Chow (1993) presented women with scenarios in the context of work and education that varied in terms of the degree and subtlety of discrimination faced by women. Even in scenarios where the discrimination was profound and blatant, women rejected "hard" forms of affirmative action that involved reverse discrimination. They were unanimous, however, in their support for "soft" programs that ensured the removal of discrimination and guaranteed equity for women.

It would seem, then, that both advantaged groups and disadvantaged groups share the same commitment to equity. Thus, on the surface, the solution for affirmative action appears obvious: where there is discrimination, a "soft" form of affirmative action will be necessary until such time as equity is restored.

Unfortunately, there are a number of complexities that need to be addressed, and these strike at the heart of the limitations to equity as a social psychological theory. The issue has to do with specifying the "inputs" that are appropriate for an analysis of equity. Equity theory has been criticized for being nonfalsifiable (see Popper, 1959) in the sense that any empirical evidence that disconfirms hypotheses arising from equity theory can be countered with the argument that important inputs were neglected in the research.

The implications for equity and affirmative action are that inputs such as ability, effort, performance, education, training, and experience that are assumed to form the basis of equity need to be researched thoroughly. For example, the hiring decisions of many police forces are partly based on inputs that specify minimum height and weight. No explicit mention is made of discrimination, yet these specific inputs indirectly discriminate against women and a variety of ethnic minority groups. Access to many educational institutions or job opportunities is, on the surface, based on recognizable inputs such as performance. Nevertheless, indirect discrimination may arise because certain disadvantaged groups have not been socialized to acquire the necessary inputs, or have not been raised in circumstances that easily allow for the necessary inputs to be developed.

Imagine that Jane Adams is an African-American female competing to enter college next year. She is the descendent of slaves, and none of her family has ever graduated from high school. Although the members of her family are supportive of her efforts, they cannot teach her the social skills or provide her with the kind of information she will need to enter and succeed at college. She is disadvantaged relative to middle-class white students, who come from a "bookish" background. In short, although in one sense she is competing on equal terms with other students, in a perhaps more profound sense she is suffering because of cultural handicaps.

Should such circumstances be considered as "negative inputs" in any merit-based analysis? If so, then a disadvantaged applicant for a job, whose qualifications on the usual criteria are less than those of an advantaged candidate, would be successful, and yet the decision would be judged as conforming to the usual equity ideal. Thus, the psychological basis of inputs and outcomes needs to be examined both for theoretical and policy reasons.

Finally, the distinction between "soft" and "hard" affirmative action may be essential to the psychological consequences of such programs for both advantaged and discriminated-against groups. From the point of view of the advantaged group, equating affirmative action with preferential treatment for minorities (hard) leads to the perception that successful members of discriminated-against groups are less qualified. In attribution terms, the ability of minority-group members is discounted (see Garcia, Erskine, Hawn, & Casmay, 1981). This interpretation is echoed by Crosby and Clayton (1991) and also explains the role that "aversive racism" (Dovidio & Gaertner, 1983) plays in the interpretation of successful minority-group candidates. Advantaged group members can easily discount the egalitarian component of aversive racism in cases of "hard" affirmative-action programs.

Equally damaging is the psychological impact of "hard" affirmative-action programs on members of discriminated-against groups. For example, women who believe that they were hired on the basis of their gender rather than merit alone report low job satisfaction, low job commitment, and high levels of stress (see Chacko, 1982; Heilman, Simon, & Repper, 1987). Minority-group members, then, fall victim to what Nacoste (1989) has labeled the "imposter syndrome." This not only is characterized by feelings of inadequacy, but motivates minority-group members to perform beyond all realistic standards in order to compensate for their feeling like imposters.

Affirmative action, then, can, under certain conditions, have negative consequences for both advantaged and disadvantaged group members alike. However, the root of these negative consequences is the belief that affirmative action violates equity by giving special treatment to certain people based on category membership. But such treatment is only true for "hard" affirmative-action programs; for the more frequent "soft" programs, the very purpose is to remove past discrimination and to introduce a genuine equity rule of justice.

In the final analysis, the socially defined "inputs" that are central to equity theory need to be addressed. As Blanchard and Crosby (1989) point out, socially defined "inputs" is a euphemism for "defined by members of the advantaged group." Perhaps what is really needed is a careful analysis of how "inputs" become defined and how they can be thereby altered and expanded to reduce the potential for discrimination.

CRITICAL REVIEW OF EQUITY THEORY

Equity theory suffers from a number of limitations, which we review in this section. The most important are that equity theory is not specific about inputs and outcomes; it tends to be culturally biased; and it is vague about the social comparison process assumed to be involved in judgments of fairness. We will review each of these limitations in some detail, since there have been a number of attempts to overcome them, and many have rather direct implications for the operation of justice in relations between groups.

Specifying Inputs and Outcomes

As we have noted, a particularly thorny problem for equity theory is its ability or lack of ability to specify the appropriate inputs and outcomes in a particular relationship (see Deutsch, 1985).

This highlights an important problem: No matter what prediction is tested, equity theory can never be proved wrong, because other inputs and outcomes can always be found later to explain whatever results were obtained. This circularity of argument poses a fundamental difficulty. It means that it is virtually impossible to predict how advantaged and disadvantaged groups will react to their situation—instead, we must wait until the reaction takes place, and then identify and calculate the inputs and outcomes that were central.

It is hard to believe that inputs and outcomes are a purely random process. The problem is that we are not yet able to predict with a significant degree of accuracy how people arrive at an understanding about which inputs and outcomes are crucial to a particular relationship. Further research is needed to clarify this process and would greatly enhance the predictive power of equity theory.

The question of specifying inputs and outcomes is also related to the types of experiments typically conducted in this area. Nowhere is the need to complement laboratory research with field studies so acute as in the testing of equity principles. The typical laboratory study is carefully designed to allow for the test of a specific hypothesis. This means that conditions are set up that severely restrict subjects. For example, in order to study the effects of inequity, researchers will place subjects in a situation where they all have the same qualifications and do the same amount of work, thereby fixing the inputs. What varies are the specific rewards that subjects in different conditions receive, and these differences are designed to produce inequitable conditions. Subjects are then given a limited range of options to deal with the inequity thus created, such as expressing negative feelings or retaliating in subsequent trials.

In real life, of course, the inputs, outcomes, and responses are not fixed in this manner. For example, few subjects in an experiment leave it, rebel against the researcher, or sabotage the experiment. After all, they agreed to participate in the experiment. In real-life intergroup relations, these are some of the more interesting strategies that groups use to cope with inequity. Beyond this, it is important to appreciate that in real life there are at least four basic elements that can be juggled either psychologically or actually in order to produce equity: one's personal or one's group's inputs and outcomes, and those of the other person or group. Experimentally the strategy is to fix three of the four options and then make predictions about how the fourth will vary systematically as a result of a number of predetermined factors.

Field studies, of course, do not permit the fixing of various inputs and outcomes. It is, therefore, impossible to make unequivocal causal statements about any results obtained. What field studies do permit is some appreciation of which elements are used naturally by people, collectively or in isolation, to deal with issues of equity. Beyond this, field studies provide hints as to which social variables may be systematically related to different inputs and outcomes. Data from such field studies can then be used as a basis for designing more controlled laboratory conditions to test certain hypotheses, hopefully with some confidence that the factors that the experimenter chooses to fix or to leave free to vary have some basis in reality.

In summary, the problem of defining inputs and outcomes makes predictions about intergroup relations from an equity perspective problematic. However, a combined field and experimental approach to the question may lead to a situation where equity can have predictive power. Then we may be better able to predict whether a disadvantaged group will accept its position, demand compensation, or lower its own inputs in response to its undesirable situation.

Culture Bias

Equity theory is conceived within a North American context and therefore tends to reflect the cultural values of that society. Specifically, equity theory and research deal with individuals rather than groups. This is not to say that groups do not conform to equity principles, but to assume so is naive. The added complexity of relationships at the group level and the nature of inputs and outcomes that are important for groups must be addressed. Indeed, the very nature of the relationship is different with groups, since much of it is not face-to-face.

Equity, through this individualistic bias, ignores a number of processes directly related to intergroup relations. Leventhal (1979) cites a number of examples that illustrate the point. He notes that when a group is in conflict, the normal concerns for justice within the group are affected. Attention focuses on the threats related to conflict rather than on fairness within the group. Further, conflict produces in-group solidarity that includes greater agreement among individuals and subgroups about the justice of how resources are distributed within the group. Finally, individual or subgroup concerns about justice are suppressed in favor of evaluating fairness in terms of what is best for the group. These issues illustrate a few of the many ways in which much is lost when principles of equity at the individual level are extrapolated directly to the level of the group.

The most compelling analysis of the differences involved in justice at the interpersonal and intergroup levels was provided by Watson (1985). She postulated that human relationships can vary along a social continuum ranging from intimate to role to group relationships, and that the operation of equity may be quite different, depending upon the type of relationship involved. Watson (1985) found that the conception of justice associated with equity theory applied only when subjects evaluated role (work) relationships; it did not apply for intimate or group contacts. Specifically, in a series of laboratory and field studies, Watson found that at the group level the rules of justice were much more strictly applied than in intimate relationships. For example, in one study

subjects who had described an injustice in their relationships with a close friend perceived these incidents as less unjust and less serious than subjects who had described injustices in a work setting. Incidents in this later context were, again, perceived as less unjust and serious than those in a group setting. (Watson, 1985, p. 275)

Beyond this, Watson also found evidence to suggest that for intimate relationships, inputs in the form of the person's intentions are a primary concern, whereas in the intergroup context the focus is more on outcomes.

Finally, at the group level attention must be paid not only to the distribution of rewards or outcomes but to procedures of justice as well. We can all think of unjust outcomes that arise from just procedures, as when an innocent defendant, because of missing evidence, is judged guilty through a fair jury trial. Conversely, unjust procedures can generate just distributions, as when a dictator is benevolent and distributes goods with fairness and compassion.

The cultural context of North America, with its individualistic bias, is reflected in the application by equity theory of economically based concepts to all human relationships. The very terms used by equity theorists—"inputs," "outcomes," "rewards," "costs," "profits," and "investments"—reflect this orientation. Deutsch (1975), in recognizing this issue, notes that "this focus is a natural one in a society in which economic values tend to pervade all aspects of social life" (p. 137). Similarly, Sampson (1975) argues that "noneconomic forms of human relationship—including, for example, relationships of liking, loving, helping, harmony, and so forth—arise from the trend to mimic the economic form" (p. 48).

One of the important consequences of such a marketplace or economic view of human relations is that the very assumption that equity forms the basis of all relationships needs to be challenged. Deutsch (1975) argues that equity operates only where the relationship is competitive and the goal is economic productivity. However, where the aim is to maintain or foster enjoyable social relations, *equality* will be operative. That is, when the aim is harmony among people, all should receive the same outcomes. Finally, a *needs* principle of justice will operate where the primary goal is personal welfare. For example, children are given not what they deserve but what they need.

Undoubtedly the nature of the distribution achieved in a society is influenced by social norms such as distributive justice. However, equity is only one of many possible rules of justice, and one that reflects North American cultural traditions. In other cultures such rules as equality and needs might have greater influence. To complicate matters further, it is clear that different rules operate even within the same society. The North American value system clearly illustrates this point. Everyone is "guaranteed" equality of opportunity to achieve whatever station in life his or her talents and efforts permit (equity), but those in genuine need will be helped by specially designed welfare and assistance programs.

The whole issue of which rule of justice operates in what circumstances is a complicated one, but an example may serve to point out its potential importance for intergroup relations. A number of experiments have examined how boys and girls distribute resources (for instance, Leventhal & Lane, 1970). The usual procedure is to have a group of boys or girls perform a group task in which individual members make differential inputs to the completion of the task. One of the members is then given a sum of money and asked to take the responsibility for dividing it among the group members. Boys typically allocate according to an equity rule, those boys who contributed most to the task receiving the most, and others receiving an amount consistent with their input. Girls, on the other hand, tend to follow an equality rule: independent of different contributions, the money is divided equally among all members.

Applying Deutsch's (1975) analysis, we might explain the results as follows. Boys are socialized to be cooperative where possible, but to put a special premium on productivity. Thus, they operate on the basis of equity. Girls, by contrast, may be more concerned with good social relationships than with productivity, and therefore use equality as the basis for resource distribution. If this is true, we have two groups whose different value systems lead to completely different perspectives on the distribution of resources. One can only speculate about the extent to which various societal, racial, cultural, or occupational groups have such different value systems, and the complexities involved when two groups whose values diverge attempt to negotiate an acceptable basis for the just distribution of resources.

CONCLUSION

These limitations notwithstanding, equity theory specifically, and justice theories more generally, make an important contribution to intergroup relations. Equity theories are to be commended for attempting a broadly based theory of social behavior. Insights into persistent puzzles are offered, and a framework is provided for addressing new issues. In the context of intergroup relations, an especially important new question must be how small groups with meager resources cope with large, powerful groups. Terrorism and hostage-taking represent creative, if frightening, solutions. Perhaps the challenge is for theorists interested in intergroup relations to examine how individualistic processes of equity apply to situations involving groups.

SUGGESTED READINGS

Blanchard, F. A., & Crosby, F. J. (1989). *Affirmative action in perspective.* New York: Springer-Verlag.

Messick, D. M., & Cook, K. S. (Eds.). (1983). *Equity theory: Psychological and sociological perspectives.* New York: Praeger.

Walster, E., Walster, G. W., & Berscheid, E. (1978). *Equity: Theory and research.* Boston: Allyn & Bacon.

6

Relative Deprivation Theory: Meeting the Challenge of Resource Mobilization Theory

A major challenge for any theory of intergroup relations is understanding the conditions that would lead disadvantaged group members to take action in order to improve their situation. Equally challenging, but less often addressed, is the more puzzling question of why members of an oppressed group might accept, with apparent contentment, their disadvantaged condition.

How are we to explain, for example, the very different perceptions of women and African-Americans, given that both are "objectively" disadvantaged? As Major (1994) notes, "Despite women's disadvantaged status in economic, political, and even family domains relative to men, there is little evidence that women in general are more dissatisfied with their situations than are men." By contrast, she notes that "unlike women as a group, Black Americans as a group appear aware of, and aggrieved about, their disadvantaged status in American life" (p. 297).

What these examples underscore is that when it comes to people's feelings, there is no isomorphic relation between their objective situation or status and subjective experience. This dictum has been recognized for centuries, but it was not until 1949 that the concept of relative deprivation was formalized by Stouffer and his colleagues.

The fundamental idea is that it is a person's relative status that determines his or her sense of satisfaction, not the objective situation. The deprivation component of "relative deprivation" signals a concern for when people feel relatively poorly off, rather than situations where they are relatively advantaged. From this description the potential value of relative deprivation theory for understanding intergroup relations is evident, especially as it pertains to disadvantaged groups responding to groups that are more advantaged.

The insights gained by recognizing the relative basis of human satisfaction lead to some particularly thorny issues. For example, a person can make comparisons with any number of others, and since a comparison with a "worse-off" other leads to a very different reaction from one with another who is "better off," it will be crucial to be able to make a precise prediction about whom a person chooses as the target for comparison. This is but one of the enduring issues associated with relative deprivation that we raise here in order to appreciate that while the relativity concept is a powerful theoretical advance, there is much yet to be done.

We begin our outline of relative deprivation theory by describing the basic findings of Stouffer and his colleagues. The purpose is to make clear, by empirical example, what types of discontent can be explained through the concept of relative deprivation. Next we focus on a 1976 article by Crosby, who provides an excellent integration of the state of the theory to that point. This is followed by a discussion of recent research that bears directly on relative deprivation in the context of intergroup relations. Finally, we present a critical analysis of relative deprivation theory. An important theme here will be the extent to which the focus of theory and research has been on the individual and his or her experiences of deprivation. All too quickly these findings from this individual perspective are extrapolated to the group level. It is also important to bear in mind that unlike equity theory (chapter 5), for example, relative deprivation theory focuses on disadvantaged individuals and groups. The interest of theorists is in the feeling of discontent that arises when comparisons are made with "better-off" others.

OUTLINE OF RELATIVE DEPRIVATION THEORY

On December 8, 1941, Stouffer and his colleagues (Stouffer, Suchman, DeVinney, Star, & Williams, 1949) initiated a large-scale research project designed to assess the attitudes of the American soldier. This was a landmark study, since for the first time the methods of social science were judged to be potentially valuable in the context of the U.S. Army, replacing the subjective opinions of military personnel who made only brief visits to the field and reported on the morale of military units on the basis of a few casual conversations. One of the most important concepts to emerge from this vast research project, published ultimately in four volumes, was relative deprivation.

The concept proved invaluable for reconciling paradoxical findings from the study. For example, complaints about promotion were expressed more vehemently in the air force than in the military police. This was a surprising finding, since the air force had numerous corporals and sergeants, whereas the vast majority of soldiers in the military police were privates. Relative deprivation provided a possible answer. Most men in the air force got promotions. Those who did not felt relatively aggrieved. By contrast, few in the military police received promotions. The result was that those who were not promoted did not feel deprived by comparison and thus were less likely to feel aggrieved.

Black soldiers in the southern United States were expected to feel particularly bitter given the history of extreme racism in that region. However, the morale of these soldiers was as good as, and at times better than, that of blacks stationed in the North. The data indicated that the high morale of those in the South was a function of comparisons they made with black civilians in the South, who were treated very poorly. But northern blacks felt relatively frustrated, because their judgments were relative to civilian blacks in the North, who were earning higher wages in the war-related factories.

These are but two of the examples from Stouffer's work that illustrate how the concept of relative deprivation can provide insights into apparently irrational feelings. It is important to note, however, that it is not possible to make a specific prediction about feelings by using relative deprivation. It is possible to explain the feelings only after the fact. How can we know beforehand that black soldiers in the South will compare themselves with civilian blacks? It is equally logical for them to compare themselves with blacks in the North or with white soldiers stationed in the South. Clearly, an important issue for the predictive power of relative deprivation is to be able to establish the mechanism by which people choose a comparison other. Pettigrew (1978) is even harsher in his criticism on this point:

Relative deprivation as an explanatory concept has often been invoked in *post hoc* fashion, its causal relationships left ambiguous, its measurement varied and questionable, and its application confused by the failure to specify precisely its operation at both the individual and social level of analysis. (1978, p. 32)

A QUARTER-CENTURY OF RESEARCH ON RELATIVE DEPRIVATION

The concept of relative deprivation flourished over 25 years following the initial work of Stouffer and his colleagues. In 1976 Faye Crosby, a social psychologist, published an important paper that not only outlined her own theoretical position but also attempted to integrate into her work other major positions on relative deprivation. Thus, reviewing certain of Crosby's propositions allows us to trace developments in the field of relative deprivation generally.

Before analyzing her model, it is important to address a definitional ambiguity about the concept of relative deprivation. The term has been used in two distinct ways. Some theorists focus on the cognitive component of relative deprivation, the perceived differential between one's own treatment and that of a comparison other. The key cognitive judgment would be the magnitude of the differential.

Other theorists emphasize the emotional component of relative deprivation, which would include feelings of anger, outrage, and grievance. From an emotional perspective, intensity would be the main variable. Our concern in this chapter is with what makes people, especially in a group context, experience hostile feelings that could potentially lead to protest or militant action. Thus, relative deprivation will be viewed here as an emotion. The cognitive aspect, the magnitude of the differential between self or own group and another person or group, can be viewed as one possible precondition for the feelings of anger and grievance we will associate with relative deprivation.

It should be stated at the outset that Crosby's model attempts to explain relative deprivation as it pertains to the individual. She makes no claims about how the process might operate in groups. The most important feature of her model is that she boldly attempts to specify the necessary and sufficient conditions for relative deprivation to be experienced. Specifically, she proposes that for the negative emotions of relative deprivation to be experienced, a person must see that someone possesses X, want X, feel entitled to X, feel that it is feasible to attain X, and not feel personally responsible for the lack of X.

The first precondition requires that a person see that someone possesses X. Obviously, it is necessary for a person to be aware that X exists in order to analyze his or her own situation with respect to X. The bigger issue here, of course, which Crosby does not address, is how to determine, among the many others who may possess X, or differing amounts of X, precisely which other will be used as a basis for comparison.

Next, the person must want X. This important precondition highlights the emotional or feeling aspect of relative deprivation. Knowing someone possesses something you don't value will not make you angry or upset. Only when someone possesses something you want will relative deprivation be experienced.

A more interesting and complex precondition is that the person must feel entitled to X. The basic idea is that even if you see someone who possesses something you want badly, this does not necessarily mean anger will be experienced. Only if you feel you deserve X, or that it is right and fair that you have X, will relative deprivation be experienced. As Crosby notes, the student who is given a D on an exam, but feels he or she deserved a D, may feel disappointment or inadequacy, but not the anger and outrage of relative deprivation. If, however, the student is given a D, but feels that he or she deserved a C or higher, then relative deprivation will be experienced.

The complexity of the entitlement precondition arises because it requires an answer to the prior question: How does a person assess the deservedness, fairness, or justice of his or her situation? As we have seen from our discussion of equity theory in chapter 5, this in itself is a complex issue.

The feasibility precondition is complex as well. If a person knows that he or she will obtain X, then no relative deprivation is experienced. At the other extreme, if there is absolutely no way that X can be obtained, then it is unlikely that relative deprivation will be experienced. This latter experience can perhaps best be described as wishful thinking. James Bond has a life-style that makes mine look dull by comparison, but it isn't realistic for me to think in his terms, so the comparison does not evoke anger in me, only envy.

The final precondition requires that the person not blame himself or herself for not having X. In one important respect this precondition is contained in precondition 3, the feeling of entitlement. If a person does blame himself or herself for not having X, then he or she is really saying that he or she doesn't deserve X or that the lack of X is just. Thus, like precondition 3, it is essential that the lack of X be judged unfair for relative deprivation to be experienced.

Empirical research to test the validity of each of these preconditions is vital for the insights it may provide into individual or, if we extrapolate, group responses to inequality. For example, think of the outrage that women, native Americans, French-speaking Québecois, gays, blacks, and Hispanics in North America have expressed. Perhaps in these cases all five preconditions for relative deprivation have been met. But think of working-class North Americans, certain Indian groups of relatively low caste, colonial Africans (until very recently), or certain newly arrived immigrant groups in Western Europe or North America. Their apparent acceptance of the unequal treatment they receive surely has nothing to do with their not seeing that others are better off or not wanting the rewards that society has to offer. Instead, it may be because there is the perception that the inequality is fair or that equality is totally unfeasible from the outset. The point here is that the presence or absence of any precondition is hypothesized to have a dramatic impact. In the highly speculative examples offered here, the range is from acceptance to collective and militant protest—in the extreme, the contemplation of the separation of a province from the rest of the country.

Crosby's initial 1976 model is the most explicit and complete in terms of spelling out the precise preconditions for relative deprivation. As such, it serves as an excellent reference point for considering other theories. Davis (1959) was the first to describe a formal theory of relative deprivation (see Cook, Crosby, and Hennigan, 1977). Adopting Crosby's format, we will translate Davis's (1959) theory to propose that the necessary preconditons are that someone does not possess X, wants X, and feels entitled to X. However, he includes certain subtleties that are important. First, he considers with whom people make comparisons, proposing that people compare themselves with similar others, a view consistent with Festinger's (1954) fundamental hypothesis of social comparison theory. Thus, members of a disadvantaged group may not compare themselves with an extremely advantaged group, simply because there is insufficient basis of similarity. Of course, questions as to precisely how people define similarity still remain (see Suls & Miller, 1977).

Because comparisons are made with similar others, Davis believed that this automatically made people feel entitled to the X in question. Thus, entitlement is contained in the fact that the first precondition is that the person sees that a similar other possesses X.

Runciman (1966) agreed on the three preconditions proposed by Davis but added the feasibility condition. Like Crosby, he felt that relative deprivation required coping with reality-based aspirations.

However, Gurr (1970) made the opposite prediction. He focused on what gives rise to a sense of grievance and believed that when people do not think that attaining X is feasible, this contributes directly to a sense of grievance and, thereby, feelings of deprivation.

Thus, various theorists include some but not all of the preconditions outlined by Crosby (1976). Beyond this, there would seem to be a fundamental disagreement about the role of feasibility. Crosby (1976) and Runciman (1966) believe that it is the perception of X as attainable, and Gurr (1970) argues that it is perceiving that the attainment of X is not feasible, that leads to relative deprivation.

Before completing discussion of relative deprivation theories, it may be instructive to examine two other theories in terms of how they would deal with the preconditions proposed by Crosby (1976). The two theories in question are frustration-aggression theory and equity theory, both of which were described in earlier chapters.

Frustration-aggression theory (Dollard et al., 1939) focuses on the individual and hypothesizes that whenever goal-directed behavior is blocked, frustration will be experienced, which will lead to aggression. The interesting aspect of the theory is its attention to the psychoanalytic concept of displacement. Thus, when a powerful person or force blocks goal-directed behavior, the frustrated person may displace his or her aggression from the rational target onto a related but weaker target. The man whose boss has made him angry may not confront the boss, but instead take out his aggression on the boss's secretary, his own wife, and even the family pet. The concept of displacement has been important in explaining why powerless minority groups are so often the target of aggression.

Placing the theory in relative deprivation terms generally, and in Crosby's model in particular, the person must want X and believe that it is feasible to obtain X. Presumably, people do not pursue goals they don't want or don't think are possible to achieve. No reference is made to seeing that others or similar others possess X, or that entitlement, deservedness, and responsibility are necessary conditions.

The essence of equity theory, which was discussed in detail in chapter 5, involves social comparison and entitlement. People judge the satisfaction of relationships on the basis of the ratio of inputs to outcomes for both participants in the relationship. Naturally a person sees the other's inputs and outcomes—in Crosby's terms, the X—and makes social comparisons. Equity theory makes very explicit predictions about whom one makes comparisons with—the other person in the relationship.

Also implied in equity theory are the preconditions associated with entitlement. Equity explicitly defines this in terms of the equality of ratios of inputs to outcomes for both partners. Thus, in Crosby's terms equity theory involves seeing that another possesses X, wants X, feels entitled to X, and does not feel responsible for the lack of X. Not mentioned is the controversial feasibility precondition.

With each theory having its own constellation of preconditions for relative deprivation, it would be crucial to put each of the theories to the test. Fortunately, Bernstein and Crosby (1980) have done just that. This research is important not only for the findings that emerged but also because the studies typify the two kinds of methods that have been used most widely in social psychological research on relative deprivation.

Before describing these methods, it may be helpful to organize and summarize the predictions about the specific preconditions that each

Table 6.1

Summary of Preconditions for Relative Deprivation Specified by Various Theories

THEORISTS	OTHER POSSESSES X	WANT X	ENTITLED TO X	FEASIBLE TO ATTAIN X	LACK OF RESPONSIBILITY FOR LACK OF X
CROSBY	✓	✓	✓	✓	✓
DAVIS	✓	✓	✓		
RUNCIMAN	✓	✓	✓	✓	
GURR	(✓)	✓	✓	–	
FRUSTRATION / AGGRESSION		✓		✓	
EQUITY	(✓)	✓	✓		✓

– means the absence of precondition

( ) means precondition necessary but with important qualifications

Source: F. Crosby & M. Bernstein. (1978). *Relative deprivation: Testing the models.* Paper presented at the meeting of the American Psychological Association, Toronto. Reprinted by permission of the authors.

theory makes. Table 6.1 uses Crosby's (1976) preconditions as a format and lists the other theories in terms of the precise preconditions each specifies.

The studies conducted by Bernstein and Crosby (1980) and Crosby (1982) are prototypic of social psychological research on relative deprivation. The first used a more experimental procedure involving 528 university students as subjects. The subjects were asked to read a number of carefully prepared vignettes about an individual who lacked a desired X. Different variations of the vignette described the individual as someone who (*a*) did or did not see another who possessed X; (*b*) did or did not feel entitled to X; (*c*) had or had not attained X in the past; (*d*) did or did not think it likely to attain X in the future; and (*e*) did or did not assume personal responsibility for current failure to possess X. After reading the vignette, subjects rated, on modified Likert-type scales, the extent to which the central character would have experienced resentment, dissatisfaction, anger, and unhappiness.

Subjects made judgments about a large number of vignettes where every possible combination of the presence or absence of each precondition was presented. In this way the effect of each precondition could be assessed in terms of its importance for relative deprivation. However, the "wanting" component was not manipulated.

An interesting pattern of results emerged. Consistent with all the theories, seeing that others possess X and feeling entitled to X were strongly related to the negative emotions of relative deprivation. However, the finding related to feasibility supported Gurr (1970), but not Runciman (1966) or Crosby (1976) herself. The findings showed that relative deprivation was not severe when it was not feasible to obtain X. Equity and frustration-aggression theory were shown to be incomplete in that they do not deal with feasibility.

Finally, the results for the personal responsibility precondition were exactly opposite to the prediction: relative deprivation was highest when people blamed themselves for not having X. Does this mean that this whole precondition must be reevaluated, or is there a possible methodological problem? One limitation of the vignette is that it tells us about the main character but not about other specific persons who might be blamed in the situation. Perhaps the self-blame finding arose because the vignette offered no real alternatives.

Bernstein and Crosby (1980) produced an elegant demonstration of how the specific preconditions of relative deprivation can be operationalized and experimentally studied. The cost of such an experimental approach is that the subjects were not asked about their feelings about a real and involving personal topic. Of relevance to this issue is a fairly comprehensive study conducted by Crosby (1982) with over 400 participants that focused on relative deprivation and working women. One of the key features of this study is the effort made to deal with issues of high personal importance to participants.

Women with relatively low- and high-prestige jobs, as well as a sample of homemakers, were asked about their feelings concerning their individual work situation, the work situation of women in general, and their own home life. The questions focused generally on their feelings of relative deprivation, and specifically on each of the preconditions that various theorists have hypothesized to be associated with relative deprivation. The comprehensive nature of the study permitted multiple tests of the role of various preconditions. Unfortunately, no clear pattern of preconditions emerged consistently, and hence none of the theories of relative deprivation received strong support. However, two themes did emerge in virtually every analysis: wanting and deserving.

This led Crosby (1982) to revise her original model, in which she hypothesized five preconditions. She now posited two preconditions for relative deprivation: (1) a discrepancy between actual outcomes and desired outcomes (want), and (2) a discrepancy between actual outcomes and the outcomes deserved. Unfortunately, the simplicity of these two preconditions hides a real complexity. The key elements in the two preconditions are actual outcomes, desired outcomes, and deserved outcomes. The first, actual outcomes, is concrete and relatively easy to deal with. Determining desired outcomes and deserved outcomes is more problematic. Assessing desired outcomes involves the complex issue of who serves as the target for social comparisons. That is, what we desire is based on what others have. However, it is not just what anyone has that is important, but what those with whom we compare have. Now we are back to the complicated question: With whom does a person compare?

Similarly, "deserved outcomes" raises the question of how justice and fairness are determined. As we saw from chapter 5, this is no small task. Thus, Crosby's two apparently simple preconditions for relative deprivation contain a number of hidden complexities.

Despite our having to weave a complex story of interacting and differing numbers of preconditions, there has been progress with the concept of relative deprivation. We have learned that though the feelings of relative deprivation are subjectively defined, it is not enough merely to have a negatively based social comparison. In addition, the concept of deservedness or fairness is central. The challenge now is to define these precisely, so we can predict when relative deprivation will be experienced.

RELATIVE DEPRIVATION AND INTERGROUP RELATIONS

Runciman (1966) was the first to explicitly address the question of relative deprivation in a collective or group context, by distinguishing between egoistical and fraternal deprivation (see also Walker & Pettigrew, 1984). Egoistical deprivation involves the traditional case, in which an individual feels deprived because of his or her position within a group. When dissatisfaction arises because of a person's group's status vis-à-vis other groups in society, fraternal deprivation is experienced. Runciman (1966) felt that a person could experience either form or, at times, both forms of deprivation. This might occur, for example, when a woman feels that her personal earnings are less than those of other women at her place of work and that women as a group earn less than men at the same place of work.

The importance of Runciman's (1966) distinction is best captured in a study by Vanneman and Pettigrew (1972). The focus was on relative deprivation and its relation to the attitudes of whites toward voting for black mayoralty candidates in major cities in the United States. The study was explicitly designed to operationalize Runciman's distinction between egoistical and fraternal deprivation. White respondents were asked to judge "their own economic gains" in relation to (1) their in-group (whites)

Figure 6.1
Four Types of Relative Deprivation

PERSONAL ECONOMIC SITUATION
COMPARED TO BLACKS

		Equal or greater	Less than
PERSONAL ECONOMIC SITUATION COMPARED TO WHITES	Equal or greater	Doubly Gratified	Fraternally Deprived
	Less than	Egoistically Deprived	Doubly Deprived

and (2) the relevant out-group (blacks). Figure 6.1 describes how respondents would be classified on the basis of their answers to these two questions.

The findings reinforce the need for a distinction between individual and collective relative deprivation. The greatest reluctance to vote for black mayoralty candidates, and the most negative images expressed regarding these black politicians, came from those who felt fraternal deprivation. Egoistical deprivation did not produce such negative attitudes; those who felt it, surprisingly, were most favorable to the black candidates.

The findings of Vanneman and Pettigrew (1972), who focused on white Americans, have been replicated with African-Americans. In separate studies, Abeles (1976) and Dibble (1981) found that fraternal deprivation, not egoistical deprivation, was most associated with discontent. In the case of Abeles (1976) this meant endorsing militancy among African-Americans, and for Dibble (1981) the focus was on approving violence as a means of gaining rights for African-Americans.

Support for the usefulness of the fraternal deprivation concept extends beyond relations between Caucasians and African-Americans in the United States. French-speaking Canadians living in the province of Quebec vary in the extent to which they support the separation of that province from Canada. Guimond and Dubé-Simard (1983) have shown that the best predictor of separatist attitudes is fraternal deprivation. Similarly, Dion, Dion, and Pak (1984) (described by Dion, 1986) report that among the Chinese community in a large Canadian city, it is fraternal deprivation that is most closely associated with satisfaction with various aspects of life in that city. Finally, Tripathi and Srivastava (1981) have found that the negative attitudes of Muslims toward Hindus are best predicted by fraternal deprivation.

Runciman (1966), however, did not deal with fraternal deprivation in any real depth, and important ambiguities remain. For example, one way to distinguish egoistical from fraternal deprivation is in terms of the target for social comparison. Thus, a comparison with members of one's own group (similar others) would be related to egoistical deprivation; a comparison with members of a "better-off" group (dissimilar others) would involve fraternal deprivation. Martin and her colleagues (Martin & Murray, 1983; Martin, Price, Bies, and Powers, 1979) examined this distinction by having secretaries view a tape and slide show depicting executives and secretaries in a company similar to their own. Secretaries were then told what pay they would receive and were asked whose pay they would be interested to learn about. The subjects were most interested in the highest-paid secretary and showed less interest in the pay of executives. Thus, comparison was egoistical, with a similar other, not with the dissimilar other (the executive). At one level such findings might be interpreted to mean that individual comparisons are primary and more frequent than group comparisons. We should not, however, be too hasty in drawing this conclusion. Instead, we should reexamine the definition of group or fraternal deprivation.

By the definition implied here, even the group comparison is individualistic, in the sense that it is the individual comparing himself or herself with another individual who happens to represent a different group. It is an individual secretary comparing with an individual executive. What about the more usual case, where, as a member of a group, I compare my group with another group? Thus, in the Martin et al. (1979) experiment, the question would not be "Does the secretary compare herself with another secretary or an executive?" but, rather, "Does she compare secretaries as a group with executives as a group in terms of salary?"

Crosby's (1982) study of working women points to the fundamental importance of this distinction. The women in her sample were asked about their personal feelings regarding their specific work situations, as well as about the situation of women in general. Surprisingly, Crosby did not obtain the same responses to these two questions. The women responded that on the whole they were satisfied with their personal work situations. However, they expressed considerable discontent about the position of working women as a group in the United States. Moreover, the women who expressed the most dissatisfaction about the role of women in general were those in high-prestige jobs. Why this should be the case, and why women report satisfaction with their own personal situations but dissatisfaction about the position of women in general, needs to be explored (see chapter 8 for a discussion of this issue in terms of discrimination). Clearly, the distinction between egoistical deprivation and fraternal deprivation has important implications for people's feelings, but experiencing one of these does not necessarily mean that the other one is experienced as well.

Finally, Martin, Brickman, and Murray (1984) expressed dissatisfaction with current definitions of deprivation in group terms and conducted interesting experiments to examine the variables affecting feelings of relative deprivation and their relation to action. Again, a business context was used. Subjects were presented with information about a fictitious company that had different salary levels for men and women. The variable manipulated was the number of women in the company whose salaries were equal to those of the men. The findings indicated that feelings of collective relative deprivation correlated with the magnitude of salary inequities. However, these feelings did not necessarily translate into collective action. Another feature of the experiment was that subjects were asked to judge the extent to which they would engage in various collective actions, such as attending meetings, engaging in work slowdowns, or making deliberate errors in work. However, the amount of felt deprivation did not produce differential willingness to engage in these forms of collective action.

Clearly, work on the feelings associated with collective deprivation is just beginning, and, at least for the immediate future, research on this topic is likely to be somewhat uncoordinated. There are a number of reasons for this. First, there will continue to be research at the individual level that is extrapolated directly to the group. Second, fundamental issues regarding the social comparison process remain to be resolved, such as when people make comparisons and which targets people choose for their comparisons. Research on these topics at either the individual or the group level will be important. Finally, there are no systematic attempts to outline the features unique to collective relative deprivation. Hence, research will, in the short term at least, be exploratory and therefore unfocused. The hope is that with an increased awareness of group issues and the insights gained from exploratory research, a clearer definition of the issues will emerge.

CRITICAL REVIEW OF RELATIVE DEPRIVATION

Any critical review of relative deprivation theory must begin by addressing the vehement attacks that have been made on social psychological theories of intergroup relations in general, and relative deprivation theory in particular, by proponents of resource mobilization theory (e.g., McCarthy & Zald, 1977; McPhail, 1980). Resource mobilization theorists argue that psychological processes are irrelevant to the study of collective behavior. For example, in a discussion of social protest, Kramnick (1972) describes research on perceived injustice as "obvious and trite, for surely only angry men turn to revolution" (p. 56).

According to resource mobilization theory, action on the part of disadvantaged group members arises when there are concrete resources to facilitate some form of action. Thus, where there are financial resources, where there is some form of social organization that includes effective communication channels among members, where there is coherent leadership, and where there are established mechanisms for protest, action is likely to ensue. Thus, from a resource mobilization theory perspective, feelings of relative deprivation do not lead to action. There is always discontent among disadvantaged peoples, resource mobilization theorists would argue, so what determines whether or not the discontent becomes translated into action is the availability of concrete structural resources.

Resource mobilization theory receives unanticipated support from a study by Martin, et al., (1984) whose theoretical perspective was sympathetic to relative deprivation theory. They used a laboratory paradigm and found that the willingness of disadvantaged group members to engage in illegitimate forms of collective action was affected only by the presence or absence of mobilization resources, and not by the magnitude of the feelings of deprivation. Variables such as the opportunity for frequent contact with other group members and the existence of previously successful examples served to increase ratings of interest in petty acts of sabotage, picketing, and pressure tactics. Increased feelings of deprivation were not effective in increasing interest in these types of actions.

It might be tempting to abandon the search for psychological processes such as relative deprivation to explain behavior in an intergroup context. But such a drastic measure might be premature. Instead, it may be more fruitful to respond to the challenges of resource mobilization theory by examining some of the limitations to theories like relative deprivation, with a view to understanding better the relationship between the emotions asociated with relative deprivation and the behaviors associated with these emotions. Three important limitations need to be addressed in this context (see Wright, Taylor, & Moghaddam, 1990a, for a review).

The first limitation is the restricted range of emotions that are normally examined in studies of relative deprivation. The focus is usually on emotions such as anger, frustration, and outrage that are obvious starting points for understanding responses to relative deprivation. This cluster of emotions is restrictive in two ways. First, the range is incomplete and needs to be expanded in future research. Moreover, selecting new emotions need not be based on guesswork. For example, Folger (1986), in the context of his referent cognitions theory, points to emotions such as "hope" and "faith in the existing system" as important determinants of behavior in an intergroup context. Thus, it is possible not only to expand the range of emotions that are included in relative deprivation research, but to base the expansion on sound theory.

The second way in which the range of emotions used in previous research has been restrictive is in the individualistic emphasis placed on these emotions. Too often resource mobilization theorists have attempted to predict collective behavior by examining feelings that are very individualistic in focus. Thus, there is a need to explore feelings such as collective anger and outrage.

Taylor, Wong-Rieger, McKirnan, and Bercusson (1982) examined the relationship between feeling threatened and whether an individualistic or collective response would be preferred. The participants were Anglophone Québecois, and the focus was on the language situation in Quebec. Potential individual threats, such as the inability to communicate in French on the phone or one's son or daughter marrying a French-speaking person, were contrasted with possible collective threats, such as the lack of opportunity for advancement at work for Anglophones, or hostility between Francophones and Anglophones. The overriding hypothesis was that individual threats would be associated with individually based coping strategies, and that collective action would be the anticipated response to group threats.

Surprisingly, this hypothesis was not confirmed. The Anglophone participants in the study consistently preferred an individualistic strategy for coping with threats even when these were defined as group based. Why might this be the case? Perhaps the Anglophone community in Quebec is not a well-defined social category that is accustomed to taking collective action. Or maybe there was, at the time of the study, no obvious leadership around which to organize collective action. Again, perhaps there is a feeling that taking collective action would only make matters worse and ultimately produce a worsening of intergroup relations. Whatever the reason, it is clear that there is no simple relationship between the feeling of relative deprivation and the response it generates.

The second major limitation to relative deprivation research is that too often behavior is not clearly operationalized. For example, dependent variables may include attitudes toward violent tactics (Abeles, 1976) or belief in violence as a means of gaining rights (Dibble, 1981). At best these may be measures of "behavioral intention," but they are more likely perceptions about what might be successful, not what subjects themselves might do.

The third, perhaps more serious limitation to research on relative deprivation is the tendency to investigate only a single form of behavior. Often the focus is on collective forms of socially disruptive behavior. Although the social significance of such behavior cannot be disputed, there are varieties of responses that someone might consider in the context of relative deprivation. These can range from individual forms of protest to collective behavior that is legitimized by society. Furthermore, these behaviors can take on various levels of severity. By focusing on a single behavior, the lack of predictability may arise not because relative deprivation is unimportant, but because subjects were not provided with behavioral options that they would endorse intuitively.

The challenge, then, is to address these limitations and test whether or not psychological processes such as relative deprivation play a role in understanding behavior. One initial attempt in this area has been made by Wright et al. (1990a), and the results are encouraging. It was possible to specify conditions where a strong association between emotions and behavior would arise. These findings dampen the enthusiasm of resource mobilization theorists who argue that any focus on psychological processes is misplaced. In the final analysis, then, resource mobilization theory, by its challenges to relative deprivation theory, will have played a constructive role if it stimulates better social psychological research on intergroup relations.

Pettigrew (1978), in addressing the question as to how a target for social comparison is selected with respect to groups, made a bold assertion that, if empirically verified, could prepare the ground for resolving the entire issue. He proposed that in the intergroup context the range of potential comparisons is very limited. He argued: "When groups are the referent, as opposed to individuals, the number of possibilities are sharply reduced. And reference groups tend to be reciprocally paired much in the manner of social roles: White-Black; native-immigrant; blue collar–white collar. Even in the polyethnic states, groups often form two political factions" (p. 36).

The predictive power of social comparison theory would be enhanced in important ways should Pettigrew's analysis be correct. But there are sound reasons for questioning his simple model of comparison choices in an intergroup context. Blacks may indeed compare themselves to whites. However, social comparisons may also reasonably be made with a variety of other groups, including blacks and whites in the past, various subgroups of blacks and whites, and any number of other visible minority groups, such as Mexican-Americans and Puerto Ricans, to cite two salient examples.

In order to address this issue directly, Taylor, Moghaddam, & Bellerose (1987) set out to examine, in the context of intergroup relations, what types of comparisons people make. Our operating hypothesis contrasted sharply with that expressed by Pettigrew (1978). Our assumption was that not all members of a group make comparisons with the same out-group. The participants in our study were Anglophones from the province of Quebec, and the focus was on the threats they feel from language legislation in the province that has made French the official language. We found eight major groups with whom Anglophones spontaneously and frequently made comparisons on the issue of language rights. These groups included, among others, Anglophones in other provinces, Francophones in Quebec today, Anglophones in Quebec in the past, and other language groups in Quebec.

Thus, our hypothesis was confirmed: in an intergroup context group members have a variety of potential groups with whom they might make comparisons. Thus, predicting whom members of a group will select for purposes of comparison, and under what circumstances, remains a fundamental issue for relative deprivation.

Fortunately there has been an upsurge of interest in the issue of social comparison in an intergroup context, and recently Major (1994) has integrated this research into the context of the social psychology of entitlement. She outlines three major factors that are likely to influence the choice of comparison target for disadvantaged group members. The first is the proximity or salience of comparison targets in the immediate environment. Major (1994) argues that since groups tend to be segregated from one another, and because there is a tendency for members of a group to affiliate with members of their own group (see Crocker & Major, 1989), then it follows that members of disadvantaged groups are likely to make intragroup, not intergroup, comparisons.

In terms of disadvantaged groups who are demarked on the basis of race or ethnicity, the notion that proximity might lead to an emphasis on intragroup comparisons is intuitively appealing. A major theme in the race-relations literature is the persistence of racial segregation, be it residential, in the workplace, or for leisure activities. Indeed, even in desegregated schools a consistent observation is that other than in the formal classroom environment, much of school life is characterized by segregation.

Less obvious is the extent to which women and men are segregated, thereby creating the conditions that might lead to intragroup comparisons. In terms of interpersonal relations and family life, women are a unique disadvantaged group with respect to the contact they have with men. However, Major (1994) argues convincingly that in the workplace gender segregation is pronounced. Within and across occupations and organizations, gender segregation is pervasive (Bielby & Baron, 1984). Indeed, while tasks and roles may differ cross-culturally, there is usually a clear distinction between "women's work" and "men's work" (Eagly, 1987). Thus, even in the less obvious situation of relations between men and women, conditions of proximity may lead women to make intra- rather than intergroup comparisons.

The second major influence on choice of comparison other that Major (1994) raises is the well-researched "perceived similarity" factor (see Suls & Miller, 1977; Wood, 1989). Since people tend to compare themselves with similar others, especially those who are similar in terms of attributes perceived to be related to the dimension being evaluated, it follows that members of a disadvantaged group have a tendency to make social comparisons with other in-group members.

Finally, the choice of comparison other very much depends upon the motivation underlying the social comparison. Taylor, Moghaddam, and Bellerose (1987) have addressed this issue in an intergroup context. They proposed three possible motivations for social comparison in an intergroup context: reality testing, group enhancement, and equity appeal.

To test these hypotheses, Anglophones were asked to indicate which, among the eight potential comparison groups described earlier, they would compare with under the three motivational conditions. The results are summarized in figure 6.2, where a striking pattern emerges. When motivated to evaluate their situation (reality testing), Anglophones reported making a variety of comparisons from a cross-section of groups. Among these groups there were equal numbers that were empirically determined to be "better-off" and "worse-off" groups. Indeed, the two most popular comparison groups included one that was empirically determined to be better off (Anglophones from other provinces) and one determined to be worse off (Francophones from other provinces). From figure 6.2 it is also clear that when they are motivated by "group enhancement," Anglophones make downward social comparisons, and when they are concerned with "equity appeal," the focus is on upward social comparisons.

The implicit assumption underlying relative deprivation theory is that social comparisons are made for the purposes of reality testing so that members of a group can evaluate their situation. The present analysis indicates that reality testing is only one of the motivations for making intergroup comparisons. Moreover, when motivated to test reality, group members do what is rational: they make comparisons with a variety of "better-off" and "worse-off" groups. Furthermore, as we discussed earlier, Major (1994) has pointed out how the variables of propinquity and similarity converge to bias disadvantaged group members toward intra-

Figure 6.2
Frequency with Which Comparison Groups Were Selected under Three Motivational Conditions

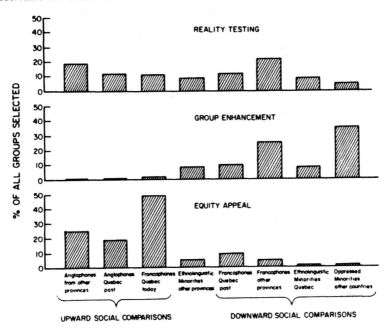

Source: Reprinted from Taylor, Moghaddam, & Bellerose, "Social Comparison in an Intergroup Context" in *The Journal of Social Psychology*, *129* (4), 499–515. Reprinted with permission of the Helen Dwight Reid Educational Foundation. Published by Haldref Publications, 1319 18th Street, N.W. Washington, D.C. 20036-1802, Copyright 1989.

group social comparisons. Therefore, it would seem that only rarely would disadvantaged group members engage in the type of social comparison that is assumed by relative deprivation—an intergroup comparison with a "better-off" out-group for the purposes of reality testing.

CONCLUSION

Relative deprivation has intuitive appeal as a theory because it offers insights into some persistent puzzles associated with intergroup relations. Specifically, it addresses two fundamental questions: Why is it that groups that are well off in terms of objective criteria sometimes feel dissatisfied, and why do disadvantaged groups sometimes accept their oppressed position?

Unfortunately, for many years relative deprivation theory languished because it could not address two issues that would give it the predictive power it needed. First, as resource mobilization theorists point out, it has little power to predict actual behavior. Second, it has not been possible to specify the target of social comparison, thereby reducing relative deprivation theory's predictive power.

As we have noted, in recent years there has been an upsurge of theoretical and empirical interest in these two issues. The result is a clear research agenda with a renewed status for relative deprivation, such that before long we can anticipate a major reformulation of the theory.

SUGGESTED READINGS

Crosby, F. (1982). *Relative deprivation and working women.* New York: Oxford University Press.

Major, B. (1994). From social inequality to personal entitlement: The role of social comparisons, legitimacy appraisals, and group membership. In M. Zanna (Ed.), *Advances in Experimental Psychology* (Vol. 26). New York, pp. 293–355.

Olson, J. M., Herman, C. P., & Zanna, M. P. (Eds.). (1986). *Relative deprivation and social comparison: The Ontario symposium* (Vol. 4). Hillsdale, N.J.: Erlbaum.

7

A Five-Stage Model of Intergroup Relations: Tokenism as a Potent Form of Discrimination

The five-stage model of intergroup relations, developed by Taylor and McKirnan (1984), can be usefully viewed in the context of the move toward nonreductionist social psychological accounts of intergroup relations. Taylor and McKirnan have attempted to produce a model of intergroup relations that is broad in scope and has theoretical underpinnings that are well established in mainstream social psychology. As such, the five-stage model can be seen as attempting to incorporate both macro and micro processes in interpreting intergroup behavior, thus aiming for a truly social psychological perspective.

In explaining the historical background to the five-stage model, it is relevant to point out that this model was developed at McGill, a Canadian university influenced by the academic traditions of both Europe and the United States. While most of Taylor and McKirnan's work is in the tradition of mainstream North American social research, their links with European social psychological theory are evident.

For example, in addition to being influenced by social identity theory (chapter 4), the five-stage model has its roots in elite theory (see Pareto, 1935, 1971; Mosca, 1939), a European-based theory that has been ignored by modern theorists. The theory proposes that all societies are composed of elites and nonelites. Where these groups are open and circulation between them is allowed, talented individuals move up into the elite and those with insufficient talent move down into the nonelite. However, where circulation is not permitted, talented members of the nonelite form counterelites and collectively attempt to overthrow the governing elite.

Thus, the European and North American influences are reflected in the scope and concerns of the five-stage model. On the one hand, the model reflects the European concern for macro social processes and the fate of disadvantaged groups; on the other hand, the theoretical underpinnings of the model, attribution and social comparison, are central to North American social psychology.

An assumption inherent in the five-stage model is that rarely, if ever, is the relationship between two groups perfectly equal. Thus, the model attempts to explain relations between groups where one is advantaged and the other is disadvantaged. The use of the labels "advantaged" and "disadvantaged" by Taylor and McKirnan (1984) should not go unnoticed, since it hints at a possible a priori bias. Some theorists use such labels as "majority" and "minority," which are neutral but misleading because numbers may not be a true indication of power. Others, such as Tajfel and Turner (1979), use the labels "dominant" and "subordinate," or "high" and "low" status, implying, however subtly, that the groups themselves are somehow responsible for their position or status. Taylor and McKirnan's use of "advantaged" and "disadvantaged" seems to imply that external conditions, rather than the traits of groups, are responsible for inequality.

Another feature of the five-stage model is its focus upon both the advantaged group and the disadvantaged group in an unequal relationship. This focus on both groups is welcome, given the rather unbalanced perspective that has characterized intergroup relations thus far. This imbalance has tended to be to the detriment of disadvantaged groups, since it is generally in Europe that research has, at least to some extent, focused upon minority-group behavior (Mugny, 1984). Interestingly, the issue of the underdog and minority-group behavior was a major concern of North American researchers, but only in the immediate postwar period. For example, this is clearly reflected in the research reviewed in Allport's classic study *The Nature of Prejudice* (1954) since the object of prejudice is generally a disadvantaged individual or group, a "minority" by definition (see Asch, 1956). However, the issue of minority-group behavior seems to have been set aside by North American psychologists since the early 1960s, and biases in favor of majority groups seem to have crept into all aspects of research (Sampson, 1981). Thus, the issue of responses to inequality, which is necessarily a minority-group concern, is a relatively neglected issue in contemporary social psychology.

As a social psychological model, the five-stage model is unusual both in its temporal expanse and in the scope of the factors it encompasses. The model deals with intergroup developmental processes that are assumed to be influenced by large-scale social changes, such as industrialization. Thus, it has a historical perspective. Moreover, the model deals with processes that can take more than the lifetime of any individual group member to complete. This implies that the processes underlying the five-stage model are in some ways more extensive than the psychology of any one generation of group members.

In the first part of this chapter, we shall review the main propositions of the five-stage model. This will be followed by a discussion of research designed to test major propositions of the model. Specifically, the focus will be on laboratory research that illustrates how tokenism serves as a subtle but potent form of discrimination. In the final major section, we present a critical review of the theory, focusing on its strengths and weaknesses.

AN OUTLINE OF THE FIVE-STAGE MODEL

Taylor and McKirnan (1984) propose five distinct developmental stages to intergroup behavior; they are presented schematically in figure 7.1. The stages include (1) clearly stratified intergroup relations, (2) individualistic ideology, (3) individual social mobility, (4) consciousness raising, and (5) collective action. It is assumed that all intergroup relations involve this five-stage development in the same sequential order. In terms of time frame, the five stages can take centuries to be completed, or they may take a much shorter period. The time required for intergroup relations to move from one stage to the next is not specified, but is assumed to be variable and dependent upon historical, social, economic, political, and psychological factors.

An important feature of the model, one that remains constant throughout the five stages, is the assumption that there are high- and low-status groups in society. That is, the stratified and differential state of society is accepted as part of social reality.

Finally, it is hypothesized that the key processes linking the sequence of stages are two mainstream social psychological concepts: causal attribution and social comparison. Beyond this, an important extension is made to both causal attribution and social comparison in order that they can be more effectively applied to an intergroup context. Specifically, two levels of causal attribution and social comparison are distinguished. In terms of causal attribution, the two levels are individual attribution, where causes and explanations are sought for individual behavior, and group attribution, where the individual seeks an explanation for the behavior of his or her own or another group.

Figure 7.1
Stages in the Dynamics of Intergroup Relations

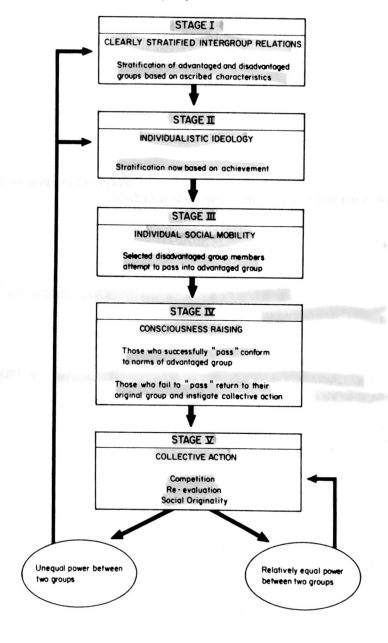

A similar distinction is made for social comparison. Individualistic social comparisons involve a person making social comparisons with other in-group members, whereas group comparisons involve the comparisons a person makes between his or her own group and some other relevant out-group.

Stage I: Clearly Stratified Intergroup Relations

At stage I, groups are stratified on the basis of ascribed characteristics, and there is an unbridged division between the advantaged group and the disadvantaged group. Examples of such societies are feudal and caste social structures, as well as what Van den Berghe (1967) has referred to as "paternalistic" societies. An example would be the relationship between slave owners and slaves in early U.S. history. A current example of this phenomenon might be the caste system in India. The basis for social stratification in such societies can be inherent, such as race and sex, or ascribed, such as religious belief and role. However, in all cases it is assumed that stratification takes place only on the basis of the selected criteria for group membership, and this division is not questioned by members of either group.

In such intergroup contexts, the pattern of social attributions and social comparisons is dictated by the power relations between the groups. Only individualistic or intragroup social comparisons are deemed legitimate, since the out-group, whether it is advantaged or disadvantaged, is seen as being so dissimilar to the in-group that social comparison with its members is judged to be illegitimate (Festinger, 1954). Group membership covaries perfectly with an easily recognizable characteristic such as race or sex, and the intergroup status situation is completely rigid.

Paradoxically, disadvantaged group members attribute their disadvantaged position to themselves, on the assumption that it is their own race or sex, for example, that has led them to be disadvantaged. Such "own responsible" attributions are, naturally, propagated by the advantaged group; and disadvantaged group members have such limited power that they have little option but to share the advantaged group's views on social reality.

Stage II: Emerging Individualistic Social Ideology

During stage II, stratification is on the basis of achievement rather than ascribed characteristics. This stage of development is reached as an outcome of modernization and the growth of a middle class. The increased importance of both occupational skill and role complexity, and the implication that individual ability and effort determine the occupational role and status of a person, gradually lead to the ideology of individual social mobility. That is, although there are still two groups during stage II, one relatively advantaged and the other disadvantaged, group membership is now assumed to be based on individual achievement rather than ascribed group characteristics.

While in stage I perceptions of the basis of social stratification correspond to the actual basis, in stage II the actual basis of social stratification may be different from the perceived basis. Thus, while the perceived basis of membership in an advantaged group might be individual achievement, the actual basis could still be race, sex, or birth into a rich family.

The key psychological difference between stages I and II is that in stage I the groups are accurately perceived as being closed, but in stage II the groups are perceived as being open. Also, the social comparisons and social attributions made in stage II legitimize the perception that individual ability and effort determine status. Members of both advantaged and disadvantaged groups attribute their status to individual characteristics for which they are assumed to be responsible, such as ability and effort. From the perspective of the advantaged group, this "person blame" ideology is particularly important, since it exonerates the advantaged group from responsibility for the disadvantaged position of the out-group members.

Since individuals are perceived as being responsible for group membership, social comparisons take place at the interindividual level. In terms of equity theory (see chapter 5), disadvantaged group members comparing themselves with members of the out-group downplay their own input until the ratio of inputs to outcomes is identical with that of the out-group. For example, working-class persons are socialized to believe that their inputs to society are less valuable than those of persons in professional positions. Through this process, they come to feel that they "get what they deserve," thereby justifying their disadvantaged position.

Stage III: Individual Social Mobility

At stage III, individual members of the disadvantaged group attempt to move into the advantaged group. This social mobility will be in two forms. The first involves an attempt by a disadvantaged group member to completely change his or her characteristics so as to "pass" as a member of the advantaged group. The second form of social mobility is less extensive and involves an attempt by a disadvantaged group member to adopt enough of the advantaged group's characteristics to be accepted as a member of that group, yet retain enough features of the disadvantaged group to maintain his or her original identity.

The motivation for an attempt to move into the advantaged group is assumed to be a need for positive social identity. In this key respect, therefore, the five-stage model is similar to social identity theory (see chapter 4), which perhaps reflects the influence of Tajfel and his associates on this model. By passing into an advantaged group, a disadvantaged group member necessarily rejects some of the features of the disadvantaged group.

The five-stage model is very specific about precisely who among the disadvantaged group are most likely to attempt upward social mobility. This move will be attempted only by a select few among the disadvantaged group, the most talented and the ones most likely to initiate interpersonal comparisons with individual members of the advantaged group.

The social comparisons encouraged by the stage II ideology lead the most talented disadvantaged group members to initiate upward social mobility. The key feature of the social comparisons encouraged by the stage II ideology is that they are interindividual. Moreover, they are not on the basis of ascribed characteristics, but of the criteria that are relevant to the requirements for entry into the advantaged group. Thus, when social comparisons are made on the basis of ability and effort, it is the most talented among the disadvantaged group who come closest to having the requirements for entry into the advantaged group.

The social attribution patterns of the stage II ideology also encourage attempts at upward social mobility by the most talented members of the disadvantaged group. Advantaged group members attribute the acquisition of their status to factors for which they are personally responsible, such as effort and ability. Disadvantaged group members who are closest to the advantaged group in terms of relevant characteristics, and who share the ideology of the advantaged group, are thus motivated to attempt upward social mobility, since they see themselves as good enough to succeed according to the rules of the system.

The key assumption made with respect to stage III is that individual attempts at upward social mobility are always the first strategy by which the most talented members of a disadvantaged group cope with inequality. According to the five-stage model, collective action occurs only after individual attempts at upward social mobility have failed. Historic examples of such behavior are the blacks in North America, various immigrant groups, and the French in Canada. In all cases, attempts were made to "pass" individually into the advantaged group by changing physical characteristics, anglicizing names, altering accents in speech, or acquiring English. Only later did collective action predominate.

This assumption that individual action will always precede collective action holds only for stage III conditions where the predominant ideology is that individual mobility is possible on the basis of ability and effort. In a recent experiment, Ellemers, Wilke, and van Knippenberg (1993) claim to have produced conditions that disconfirm this assumption of the five-stage model. They report that under certain conditions, subjects will prefer collective action without first considering, or apparently exploring, the possibility of individual action. However, in Ellemers et al.'s laboratory condition, subjects were explicitly told that individual mobility was not a possibility. Naturally subjects will gravitate to a collective alternative when there is no possibility for individual mobility (stage I). The challenge, then, is to find conditions where, as in most Western cultures, individual mobility according to a "meritocracy" is the stated ideology, and yet people show an initial preference for collective over individual action.

Stage IV: Consciousness Raising

The talented members of the disadvantaged group who attempt upward social mobility are not always successful. However, the few who do succeed play an important role in strengthening the social system. They do this in two ways. First, their success reaffirms their belief in the ideology and justice of the system and leads them to assimilate in the extreme into the advantaged group. According to the dominant ideology, it was hard work and talent that moved them up into the advantaged group, and they are justified in feeling proud of their success.

The disadvantaged group members who do succeed in moving up into the advantaged group serve as evidence that the system works, that it is just, and that anyone with the required abilities can "make it." Also, since these individuals are the potential leaders of the disadvantaged group, their upward social mobility serves to weaken the disadvantaged group and strengthen the advantaged group.

There will also be some disadvantaged group members who attempt upward social mobility but fail to gain entry into the advantaged group. They may, in accordance with the prevailing ideology, attribute their failure to their own personal characteristics. Thus, the notion "I am just not good enough" or "I should have tried harder" could be used to explain their failure to gain entrance into the advantaged group. However, Taylor and McKirnan (1984) argue that this is unlikely, since these individuals will probably be influenced by self-serving biases in attribution. Thus, they will look to external factors to explain their failure to move into the advantaged group. Specifically, they will see the actions of the advantaged group as having unjustly prevented their upward social mobility. Furthermore, they will switch from seeing their own personal characteristics as being the cause of their disadvantaged position to seeing the actions of the dominant group as being causally responsible. Thus, they will gradually see events in intergroup rather than in individualistic terms.

Those disadvantaged group members who fail in their attempt at upward social mobility will come to believe that their personal esteem is tied up with that of the entire disadvantaged group, rather than being based on their personal characteristics. That is, the only way in which the position of the self can be improved is by improving the position of the entire group. This transition in perspective involves a shift from interpersonal to intergroup social comparisons.

However, a move toward collective action by the disadvantaged group requires that a large number of disadvantaged group members come to believe that the ideology linking ability and effort to station in life is invalid. Specifically, they must come to believe that social status is not in fact determined by individual characteristics, but is unjustly determined on the basis of characteristics such as race or sex; in short, discrimination. Those disadvantaged group members who have failed to achieve upward social mobility play a key role in bringing about this awareness by embarking upon consciousness raising among the disadvantaged group. These "consciousness raisers" attempt to convince all the members of their group that membership in a disadvantaged group is not based upon such individual characteristics as ability and effort, but is unjustly determined by discrimination on the basis of ascribed characteristics such as ethnicity and race.

Stage V: Collective Action

Consciousness raising among the disadvantaged group members leads to collective attempts to improve the group's position vis-à-vis the advantaged group. The collective strategies envisaged in the five-stage model are those outlined by Tajfel and Turner (1979) in social identity theory (see chapter 4). The first collective strategy is collective competition, which involves attempts to compete with the advantaged group along particular dimensions of competence or status in a given society. This is competition according to the existing rules of the game. A second collective strategy involves redefinition. That is, characteristics of the group that were previously defined as negative are redefined as positive, and attempts are made to obtain acceptance for this reevaluation. A classic example would be the "Black is beautiful" movement among North American blacks. A third collective strategy is referred to as "social originality" and involves the creation of new dimensions for social comparison by the disadvantaged group. For example, a disadvantaged group might emphasize not the outcome of a performance but the environmental hardships that have to be overcome in order to achieve the outcome. By implication, those persons who are less advantaged in terms of environmental conditions are now seen as higher achievers, even if they do not do quite as well as advantaged persons who enjoy good environmental conditions.

At this stage, the disadvantaged group encourages intergroup comparisons, while the advantaged group attempts to show that only individualistic comparisons are legitimate. That is, the advantaged group will argue that there is free movement between groups, and anyone who has the necessary entry requirements will be able to achieve upward social mobility into the advantaged group. By contrast, the disadvantaged group will attempt to show that social categorization is on the basis of ascribed characteristics, and movement between groups is not possible.

The pattern of attribution at this stage is particularly interesting. While disadvantaged group members attribute responsibility for past subordination to the advantaged group (external attribution), hope for the future is attributed to the disadvantaged group in the form of controllable internal characteristics of the disadvantaged group (internal attribution). This pattern of external attributions for past status and internal attributions for future status has been found, for example, among North American blacks (Rappaport, 1977).

Once the stage of intergroup competitive relations (stage V) has been reached, three possible outcomes are hypothesized. The first and second of these lead the groups back to stage I or II, with the cycle beginning anew. That is, first, the relative power between the advantaged and disadvantaged groups may remain unchanged, resulting in a return to stage II relations. Second, the previously disadvantaged group may emerge as dominant, resulting in a return to stage II relations with the status position of the groups now reversed. Third, the groups may become relatively, although never completely, equal in status and power. In this situation, constant intergroup social comparisons, with no clear-cut victor, will keep the intergroup situation in a healthy state of competition.

RESEARCH ARISING OUT OF THE FIVE-STAGE MODEL: TOKENISM AS A MECHANISM FOR DISCRIMINATION

Wright and his colleagues (see Wright, Taylor, & Moghaddam, 1990) have completed a series of experiments, stimulated by the five-stage model, that focus on "tokenism" as a subtle but powerful form of discrimination. Tokenism is a structural reality that may be encountered by members of virtually every disadvantaged group, including women, the disabled, and all racial, ethnic, and language minorities. Tokenism is a social strategy whereby a few capable members of a disadvantaged group are accepted into advantaged positions while access is systematically blocked for the vast majority of qualified disadvantaged group members. This structural strategy represents a particularly subtle form of discrimination (see Laws, 1975; Moreland, 1965).

In order to address the issue of tokenism it was necessary first to develop a framework for categorizing the numerous behaviors that might be instigated by members of a disadvantaged group, and then design an experimental paradigm to test the effects of tokenism (see Taylor, Moghaddam, Gamble, & Zellerer, 1987). The need for a behavioral framework arises because of methodological limitations to research on intergroup relations we highlighted in our discussion of relative deprivation theory (chapter 6). Usually research is restricted to the perceptions and feelings of disadvantaged group members and does not examine behavior per se. Moreover, even when behavior is the focus, subjects are usually presented with the options of either taking no action or choosing the one behavior offered by the experimenter.

The behavioral framework proposed by Wright et al. (1990b) involves categorizing the behavior of disadvantaged group members along two dimensions: the extent to which the behavior is individual or collective, and the extent to which it is normative or antinormative from the perspective of the advantaged group. From these dimensions, five broad categories of behavior arise: (1) apparent acceptance of one's disadvantaged position, (2) attempts at individual upward mobility through normative channels, (3) individual action that is counter to the norms specified by the advantaged group, (4) instigation of collective action that is within the prescribed norms, and (5) instigation of collective action that is contrary to the norms.

The behaviors described by these categories have dramatically different societal consequences. For example, collective antinormative action (e.g., riots) directly threatens the existing social order, whereas acceptance and individual normative actions serve to protect the status quo.

The experimental paradigm developed to test hypotheses derived from the five-stage model, and tokenism more specifically, involves reproducing in the laboratory certain features of the "meritocracy" ideology that is central to Western democracy. Participants are told that "as in the real world," they will begin the experiment as a member of a low-status decision-making group, but, again as in the "real world," their performance on a decision-making task may earn them a promotion to a high-status decision-making group. Participants are also told that as in real-life organizations, it is members of the high-status group who set the decision-making test and decide on the performance criteria for promotion to the high-status group. Finally, it is explained that because of their proven performance, members of the high-status group participate in a $300 lottery, whereas members of the low-status group are relegated to a $30 lottery. (In fact, all participate in the $300 lottery.)

Following these instructions, participants complete a test for effective decision making, a test, it is explained, that, while not favoring any faculty over another, measures a skill that is essential for anyone who aspires to a position of status and leadership. Participants are given 15 minutes to complete the test, which requires them to read the evidence from a criminal case and to answer three short essay questions, ostensibly designed to assess their decision-making skills. Upon completion, their answers are taken by an assistant to another room, where presumably a panel of high-status-group members grades the participant's work.

After an appropriate delay, the assistant returns to the laboratory room with written feedback for each participant from the panel of judges. This written feedback is in fact prepared by the assistant and is the major mechanism by which different experimental conditions are created. For example, through the written feedback, participants can be led to believe that they have succeeded or failed in their bid to be promoted to the high-status group. The legitimacy of their fate can also be manipulated, as can information about the fate of others from the low-status group who are aspiring to upward mobility. Thus, the paradigm mirrors the meritocratic structure of most real-world institutions. However, it allows for any number of experimental manipulations in order to examine the conditions under which participants will prefer one or more of the five categories of behavior in response to their attempts at upward mobility.

The experimental paradigm, coupled with the framework for behavior, allows for a test of how disadvantaged group members respond to tokenism. Four experimental conditions were created (see Wright et al., 1990b) by varying the written feedback that participants received from their effort to gain entry to the high-status group. All participants were told that a grade of 8.5/10 was the mark required to be successful. In the "meritocracy" condition, participants failed in their quest because they achieved a score below the required 8.5. In the "closed" condition, participants received a grade above the required 8.5, but were told in writing from the panel of high-status-group members that despite their good performance the panel had arbitrarily decided, after the fact, not to allow any member of the low-status group into the high-status group. In the "partially closed" condition, participants again received a grade above the 8.5 cutoff, but were told that access to the high-status group was denied because the panel of judges had instituted a 30 percent quota. Of particular interest was the "tokenism" condition, where a 2 percent quota was arbitrarily introduced by the high-status panel. Thus, from all low-status group members who received a grade above the 8.5 criterion, only 2 percent would be permitted entry to the high-status group.

Participants' behavioral responses to the four experimental conditions were particularly revealing. For the meritocracy condition, participants responded to their failure by either accepting their fate or taking individual/normative action, which took the form of requesting a retest. Even those in the partially closed (30 percent) condition avoided any collective or antinormative actions. Despite the arbitrary introduction of the quota that led to their failure, participants behaved very much like those in the meritocracy condition.

The situation was very different for those in the closed condition. Here participants favored collective/antinormative action, the most disruptive form of action from the point of view of the high-status group. Of particular interest were the responses of those in the tokenism (2 percent) condition, who confronted failure because of an imposed quota that made access to the high-status group almost impossible. Yet participants in this condition did not respond as did those in the closed condition. Instead of opting for collective action, participants in the tokenism condition chose individual/antinormative action, an action that is not particularly threatening to the status quo.

These findings, which have been subsequently replicated (see Wright & Taylor, 1993; Lalonde & Silverman, 1994), are both unexpected and disquieting. The findings are unexpected because the tokenism and closed conditions are virtually identical in terms of personal and collective outcomes. At the personal level they are identical; despite performance that surpasses the stated criterion, the individual is robbed of a substantial personal gain because of his or her group membership. At the group level, both the closed and tokenism experiences are clearly discriminatory. In both conditions, many capable members of proven ability are being discriminated against. Yet when disadvantaged group members were faced with tokenism, they preferred individual action rather than the collective behaviors preferred by those confronted with a completely closed intergroup context.

The results are disquieting because of their societal implications. If, indeed, advantaged group members engage in tokenism with the express purpose of discriminating against members of a disadvantaged group, then their strategy appears to be highly effective. Permitting a token few members of a disadvantaged group access to upward mobility appears to ensure that the rest of the disadvantaged group members limit their reaction by engaging only in individual forms of behavior, a class of behaviors that are not especially disruptive of the status quo in general and the privileged status of the advantaged group in particular.

In order to comprehend both the theoretical and societal implications of tokenism, the psychological processes of two subgroups within the disadvantaged group need to be understood: those few disadvantaged group members who are the "tokens" and thus are permitted access to the high-status group, and the majority of disadvantaged group members who suffer the negative consequences of tokenism. Wright and Taylor (1992) conducted an initial series of experiments on successful tokens, where two contrasting hypotheses were explored. On the one hand, advocates for the promotion of talented minority-group members view such promotions as a breakthrough. The minority-group member who has achieved high status is in a strategic position to facilitate the upward mobility of all minority-group members. In direct contrast, the five-stage model proposes that successful tokens are likely to shift their identity quickly to the high-status group (stage III) and distance themselves from their prior group.

The results of the experiments consistently supported the five-stage model. Low-status-group members who were successful in gaining entrance to a high-status group despite a 2 percent quota were asked to support various actions on the part of the low-status group. Successful tokens did not support collective and antinormative actions by low-status-group members, which might have prompted a real change in status for the low-status group. Instead, successful tokens immediately shifted their allegiance from the low-status group to their new high-status group and would only allow low-status-group members to take actions that would not threaten the status quo (no action or individual/normative action).

The theoretical challenge is to understand why unsuccessful tokens avoid the socially disruptive actions (collective and antinormative) that are preferred by those who confront a completely segregated intergroup context where there is no room for upward mobility. A hypothesis proposed by Wright and Taylor (1993), which has received some initial support, is that unsuccessful tokens are confronted with an ambiguous situation that leads them to behave in a unique way. That is, on the one hand, tokenism contains elements of complete segregation in that access to the high-status group is almost impossible. On the other hand, there is an element of meritocracy, albeit a small one, in the sense that there are a token few among the low-status group who do achieve successful entry to a high-status group, and the success of the token few is based on extraordinary performance. Faced with such an ambiguous situation, low-status-group members seem to prefer individual action because of the vestiges of a meritocracy, but prefer antinormative behavior because of the obvious discrimination inherent in tokenism.

One reason why the student subjects acting as minority-group members in the laboratory study by Wright et al. (1990b) could abandon their groups fairly readily was perhaps the fact that ties of sentiment with the in-group had had little opportunity to develop. In essence, affective group ties are almost minimal in such laboratory conditions, because such groups have a very short history (e.g., one hour) compared to many minority groups in the world outside the laboratory, such as those with common cultures and ethnic histories. The issue of ecological validity is obviously of particular importance in this discussion.

Studies of first-generation immigrants from South Asia, China, the West Indies, and Iran suggest that an important segment of such groups gives priority to collective rather than individual mobility (Moghaddam, Taylor, & Lalonde, 1987; Moghaddam & Perreault, 1992). This preference for collective action seems to be associated with a desire to retain the heritage culture and language. One interpretation of these results is that the long and rich histories shared by members of such "real-life" groups lead to greater in-group ties and stronger loyalty on the part of members. Consequently, the members of such groups will give more priority to collective action and less to individual mobility, relative to the "members" of temporary laboratory groups.

However, an alternative interpretation of the results from such field studies is that the respondents are showing a preference for collective action because their attempts at individual mobility had been blocked at some earlier time. Thus, for example, it could be argued that these respondents are in transition from stage III, where their attempts at individual mobility had been blocked, to stages IV (consciousness raising) and V (collective action). In order to test this possibility, researchers might attempt to check the personal histories of minority-group members and in this way determine whether these individuals did at one time give priority to individual mobility but were blocked on that route. However, it is clear that the five-stage model is very difficult to test empirically in the field setting, because of the complexities involved in determining the exact stage at which a group is and in which direction it is actually moving in the five-stage process.

In the final analysis, tokenism emerges as a subtle but very powerful form of discrimination. Successful tokens quickly abandon their former disadvantaged group colleagues and shift their identity to the high-status group. Unsuccessful tokens, confronted with an ambiguous intergroup situation, consistently react in a manner that maintains the status quo and thereby the best interests of the high-status group. This research, then, is in line with a number of other studies that suggest that tokenism has negative consequences for minority-group members. Other studies from the literature suggest that tokens are conveyed the message "We expect you to perform poorly" (Garland & Price, 1977; Hall & Hall, 1976), and research by Delia Saenz and Charles Lord (Lord & Saenz, 1985; Saenz & Lord, 1989) suggesting that tokens can suffer cognitive handicaps as a result of recognizing themselves as tokens even when they are not treated differently.

CRITICAL REVIEW OF THE FIVE-STAGE MODEL

The most important strength of the five-stage model is probably that it encompasses both macro- and micro-level processes. That is, Taylor and McKirnan (1984) have attempted to explain intergroup relations by referring to social processes that function at the intergroup level as well as to psychological processes that function at the intra- and interpersonal levels. For example, the transition they envisage from stratification based on ascribed characteristics (stage I) to stratification based on achievement (stage II) is assumed to involve, and partly derive from, large-scale processes of industrialization and the emergence of a middle class in society. At the same time, this transition is assumed to involve psychological changes related to social attribution and social comparison at the intra- and interpersonal levels. This incorporation of micro and macro processes is surely a feature toward which social psychological accounts of intergroup relations should strive.

Second, the five-stage model has the strength of being realistic, in that it presents a picture of unequal groups in situations of actual or potential competition for scarce resources. This model also seems to take an ideological stand, in that it focuses upon responses to inequality and minority-group behavior. Despite the increase of interest in minority-group behavior during the 1980s (see Moscovici et al., 1984; Mugny, 1985), there is still little research on the behavior of disadvantaged groups, and this neglect is especially apparent in North America. The five-stage model should prove useful in redressing this imbalance.

Third, by outlining a historical development of intergroup relations, the five-stage model attempts to avoid working in a historical vacuum. By linking the five stages of intergroup development to evolutionary stages in social history, such as feudalism and industrialization, it goes some way toward placing intergroup behavior in a historical context.

Fourth, although it is a broad-based theory, the five-stage model has generated specific hypotheses that can be tested through the methods of experimental social psychology.

However, the five-stage model also seems to have a number of weaknesses. First, stages I and II represent two different social systems, the first based on ascribed characteristics and the second on achieved characteristics. However, only the second of these, the one based on achieved characteristics, is elaborated in stages III through V. That is, stages II through V all revolve around the validity of an ideology based on achieved characteristics. It might be expected that the ideology of ascribed characteristics depicted in stage I could lead to a series of dynamic relations between groups. However, this possibility has not been explored by Taylor and McKirnan (1984).

Second, the five-stage model deals with collective action by a disadvantaged group led by talented members who have failed to achieve upward social mobility. However, it does not deal with what the historical evidence would suggest is an equally important phenomenon in terms of collective responses to inequality: collective action by a disadvantaged group led by disenchanted members of the advantaged group. Such revolutionary leaders as Mao, Gandhi, and Castro serve as possible examples of how disenchanted members of advantaged groups can desert their original social class and lead disadvantaged groups to rebellion. Thus, the five-stage model needs also to deal with movement from the advantaged group to the disadvantaged group, particularly in terms of individuals who reject the dominant ideology.

Similarly, the model would benefit from an extension that would allow it to explain advantaged group reactions to rebellion by disadvantaged groups or individuals. This omission in the model might be explained by claiming that it is designed to deal mainly with responses to inequality rather than with responses to superiority. However, the responses of disadvantaged groups must, to some extent at least, be influenced by reactions on the part of the advantaged group.

Third, the model does not adequately explain the processes that enable interstage transitions to take more time than the lifespan of an individual person. A central assumption in the model is that a transition from each to the next could take several centuries. However, it is also assumed that the social psychological processes of social comparison and social attribution are influential in these transitions. The assumption implicit in the model is that there can be a transfer of the necessary perceptions, values, and ideas from one generation to the next, so that the social and psychological links between one stage and the next remain intact across generations. This assumption needs to be elaborated and supported.

Finally, the five-stage model shares with equity theory the problem of being in some ways circular and nonfalsifiable. That is, just as inputs and outputs are almost impossible to pin down exactly in equity theory, the time frame for intergroup developments has not been specified in the five-stage model. Thus, predictions regarding transition from one stage to the next might be almost impossible to test in the real world, since the model does not specify any time limits for their development.

CONCLUSION

The five-stage model of intergroup relations attempts to sketch a heuristically useful model of relations between groups. There are several features of the model that are noteworthy, given the major themes that have recurred in this volume. First, an attempt is made to provide a descriptive framework in the form of five relatively discrete stages and a fixed sequence to these stages that can be applied to any intergroup situation. The aim is to provide a set of guidelines so that research can be integrated and cumulative. Second, it is hypothesized that a true understanding of intergroup relations requires an appreciation of basic social psychological processes, with special concern for how they are influenced and modulated by the larger social, political, and economic contexts. It is proposed that causal attribution and social comparison are two basic processes that explain the maintenance of any particular stage and the transition from one stage to another. Moreover, explicit account is taken of the need to consider causal attribution and social comparison at both the individual and the collective level. Although it is perhaps too early to determine its heuristic value, the five-stage model does represent an attempt to deal with some of the recurrent limitations we have noted in many current theories, and it does attempt to meet the demands of a truly social psychological theory of intergroup relations.

SUGGESTED READING

Taylor, D. M., & McKirnan, D. J. (1984). A five-stage model of intergroup relations. *British Journal of Social Psychology, 23*, 291–300.

8

Stereotypes, Attributions, and Discrimination

In this chapter we discuss three concepts or processes that have played a central role in the social psychology of intergroup relations. Individually, or in combination, they do not constitute full-blown theories of intergroup relations. That is, they do not systematically address the genesis of intergroup conflict, its unfolding, and its resolution. Instead, they represent central psychological processes that focus on a particular dimension of intergroup relations, most notably the mechanisms by which advantaged and disadvantaged group members perceive and interpret interactions that appear to be based on their category membership rather than on their individual characteristics.

Each of the three concepts or processes has had an important and unique history in the social psychological literature. Thus, each has its own theoretical and empirical domain. In this sense there is no obvious overlap among the concepts. They are presented here in the same chapter because while they do not qualify as broadly based theories of intergroup relations, they have each offered important insights into intergroup relations, and any serious theory of intergroup relations must integrate the insights that arise from the rich tradition of research in stereotypes, attribution, and discrimination.

STEREOTYPES

The stereotype is a fundamental cognitive process in mainstream social psychology that, more than any other, is directly linked to intergroup relations. If any concept could have emerged as the basis for a broad framework for intergroup relations, it is the gender/racial/ethnic stereotype. A brief history of the development of the concept within mainstream social psychology may provide some explanation of why it remains an important and influential concept, but one that at present cannot form the basis of a theory of intergroup relations.

The definition of stereotype generally adopted by researchers reflects the strong link that this concept has had with ethnic groups (for major reviews of the stereotype literature, see Brigham, 1971; Campbell, 1967; Cauthen, Robinson, & Krauss, 1971; Fishman, 1956; Gardner, 1973; Hamilton, 1981; A. G. Miller, 1982; Tajfel, 1969; Taylor, 1981; Taylor & Lalonde, 1987. Brigham's (1971) representative definition is that a stereotype involves "a generalization made about an ethnic group, concerning a trait attribution, which is considered to be unjustified by an observer" (p. 29). Others have added further clarifications and, indeed, explicit moral judgments by noting that stereotypes are rigid impressions conforming very little to the facts (Katz & Braly, 1935), exaggerated beliefs (Allport, 1954), and inaccurate and irrational overgeneralizations (Middlebrook, 1974). In the same tradition, Baron and Byrne (1977) have argued that stereotypes are "clusters of preconceived notions regarding various groups" in which there are "strong tendencies to overgeneralize about individuals solely on the basis of their membership in particular racial, ethnic, or religious groups" (p. 155).

There are two aspects to these definitions that particularly warrant comment in the present context. First, the stereotype, unlike attitudes, attributions, values, schemata, and other cognitive predispositions, refers directly to the perception of societal groups or at least to the perception of individuals as members of groups.

But there is also a second way in which the stereotype is a truly group or collective process, and this has gone virtually unrecognized. This is best exemplified by the manner in which stereotypes are operationalized, that is, in terms of the methods that have been developed to measure stereotypes. The basic procedure was introduced by Katz and Braly (1933), and while there have been several more recent innovations (Brigham, 1971; Gardner, Wonnacott, & Taylor, 1968; Triandis & Vassiliou, 1967), the underlying rationale remains unchanged. Subjects are presented with an ethnic-group label and are asked to check off or rate the extent to which each of a long list of trait adjectives best describes the ethnic group in question. Thus, the stereotype is operationally defined by those characteristics that are chosen or endorsed most frequently.

By definition, then, the stereotype is a collective process, since only when there is consensus among members of one group about the attributes of another can an attribute be included as part of the stereotype. In this sense the stereotype is very different from an attitude or an attribution. With attitudes, the aim is to assess an individual's evaluative response to a social object. The stereotype is concerned with group perceptions of a social object in such a way that it is theoretically impossible to determine the stereotype from the perceptions of one individual.

We might have expected this collective feature of stereotypes to be a major focus for theory and research. However, it has received little attention from researchers. For example, Gardner, Kirby, and Finley (1973) and Lalonde (1985) are among the few even to explore the implications of the consensual aspect of stereotypes by examining how the shared features of stereotypes facilitate in-group communication.

Until very recently, the study of stereotypes has been largely a descriptive exercise, aimed at identifying the stereotype that one particular group has of another. The emphasis on the negative implications of the traits often identified by research on stereotyping is probably one of the reasons why the stereotype has been viewed as morally wrong. For example, we learned that college students from the United States stereotype Jewish people as intelligent, industrious, and shrewd; Turks as treacherous; Germans as industrious and scientifically minded; and blacks as musical, happy-go-lucky, and lazy (Karlins, Coffman, & Walters, 1969). In Canada, English Canadians stereotype French Canadians as talkative, excitable, and proud (Gardner et al., 1968), and French Canadians describe English Canadians as educated, dominant, and ambitious (Aboud & Taylor, 1971). Although this legacy of descriptive research is a useful point of departure, it has done little to thrust the concept of stereotype to center stage in social psychology. Nor has it advanced our understanding of the dynamics of intergroup relations.

Recently, however, two major developments have taken place within the field of stereotypes, the first no doubt paving the way for the second. First, there has been a change in the way stereotypes are conceptualized and defined. Traditionally, the stereotype was defined as an undesirable process because it was either an inferior cognitive process in the form of an overgeneralization or oversimplification, or a process that was morally wrong because it categorized people who had no desire to be so categorized.

More recently, the trend is to view stereotyping as a basic cognitive process that is neither desirable nor undesirable in and of itself (see, for example, Berry, 1970; Tajfel, 1969; Triandis, 1971). So, for example,

Hamilton (1979, 1981) describes the stereotype as a schema about members of an identifiable group. Taylor (1981) has defined the stereotype as consensus among members of one group regarding the attributes of another, thereby explicitly rejecting the view of the stereotype as an inferior process or morally wrong. The social psychology text by Deaux and Wrightsman (1984) underlines this point. They remark that "although stereotypes may have certain negatively valued characteristics, most psychologists today would not consider them automatically bad things to have" (p. 90).

This change in evaluative judgment about the stereotype has had the effect of shifting attention away from the descriptive aspects of the stereotype and to understanding how it operates as a basic cognitive process. So, for example, Hamilton and his colleagues (Hamilton, 1979; Hamilton & Gifford, 1976) have focused on the illusory correlation arising in stereotypes whereby a group becomes associated with a particular characteristic, not as a function of explicit prejudice but out of a basic cognitive process. This process involves people perceiving a relation between events that are distinctive, even when the relation is not warranted on the basis of the actual frequency with which the event occurs. For example, when a newspaper reports that a minority-group member committed a brutal murder, the illusory correlation process is set in motion. To be a member of a minority group and to commit murder are both unusual or very distinctive. Thus, an association is made between that minority group and the brutal behavior in the form of a stereotype, even if the frequency with which members of that minority commit such acts does not warrant such a generalization.

The current drama associated with international terrorism no doubt lends itself precisely to this process and indeed may be responsible for the ongoing "Arab-bashing" in America. A representative *Newsweek* article (Newell, McKillop, & Monroe, 1986) on the harassment experienced by Arab Americans notes that while youngsters cope with being labeled "camel jockey" and "rag head," and the Arab community is stereotyped as "terrorists," most are "themselves victims of terror: war-weary expatriates from the Middle East who hoped to find safety in America." Despite these implications for group perception, this focus on stereotypes as a basic and normal process represents an important new level of inquiry, but one that is still not sufficiently intergroup in its emphasis.

Research in the cognitive tradition has begun to implicate relations between groups more directly. For example, Rothbart and his colleagues have been examining systematic differences between in-group and out-group stereotypes (Park & Rothbart, 1982; Rothbart, Dawes, & Park,

1984). One key hypothesis in this domain is that people perceive more variability in the characteristics of their own group than in the characteristics of out-groups. This "out-group homogeneity" effect is captured in popular phrases such as "I can't tell one from the other" and "They all look the same to me." Of greater interest from an intergroup perspective will be the pinning down of explanations for this "out-group homogeneity" effect, with which subsequent research will probably deal in greater depth. Is this effect, as Wilder (1984) suggests, a desire to maintain individuality within the in-group while preserving or enhancing in-group favoritism by deindividualization of the out-group? Or is it strictly a question of familiarity such that the less familiar we are with a group, the more likely we are to have a uniform stereotype of that group?

Studies on the out-group homogeneity effect are representative of research that is designed to understand the stereotype as a process having more direct implications for intergroup relations. But in order for stereotypes to become the basis for a theory of intergroup relations, the intergroup feature of stereotypes must serve as the research focus.

One such attempt has been made by Taylor (1981) and Taylor and Simard (1979). They began with the intergroup implications of the traditional view of the stereotype as an inferior and morally wrong process. This view implies that group stereotypes should be eliminated to the extent possible—for example, through educational programs and cooperative exposure to members of the other group. However, Taylor (1981) has argued that there are intergroup situations where stereotyping may in fact be desirable as might be postulated by social identity theory (chapter 4). Specifically, to the extent that a group wishes to maintain its distinctiveness, it would be proud to be stereotyped, as long as the stereotype attributed to it was accurate and was respected by members of another group. From this perspective, then, harmonious intergroup relations would arise when the pattern of stereotypes is consistent with that depicted in figure 8.1.

Figure 8.1
Schematic Representation of Situation Where Stereotyping May Have Desirable Consequences

		Group doing stereotyping	
		I	II
Group being stereotyped	I	ABC +	ABC +
	II	XYZ +	XYZ +

The column classification represents the group (I or II) doing the stereotyping, and the rows refer to the group being stereotyped. The capital letters in each case represent specific stereotype attributes, and the (+) sign is used to indicate a positive attitude toward the stereotype attribute. What is depicted in figure 8.1, then, is a situation where each group stereotypes the other in a manner consistent with each group's stereotype of itself. Further, members of each group value their own attributes as well as those of the other group. Thus, we have a socially desirable intergroup situation where each group retains its own cultural distinctiveness but is respectful of the attributes that are distinctive of the other group.

Such a socially desirable configuration is, of course, difficult to achieve, and peaceful coexistence among groups, idealized here, remains one of society's most pressing challenges. Nevertheless, certain examples come to mind as attempts to approximate such an ideal. Some subgroups of women take the stand that they bring to high-status professional positions certain characteristics (such as sophisticated interpersonal skills), in addition to their basic qualifications, that make them particularly valuable. Ethnic minority groups in the United States and Canada strongly endorse the concept of multiculturalism (Taylor & Lambert, 1985), whereby groups maintain their heritage, language, and culture while participating fully in mainstream society.

These encouraging examples notwithstanding, there remain the vast majority of relations between groups that are less than desirable in terms of the ideal depicted in figure 8.1. These less desirable situations can be presented schematically in the form of systematic departures from the ideal (see figure 8.2). For example, intergroup conflict would be represented by a situation where the intergroup perceptions contain minus (−) signs instead of the plus (+) signs (figure 8.2A). An inferiority complex would involve a minus sign for a group's stereotype of itself (figure 8.2B), and misunderstandings would arise when the letters depicting the attributes are inconsistent (figure 8.2C).

The orientation described here views stereotyping as a social or intergroup process. Thus, it is the type of approach that might give rise to a theory of intergroup relations having the stereotype as its central concept. However, for the moment, the stereotype retains the status of a very important concept in the discipline of social psychology, one that has special links to intergroup relations but does not by itself represent a broadly based theory of intergroup relations.

In terms of the theories reviewed in this volume, the stereotype has the status of an important outcome, result, or dependent variable related to the status of the relationship between two groups. The stereotype is not usually

Figure 8.2
Schematic Representation of Less-Than-Desirable Patterns of Intergroup Stereotyping

A. INTERGROUP CONFLICT

Group doing stereotyping

		I	II
Group being stereotyped	I	ABC+	ABC –
	II	XYZ –	XYZ +

B. INFERIORITY COMPLEX

Group doing stereotyping

		I	II
Group being stereotyped	I	ABC+	ABC+
	II	XYZ –	XYZ –

C. STEREOTYPE MISATTRIBUTION

Group doing stereotyping

		I	II
Group being stereotyped	I	ABC	DEF
	II	UVW	XYZ

presented as the cause or independent variable in the context of relations between groups. Thus, for realistic conflict theory (chapter 3), stereotypes develop as a result of group formation, become particularly consensual and derogatory during the conflict stage, and grow less prominent as a result of the introduction of superordinate goals.

Indeed, this same analysis can be applied to each of the five major theories reviewed, except for social identity theory (chapter 4). The stereotype plays an especially significant role in social identity theory. The important motivation for group categorization is social identity. It is postulated that the need for social identity leads to a striving for group distinctiveness along positively valued dimensions. Group distinctiveness refers to those characteristics of a group that make it different from other groups—in other words, a stereotype. According to social identity theory, then, groups strive for a distinctive own-group stereotype that is valued positively by other groups. Thus, the creation and maintenance of a positively valued stereotype are postulated to be a fundamental human need. From this perspective, the view proposed by Taylor (1981) that intergroup stereotypes can be socially desirable is consistent with social identity theory.

In summary, the stereotype continues to play a central role in our understanding of intergroup relations. The current interest in stereotypes as a basic cognitive process is already providing new insights, and if this development can be coupled with a perspective focusing more on intergroup processes, an integrated theory of intergroup relations may emerge.

ATTRIBUTIONS

Not since the emergence of cognitive dissonance theory in the 1950s (Festinger, 1957) has an approach to social behavior had such a dramatic impact as that of causal attribution. The important influence of causal attribution is not limited to the field of social psychology, but has extended to the domain of developmental and clinical psychology and to the study of personality. Like other basic concepts in social psychology, attribution principles are applicable to virtually all aspects of social behavior. Theorists interested in group and intergroup processes, then, cannot reasonably ignore attribution processes, even though to date most of the research has been approached from an individualistic perspective.

Attribution processes are concerned with how we make judgments about people, ourselves as well as others. The popularity of attribution, we believe, arises because of the intuitive appeal of certain key assumptions that underlie attribution principles. First, there is the assumption that people seek to make sense of the world, and specifically that making sense of or understanding the world involves making a judgment about the cause or causes of behavior. Second, unlike more traditional approaches to person perception, it is assumed that the raw material from which judgments are made is the actual behavior of another, or one's own behavior. This is in contrast with earlier approaches that took as the starting point abstract traits rather than concrete behavior. Finally, it is assumed that the potential causes of any behavior can be classified, and that the particular classification of a cause that is selected as the explanation for behavior will have a profound impact on subsequent behavior.

The most basic classification for causes is internal and external, and it is assumed that this distinction has important implications. As a teacher, my reaction to a student who has failed an examination will be quite different if I attribute the cause to a lack of studying (internal) rather than to an unexpected illness in the family (external). Or, to give an example from the intergroup context, the attribution for the low status of South African blacks in terms of the internal-external classification has profound implications. An internal attribution (such as lazy, unintelligent) provides the perfect justification for apartheid. An external attribution (such as exploitation) demands that there should be fundamental sociopolitical changes in South African society.

The foundations for various attribution principles were laid by Heider (1958) and elaborated in various ways by theorists such as Kelley (1973), Jones and Davis (1965), and Weiner, Frieze, Kukla, Reed, Rest, & Rosenbaum (1972). The key question addressed by attribution theorists is how the individual comes to focus on one or more causes from among the many possible causes for an instance of social behavior.

Reviewing the principles that have been articulated to answer this question is beyond the scope of the present chapter. For our purposes, it is useful to consider two broad categories of principles: rational and emotional. The rational category involves the logical use of information that people employ to arrive at decisions about the cause of an instance of behavior. For example, to return to the student who has failed an examination, if he or she had consistently earned high marks in the past, the teacher might rationally be inclined to make an external attribution for the failure, believing that family illness was indeed the cause of the poor performance.

The emotional category involves ignoring information that might lead to a rational judgment and, instead, making attributions designed to meet the perceiver's needs. Foremost among these more "irrational" or emotional processes is the self-serving bias. Current controversies notwithstanding (see Bradley, 1978; D. T. Miller, 1978; Miller & Ross, 1975; Weary, 1979), there is a tendency for individuals to make attributions that protect or enhance their ego. That is, individuals have a tendency to take undue credit for success and to deny responsibility for failure.

As might be expected, attribution processes have been addressed from an individualistic perspective, focusing almost exclusively on how the individual arrives at causal explanations about the behavior of another individual. Thus, we would expect attribution processes to play an important role in any broadly based theory of intergroup relations, but we would not expect attribution by itself to be the framework for a theory of intergroup relations.

Attribution theory could play an even greater role in explaining behavior in intergroup contexts once attention begins to focus more directly on how attribution processes operate at the intergroup level. Fortunately, there are signs that interest in this area may be developing.

Pettigrew (1978, 1979) has made an important application of attribution processes to the intergroup context. His starting point was a basic attribution phenomenon labeled the "fundamental attribution error" by Ross (1977). The error involves an inherent bias to individuals' attributions: when attributing behavior, individuals tend to underestimate the impact of situation (external) and overestimate the importance of the actor's traits and attitudes (internal). Pettigrew (1978, 1979) suggests that this "fundamental attribution error" becomes the "ultimate attribution error" when applied to attributions made in an intergroup context. Like the self-serving bias, the error in this case operates in such a way that when members of an in-group make attributions about the socially desirable behavior of their own group, they focus on the positive traits (internal), but when they attribute the same desirable behavior to an out-group, an external cause is the focus.

Conversely, for socially undesirable behavior, external causes are the focus for the in-group. However, when the undesirable behavior is performed by an out-group, the focus is an internal factor, such as the negative traits of the out-group. This "ultimate attribution error" builds on an initial experiment by Taylor and Jaggi (1974), which demonstrated this basic intergroup bias in group attribution, and has been elaborated by Hewstone and Ward (1985). This process can be further clarified by considering the context of a race riot. The authorities are likely to attribute the antisocial behavior to the irresponsible and wicked intentions of the rioters (internal), whereas the rioters might view their behavior as caused by the oppression they have experienced (external). In each case, the attributions made serve to justify the behavior of the group making the attributions and to condemn the opposing group. Or, to coin a phrase, "One group's terrorist is the other's freedom fighter."

Pettigrew's analysis involves taking a process that has been articulated at the individual level and extrapolating it to groups. Taylor and his colleagues (Taylor & Doria, 1981; Taylor, Doria, & Tyler, 1983) have taken the attribution process as it has been applied to groups one step further. They argue that when examining the usual internal-external distinction in a group context, it is necessary to expand this bipolar classification to include a third important possibility. Specifically, Taylor et al. (1983) posit three attribution categories: internal, in which the individual attributes group behavior to the self; external within group, in which the individual attributes group behavior to other members of his or her own group; and external, in which the individual attributes group behavior to forces that lie not only outside the self but outside the ingroup as well.

This tripartite distinction has important implications for group cohesion. For example, if, in order to protect the self, individual group members make an external attribution for group failure, cohesion is maintained. However, if instead an external-within-group attribution is made, group cohesion would be adversely affected. Conversely, avoiding external-within-group attributions for group failure, and focusing on external-within-group attributions for group success, should lead to increased cohesion in a group. This was precisely the attribution pattern found by Taylor et al. (1983) to predominate in the case of naturalistic groups that are extremely cohesive.

The context for this study was an athletic team that experienced an extremely poor season within its league. Despite consistent failure, team cohesion was extremely high. An attribution analysis indicated that individual team members took personal responsibility for team failures and, on those few instances of team success, shared responsibility with their teammates. This pattern was labeled "group-serving bias" in attribution since, on the surface at least, group cohesion was being maintained at the expense of the individual.

In general, how processes of attribution operate in an intergroup context is still a relatively understudied topic. However, there would seem to be sufficient evidence to suggest that the processes of attribution that have been delineated at the individual level cannot always be applied directly to the group level.

Nevertheless, given the importance of attribution processes in modern social psychology, we would expect to see evidence of their operation in any major theory of intergroup relations. For example, attribution is explicitly described as one of the key processes for the five-stage model of intergroup relations (chapter 7). Because attribution is so basic to that theory, and is so explicit, its role need not be elaborated here.

Another theory that is quite explicit about the importance of attribution is relative deprivation theory (chapter 6). Our analysis of that theory revolved around a set of necessary and sufficient conditions for relative deprivation to be experienced (Crosby, 1976). An important condition specified by Crosby was that the individual not feel responsible for not having, or having less of, a desired commodity. In fact, this is a fundamental attribution assertion. If the individual makes an internal attribution of the form "It is my fault," then no relative deprivation will be experienced. If, however, the cause is perceived to be external, "It is not my fault," then all of the negative emotions associated with relative deprivation will surface.

Equity theory (chapter 5) involves important applications of attribution. For example, attribution is especially prominent when, in an inequitable relationship, advantaged or disadvantaged group members attempt the psychological restoration of equity. Under certain conditions, advantaged group members will alter their perceptions of inputs and outcomes in order to propagate the belief that the outcomes of disadvantaged people are equitable. How can advantaged group members come to believe that their position is justified? The answer is to develop the belief that disadvantaged persons make fewer inputs than advantaged persons, and so their disadvantaged position is just and fair—in short, "blame the victim." This term reflects the attribution implications—the cause of poor outcomes is internal; the disadvantaged group member is the cause of his or her situation. For example, when it is pointed out that women and blacks account for the greatest number of the unemployed, this might be justified by propagating the idea that this situation is a result of their own laziness and lack of training.

Attribution is also implicated in equity theory's explanation of why disadvantaged persons or groups may take no action in the face of inequity. It was noted that despite their motivation actually to restore equity, disadvantaged persons may lack the power or resources to do so. Thus, they may come to restore equity psychologically by perceiving the inputs and outcomes of their own group and the advantaged group in such a way that equity is restored. Again, such a judgment requires that the self or own group (internal) be perceived as the cause of poor outcomes rather than holding the advantaged group responsible. It is hard to take action against another group when one's own group is to blame for a poor situation—and such a conclusion requires a very specific attribution about the cause of unequal outcomes.

The remaining theories—realistic conflict theory (chapter 3) and social identity theory (chapter 4)—also allude to attribution processes, but only indirectly and in a way that shows the breadth of attribution as a process. These theories focus on the trait characteristics of low-status and high-status groups, and the terms "attitude" and "stereotype" are used in this context. However, an attribution approach would interpret the perception of a group in terms of a specific trait as merely the internal attribution for a specific behavior. So when, in terms of realistic conflict theory, one group judges the other to be "cheaters" or, in terms of social identity theory, group members define their identity in terms of being "technologically sophisticated," this involves an internal attribution. That is, the focus for the explanation of the group behavior is the personality of its members, not external circumstances.

In summary, attribution processes are fundamental to all social behavior, and as we have seen, they surface explicitly or implicitly in every major theory of intergroup relations. However, to date the tendency has been to extrapolate attribution principles at the interindividual level to the level of groups. The aspects of attribution that are unique to group contexts have only begun to be explored, and it is these unique features that are sure to play an even more central role in theories of intergroup relations.

DISCRIMINATION

Discrimination involves behavior directed at a person on the basis of his or her category membership. At times people want to be treated differently on the basis of their category membership, as when they wish to have their social identity acknowledged (social identity theory), or when affirmative-action programs come into play. For the most part, however, discrimination is a particularly ugly experience since it usually involves behaving toward others exclusively on the basis of their category membership, in a negative manner, and without the consent or desire of the group being discriminated against.

Until very recently, social psychological theory and research in the area of prejudice and discrimination were, for the most part, self-serving in their orientation. The focus was on members of the dominant group and what might lead a member of the dominant group to become prejudiced or to engage in discrimination. Thus, authoritarian, dogmatic, poor, uneducated, highly religious, and cognitively simple people with low self-esteem were found to be prone to engage in discrimination.

On the surface, this would seem to be a socially responsible focus since it implies that the problem of prejudice and discrimination lies squarely with the dominant group. But a closer inspection reveals a much less altruistic motive for such a research emphasis. In typical individualistic style, the thrust of most research was to reveal which few dominant group members were sufficiently psychologically deranged that they engaged in irrational forms of discrimination toward disadvantaged groups. The implication, of course, was that the vast majority of dominant group members were psychologically healthy beings who would never engage in pathological behavior like discrimination. Once the small minority of "bigots" could be identified, the rest of the dominant group could be absolved from guilt. What better theoretical orientation could there be for a discipline dominated by middle-class, Caucasian, male scientists?

Recently, theoretical interest has shifted from the perpetrators of discrimination to the experiences of potential victims. This shift has generated new theoretical insights that challenge the traditional view of the consequences of discrimination for stigmatized group members. The theoretical and empirical work of Crocker and Major (1989) and Major and Crocker (1993) has been pivotal in charting this new course.

Despite the traditional preoccupation with an individual difference analysis of predispositions for discrimination among advantaged group members, there has always been a small cadre of social scientists who pursued the topic of discrimination from the point of view of potential victims. The seminal work by the Clarks (Clark & Clark, 1947), the laboratory research of Dion and his colleagues begun in the mid-1970s (Dion, 1975; Dion & Earn, 1975), and a long-standing tradition of research in sociology paved the way for current theory and research.

The major theme to emerge from much of the early research was that members of discriminated-against groups suffer from low self-esteem. This conclusion was supported by a variety of theoretical perspectives, ranging from "symbolic interaction" theorists (e.g., Cooley, 1956) to proponents of a self-fulfilling prophecy (e.g., Merton, 1948) to those interested in self-efficacy (e.g., Gecas & Schwalbe, 1983). The conclusion that members of discriminated-against groups would suffer from low self-esteem seemed intuitively obvious. First, their objectively defined outcomes were relatively poor, and second, perpetrators of discrimination would have both the motivation and the power to promote a "victim-blame" explanation to rationalize discriminatory treatment toward, and poor outcomes for, disadvantaged group members.

Moreover, there was empirical evidence to support the notion of pervasive low self-esteem among disadvantaged group members. The preference of black children and Maori native children for white dolls (Clark & Clark, 1947; Vaughan, 1972), the identification of some concentration-camp prisoners with their aggressor (Bettelheim, 1958), and the positive reaction of French-speaking schoolchildren in Quebec to English-speaking voices (e.g., Lambert, Hodgson, Gardner, & Fillenbaum, 1960) were all interpreted as evidence of low self-esteem among minority-group members. So strong was the phenomenon that as early as the 1950s, the label "self-hate" was invoked to describe the extremes of low self-esteem among members of disadvantaged groups (Allport, 1954).

In 1989 Crocker and Major published an important theoretical article that challenged the traditional wisdom that associated low self-esteem with membership in a stigmatized group. They reviewed the literature only to discover that for a variety of disadvantaged groups, including racial and ethnic minorities, women, the physically disabled, the learning disabled, homosexuals, the mentally ill, and juvenile delinquents, there was no evidence of pervasive low self-esteem. This prompted Crocker and Major (1989) to conclude that "this research, conducted over a time span of more than 20 years, leads to the surprising conclusion that prejudice against members of stigmatized or oppressed groups generally does *not* result in lowered self-esteem for members of those groups" (p. 611).

In order to explain these unexpected findings, Crocker and Major (1989) theorized that members of stigmatized groups constantly face attributional ambiguities that are not faced by advantaged group members. The ambiguity arises because every time a stigmatized-group member receives negative, or indeed positive, feedback from an advantaged group member, there is the usual array of attributional judgments to make along with one important addition: the possibility that the feedback was due to discrimination.

While this ambiguity is itself disquieting for disadvantaged group members, it does offer them the opportunity to engage in self-protection and self-enhancement. Specifically, attributing negative feedback to discrimination rather than to inadequate personal qualities can bolster self-esteem in the face of failure. Similarly, when a person is experiencing success, it would be highly ego-enhancing to have achieved the success despite having to face the hurdle of discrimination. In both instances, then, discrimination allows the stigmatized-group member to maintain high self-esteem and thereby challenge the traditional notion that stigmatized-group members on the whole suffer from low self-esteem.

Evidence for this link between attribution to discrimination and maintenance of self-esteem was first obtained by Dion (1975) and Dion and Earn (1975), but has been tested most directly in a series of experiments by Crocker and Major and their associates. Prototypic of such experiments is one reported by Crocker, Voelkl, Testa, and Major (1991) involving black students who received very negative or positive feedback, ostensibly from another subject who was white. The key manipulation involved having the black student receive negative feedback from the white subject, who was seated in a separate room. The two experimental conditions were (1) the blinds on the one-way mirror separating the subjects were down; (2) the blinds were up. The results supported their hypothesis: for black students, the feedback was more likely to be attributed to discrimination when it was negative, rather than positive, and when the blinds were up (and the white student could see them) than when the blinds were down. Furthermore, for black students who received negative feedback, self-esteem decreased if they could not be seen by the white student, but did not decrease when they could be seen.

The implications of Crocker and Major's work are challenging. The suggestion is that at times members of groups who are potential targets for discrimination will be motivated to attribute their outcomes to discrimination so that they can protect their self-esteem.

This new perspective on discrimination is especially interesting in light of another phenomenon associated with perceived discrimination that Taylor, Wright, Moghaddam, and Lalonde (1990) have labeled *the personal/group discrimination discrepancy*. The phenomenon involves members of disadvantaged groups rating discrimination directed at their group as a whole substantially higher than discrimination aimed at themselves personally as a member of that group.

The personal/group discrimination discrepancy is a particularly robust phenomenon. The tendency to rate discrimination higher at the group level, as compared to the personal level, was first documented by Crosby (1982) in her study of working women in the Boston area. Since then, the discrepancy has arisen without exception among a wide array of disadvantaged groups. By way of examples, figure 8.3 presents ratings of personal and group discrimination for different samples of women, inner-city African-American men living in subsidized housing projects, visible minority immigrant women, and a sample of native peoples (see Taylor, Wright, & Porter, 1993).

Indeed, the personal/group discrimination discrepancy is so robust that Moghaddam and Hutchenson (1993) have argued that it may be more accurate to refer to a "general personal/group discrepancy," because the phenomenon may not be domain-specific. Moghaddam and Hutchenson (1993) asked respondents to rate the extent to which respondents were "personally" affected by a wide range of issues and events, including "the current economic recession," "ecological issues," "the threat of AIDS," "sexual harassment," "rising health costs," "the end of the cold war," and "racial discrimination." Respondents were also asked to rate the extent to which their close friends, persons of their gender, and the population in general were affected. A "general personal/group discrepancy" was con-

Figure 8.3
Examples of the Personal/Group Discrimination Discrepancy

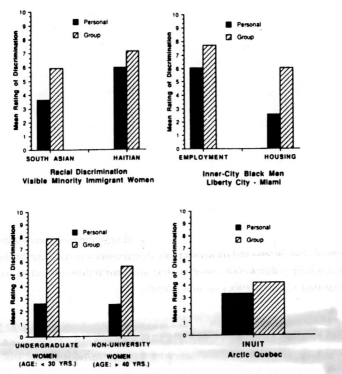

Source: Reprinted from Taylor, Wright, & Porter (1993), "Dimensions of Perceived Discrimination: The Personal/Group Discrimination Discrepancy," in *The Psychology of Prejudice: The Ontario Symposium*, eds. Mark P. Zanna and James M. Olson, Volume 7, p. 235. Used with permission of Lawrence Erlbaum Associates, Publishers.

sistently demonstrated, with respondents seeing the population in general and their gender group as always being affected more than themselves personally, and their close friends more affected than themselves on most issues. These results suggest that judgments about the self are consistently lower than those directed at the group level, whatever the domain of negative experience.

Not only is the personal/group discrimination discrepancy a robust phenomenon, but it also does not appear to arise from any artifact due to the wording of the questions about discrimination. For example, Taylor et al. (1993) report that several samples of university women were asked to rate their experiences with discrimination using a variety of different wordings. In addition to answering the two standard questions, different samples of women were asked to rate the "frequency" of discrimination at both the group and personal levels and the "severity" of discrimination at the two levels. Finally, one sample had the standard group question (North American women as a group) replaced by the phrase "average North American woman." The results were conclusive. Despite variations in the wording, respondents consistently rated discrimination directed at women as a group higher than ratings of discrimination aimed at themselves personally as a woman.

The personal/group discrimination discrepancy, then, is a legitimate phenomenon of potential social and theoretical importance. To date, however, there has been little research designed to address its underlying cause. Despite the paucity of research, many and varied explanations have been proposed (see Taylor et al., 1990, for a review). Foremost among these is that the discrepancy in perceived discrimination arises because disadvantaged group members deny or minimize the discrimination that is directed at them personally (see Crosby, 1984). Moreover, recent experiments in our own laboratory (Ruggiero & Taylor, 1993) support the view that women tend to minimize discrimination that is directed at them personally.

This minimization proposal is especially interesting in light of Crocker and Major's (1989) thesis that disadvantaged group members are motivated to perceive discrimination as a mechanism for protecting self-esteem. Research is needed to address this theoretical paradox: according to attributional ambiguity theory (Crocker & Major, 1989), disadvantaged group members are vigilant in terms of perceiving discrimination, whereas the personal/group discrimination discrepancy (Taylor et al., 1990) proposes that disadvantaged group members minimize discrimination directed at them personally.

CONCLUSION

In this chapter we have attempted to briefly describe three important concepts that are often associated with the topic of intergroup relations, but do not by themselves constitute a major theoretical orientation to intergroup relations. This is not to belittle the importance of these concepts. Their general importance in the field of social psychology virtually demands that they be included in any volume associated with intergroup relations.

SUGGESTED READINGS

Crocker, J., & Major, B. (1989). Social stigma and self-esteem: The self-protective properties of stigma. *Psychological Review, 96*, 608–630.

Hamilton, D. L. (Ed.). (1981). *Cognitive processes in stereotyping and intergroup behavior.* Hillsdale, N.J.: Erlbaum.

Hewstone, M. (1990). *Causal attribution: From cognitive processes to collective beliefs.* Oxford: Blackwell.

9

Intergroup Contact: From Desegregation to Multiculturalism

Contact between groups is an implicit theme underlying most theories of intergroup relations. The nature of the contact that gives rise to conflict, and the contact associated with superordinate goals, are central to realistic conflict theory. Theories that revolve around intergroup social comparisons, such as social identity, relative deprivation, equity, and the five-stage model, all presume some level of contact.

Intergroup contact has evolved into an important theoretical focus in its own right, but not because of its implied role in other theories. Intergroup contact, as a major topic in the social psychology of intergroup relations, has evolved because of two influential political policies that have impacted Western societies in general and the United States in particular. The first has to do primarily with race relations in the United States. An observer of the American "persona" once described the United States as having three major preoccupations: war and peace, bread and butter, and black and white. It is this latter preoccupation that has made intergroup contact such a prominent issue, since the underlying rationale was that contact between the races, in the form of desegregating society, would inevitably lead to racial harmony (see Pettigrew, 1986).

The second political policy involves an extension of the tripartite preoccupation. As Lambert and Taylor (1990) argue in their analysis of the American "persona": "Interesting as this overview is, we feel it misses what may be the most distinctive feature of all: a preoccupation and underlying concern in the United States with what is or is not 'American'"

(p. 1). The basis of this preoccupation is the contact that arises between immigrants and refugees, on the one hand, and mainstream members of the host society, on the other. Immigrant-receiving nations around the world confront the overwhelming challenge of welcoming and integrating large numbers of people representing diverse groups and cultures. Immigrant and refugee groups, in turn, face intergroup contact that is characterized by unequal status and cultural and linguistic adjustment to an oftentimes strange, and sometimes hostile, social environment. The preoccupation with what is, and what is not, "American" arises from political policies and social psychological theories that revolve around issues of assimilation and multiculturalism. In the minds of many Americans, this leads to questions about the extent to which it is "American" to speak languages other than English, to pursue a variety of cultures, and to maintain social solidarity with members of one's own cultural community. In this chapter, then, we explore the social psychological issues associated with intergroup contact that grow out of these two profoundly important political policies.

RACE RELATIONS IN THE UNITED STATES AND CONTACT BETWEEN LANGUAGE GROUPS IN CANADA

A cursory review of the literature on the contact hypothesis reveals that from its initiation by R. M. Williams (1947) and Allport (1954) to the seminal works of Cook (1978) and Pettigrew (1971) and the comprehensive reviews of Amir (1976), the themes have remained unchanged. Briefly stated, intergroup contact will be associated with harmony to the extent that it involves interaction that is intimate, where there is equal status between the interlocutors, where the surrounding social climate is supportive, and where the purpose of the interaction is cooperative rather than competitive.

Pettigrew's (1986) review of the contact hypothesis helps explain both why the theoretical issues have remained unchanged for 45 years, and why the conditions associated with successful intergroup contact have remained largely unchanged throughout this same period. Consistent with our analysis, he notes that the contact hypothesis arises out of a unique context, race relations in the United States. More important, the ideological assumption underlying racial conflict during this period was, and is, that the primary cause of racism is intergroup ignorance. The solution, therefore, is the promotion of intergroup contact under conditions that will allow members of both groups to "get to know each other" and thereby eliminate intergroup ignorance and, by extension, intergroup conflict.

The argument to be made in this chapter is that the issue of contact and conflict should be approached differently. The traditional approach assumes that relations between individual members of different groups are normally conflictual, since when individuals representing two conflicting groups interact, they presumably act out at the individual level the conflict that is characteristic of the relationship between the groups. Research is then directed at specifying the conditions of individual contact that can reduce this conflict, first between individuals and then, by extension, between the two groups. Our own position is different. We begin with the assumption that at the interpersonal level, relations between members of different groups are for the most part surprisingly amicable. Thus, the orienting question becomes, What are the normal mechanisms by which harmony is maintained among individual members of different groups when the groups they represent are in conflict with one another?

Our analysis of this question begins not with a focus on intergroup relations per se, but with everyday observations of individuals and their interactions. Often individuals must interact with each other on a one-to-one basis despite conflict between the groups they represent. Individuals may represent conflicting work groups, families, or professional groups, and yet role demands or proximity require them to interact frequently. Romeo and Juliet, and Olympic athletes in the same discipline but from competing nations, are salient examples. They cannot, or do not want to, avoid each other, and so to a large extent they interact in apparent harmony, despite the underlying intergroup conflict.

The same observations can be made of members of rival societal groups who share the same social environment. The point here is that the highly salient examples of intergroup violence in the world that seem to dominate the news media may well mask a more pervasive phenomenon: the countless everyday interactions between individual members of conflicting groups that are carried out in apparent harmony. For example, intergroup violence involving Francophones and Anglophones in Quebec is rarely heard of, and racial clashes in the United States and Britain, while dramatic, may well be atypical. While the importance and horror of these occurrences cannot be overemphasized, it is also true that they can be misleading. The salience of such violence leaves us with the impression that it is the norm, whereas quite the opposite may be true. For example, Cook (1979), in reviewing the desegregation experience in the United States, comments that while attention has focused on the violence associated with desegregation, the "near miraculous orderliness" with which 82 percent of the communities managed this process is forgotten.

It would seem that individuals, of necessity, have developed a variety of mechanisms for interacting effectively with members of a different group despite underlying conflict between the two groups. It is these processes that must be explored. Conflict presumably would surface when these usual mechanisms break down. What are these mechanisms for maintaining harmony? Three hypotheses will be examined in this chapter. The first is that where intergroup interaction is apparently frequent and necessary, individuals nevertheless subtly bias their contact toward members of their own group such that intergroup contact is more illusory than real. The second hypothesis is that when intergroup contact does occur, the interactions are qualitatively different from those with in-group members. Finally, when contact is frequent and intimate, individuals psychologically define themselves, the other person, and the context in other than intergroup terms.

The Illusion of Contact

Practically speaking, much of the research on contact has attempted to capitalize on realistic social situations where variations in contact occur naturally. For example, the landmark decision to desegregate schools in the United States represents such an opportunity for the study of contact; racially and ethnically mixed cities, states, or nations also provide a natural laboratory for the study of intergroup contact.

Crucial to these studies is whether or not the independent variable truly represents increased contact as opposed to apparent increase in contact. Desegregating schools certainly places whites and blacks in close proximity, but does it truly alter the extent and nature of intergroup contact? This question is important since the ambiguity of results that have emerged in terms of whether the self-image of blacks is altered, their school performance is improved, and intergroup prejudice is reduced may be owing to a lack of any real change in contact, rather than an understanding of what effects contact has. A study by Schofield and Sagar (1977) raises precisely this issue. They examined the pattern of interaction between black and white students in a desegregated school, involving 1,200 students aged 10 to 13. The school authorities strongly supported a program of activities designed to help students get to know one another. The results clearly indicated a strong predisposition for both black and white students to prefer, and to interact with, others of their own race. This segregation was most noticeable in situations where freedom of choice was available, such as in the cafeteria during lunch and in the school yard. However, segregation even occurred in the classroom, especially when teachers streamed the students on the basis of assumed academic performance and thereby arranged seating along racial lines (see Schofield, 1986).

These results are not unique to race relations in the United States or to school desegregation. A study by Bellerose and Taylor (1984) in the French-seaking Canadian province of Quebec supports this illusion-of-contact phenomenon. They examined intergroup interaction in a context that maximized the opportunities for interaction between Anglophones and Francophones. The setting was McGill University, an English-language institution in a province where French is the official language. Francophone enrollment at McGill has been increasing to the extent that approximately one-quarter of the students are currently French-speaking. Francophone students have a number of French-language universities from which to select, and hence those who come to McGill have actually opted for an English-language education. This fact, coupled with the liberal attitudes usually associated with university students, suggests that if ever there was a social environment conducive to intergroup contact, it is among such Anglophone and Francophone students.

Samples of students from the two groups were asked to keep detailed daily records of every one of their interactions for a period of one week. Francophones constituted 24 percent of the student body, Anglophones 76 percent. Thus, if contact was not influenced by group membership, there should have been comparable figures in terms of the students' pattern of interaction. However, of the 1,419 interactions recorded by Francophones, they interacted with members of their own group 49.7 percent of the time, significantly more than the expected 24 percent. Similarly, of the 820 interactions reported by the slightly smaller sample of Anglophones, 87.3 percent were with members of their own group, again more than the expected 76 percent.

The results from quite different contexts converge to suggest that intergroup contact may not be as prevalent as believed. Even in situations that are apparently conducive to contact because of physical proximity and positive attitudes, there is less interaction than would be expected. This bias in favor of in-group contact may explain a primary mechanism by which conflict between competing groups can be avoided, that is, simply by reducing intergroup contact.

Does this mean that contact is subtly biased in favor of the in-group as a mechanism for avoiding conflict? The research to date does not allow for a conclusion about people's motivation. It may be that people just feel more comfortable with members of their own racial or ethnolinguistic group. However, regardless of motivation, where contact is only an illusion, interpersonal confrontation is neatly avoided.

Quality of Intergroup Contact

Biasing contact in favor of the in-group is an important but nevertheless primitive mechanism for avoiding conflict. In the studies reporting this contact bias, there remains a smaller, but substantial number from both groups who do have contact with members of the other group. An examination of the nature of this contact may provide further insights into how interpersonal harmony is maintained despite tension at the group level.

One study that has explicitly addressed this issue is that of Bellerose and Taylor (1984). Francophone and Anglophone students were asked to rate every interaction they had in terms of its "intimacy," its "importance," and how "agreeable" it was. The ratings were made separately for every interaction at a time when it was still fresh in their minds. The same pattern emerged for both Anglophone and Francophone students. Interactions with in-group members were significantly more "intimate" and "important" than those with out-group members. It would seem that when cross-cultural contact does take place, it is at a more superficial level.

What effect does this superficiality have on the harmony of intergroup encounters? Respondents made ratings of how "agreeable" each of their interactions was with members of both groups. Both Anglophones and Francophones found their interactions with out-group members as agreeable as those with members of the in-group. At the same time, interactions with out-group members were judged to be relatively superficial. It would seem, then, that a second mechanism for ensuring that cross-cultural contacts are harmonious is to limit them to relatively superficial encounters.

Denial and Dissociation in Intergroup Contact

Once the bias toward in-group contact and the superficial quality of cross-group contact, when it does occur, are taken into account, there still remain a number of cross-group interactions that may be frequent and intimate. Indeed, intergroup marriages, while not the norm, are nevertheless not uncommon. Moreover, many work, leisure, and neighborhood situations lead to cross-group friendships. Thus, for these relationships, there must be important psychological processes operating that guard against interpersonal contacts becoming repeated enactments of the tensions underlying the groups they represent. There are two major categories of mechanisms that would allow individuals from competing groups to interact peacefully: (*a*) the denial by individuals of tensions between the two groups and (*b*) the dissociation of individuals from their respective groups.

Denial of Tensions. At least two forms of denial must be distinguished. An individual may simply not acknowledge any tension between the groups. Such an individual might say, "Everybody, and especially the media, is always looking for conflict between our groups [e.g., blacks versus whites or Francophones versus Anglophones]. There is really no conflict, and I wish everyone would stop trying to invent or instigate one." A second form of denial would be to acknowledge tension but not to interpret the tension as a conflict between the respective groups. The opinion that it is, for instance, the government that is the enemy, not the other group, illustrates this process. Either of these forms of denial would put interaction between individual members of the two groups in a cooperative context, despite tensions at the intergroup level.

Dissociation of Individual from Group. There are a number of ways an individual may be dissociated from his or her group in the context of interaction. The most basic probably involves defining the relationship such that one's own or the other person's ethnic or racial identity is minimally salient. Focusing on individual traits, roles, or other social identities effectively reduces the importance of a person's racial or ethnic identity. This is precisely the mechanism that Brewer and Miller (1988) emphasize in their discussion of how harmonious intergroup contact may be facilitated by "decategorizing" the interaction. By "decategorization" they mean cross-group interactions that are personalized rather than category based.

That individuals will, at different times, in different situations, place different emphasis on their group identity and their unique self-identity has been described in some detail by Tajfel (1978b) and Brown and Turner (1981). The Bellerose and Taylor (1984) study, which examined the interaction patterns of Anglophones and Francophones at an English-speaking university, indirectly exemplifies this process. Participants were asked to review every interaction they had recorded for the week and to note those that made them aware of their ethnic identity. It was anticipated that Francophone students would be especially aware of their ethnic identity as they met the challenge of adjusting to an English-language institution for the first time. However, of the 1,419 interactions reviewed, only 9.9 percent made the participant aware of his or her identity as a French Quebecer. For Anglophones, only 6 percent of the 820 interactions reviewed involved their ethnic identity as English Quebecers. One interpretation of these findings is that both Anglophones and Francophones studiously avoided defining their interactions in ethnic-group terms. Thus, intergroup tensions would not intrude on the interaction, and instead the focus would be on other dimensions of self-identity, those perhaps that interlocutors had in common.

A second form of dissociation has already been noted in the literature associated with ethnic stereotypes. The dissociation involves perceiving an individual member of an ethnic group as different from "typical" members of that group, a phenomenon that has been labeled "fence mending" (Allport, 1954) or "the exceptional case" (Pettigrew, 1979). This process has been described in the context of how prejudiced individuals maintain their bigotry in the face of socially desirable behavior on the part of individual out-group members: they merely exclude the out-group individual from the disliked group. As Pettigrew (1979) notes, "This resolution can even lead to generous, if often patronizing, exaggeration of the positive qualities of this exceptional person in order to differentiate this 'good' individual from the 'bad' outgroup" (p. 468).

This form of dissociation, we believe, has more general application. It is not merely a mechanism for prejudiced individuals to deal with discrepant information. Rather, it may be a fundamental process whereby cross-group interaction can occur at the interpersonal level in the context of conflict between groups.

This section of the chapter represents an approach that complements the traditional orientation to the study of intergroup contact. Instead of emphasizing the necessary contact conditions for harmonious interaction to occur, we propose that most cross-group interactions at the personal level are, on the surface at least, harmonious. Addressing the issue from this perspective shifts the avenue of enquiry and leads to two questions. First, what are the normal mechanisms used by individuals to maintain interpersonal harmony in cross-group contact? Second, what causes the breakdown of these mechanisms such that the intergroup conflict does become actualized in the situation of one-to-one contact? Research on these questions is only just beginning, but it is hoped that by addressing issues in this complementary fashion, new insights into contact and intergroup relations can be gained.

MULTICULTURALISM IN THE UNITED STATES AND CANADA

Assimilation

The second social and political policy to preoccupy the United States is how immigrants, refugees, and majority-group members should accommodate each other. The United States characterized the appropriate form of contact to be one of assimilation. Moghaddam (Moghaddam & Solliday, 1991; Moghaddam, in press) has used the terms "minority-group assimilation" and "melting-pot assimilation" to distinguish between two historically important approaches to assimilation. Minority-group assimilation involves a one-way process through which groups are forced to abandon their heritage cultures and totally take on the majority-group culture. This form of assimilation is assumed to require the "proper" management and "correct" schooling of minorities, according to standards established by the majority.

Melting-pot assimilation, on the other hand, is assumed to be a bidirectional process involving a give-and-take between all minority and majority groups. Thus, all groups contribute to a newly emerging culture and share the outcomes of such melting. Historically, it has been assumed that melting-pot assimilation occurs spontaneously when the necessary social and ecological conditions are present. For example, it has been proposed that the highly challenging conditions of the American West formed a "pressure-cooker" melting pot, out of which emerged a new people: Americans (F. J. Turner, 1920).

Theory in the social sciences was entirely consistent with political policy in the United States. Assimilation of the minority-group form was viewed as inevitable (e.g., Park & Burgess, 1969; Park, 1950; Gordon, 1964), indeed so inevitable that researchers did not focus on whether assimilation would take place, but rather how it would unfold.

While social policy issues associated with immigration have never been a particular focus for theory and research in mainstream social psychology, there are two long-standing traditions of research in social psychology that are compatible with assimilation policy. The first is the literature on interpersonal attraction (e.g., Byrne, 1971; Newcomb, 1961). The dominant theme revolves around a robust relationship between similarity and attraction. The relationship holds true for a wide variety of dimensions, including similarity of attitudes, physical attraction, and, of relevance to the present context, ethnic groups (Kandel,

1978). The implication is clear: the cultural homogeneity that arises from assimilation is conducive to interpersonal harmony.

A study of cross-group friendships by Simard (1981) illustrates the role of ethnic diversity as a potential barrier to interpersonal harmony. Anglophone and Francophone students were required to actually make new friends and to keep a detailed record of the process. Half the students made friends with someone of the same ethnolinguistic group, the other half with members of the other group. The results indicated that students did make friends with those who were similar to them. Of particular importance for the present context, those making cross-group friendships required that potential friends be more similar to them on a variety of other dimensions than potential friends from the same group. It was as if potential friends who are different in terms of ethnic-group membership can only achieve friendship status if they compensate by being more similar on other dimensions, such as attitudes and values. Clearly, with this more stringent criterion for out-group members, assimilation processes that remove group differences should enhance the potential for harmony in cross-group interactions.

A second traditional area of research in social psychology that supports the assumption of assimilation is that of ethnic and racial stereotypes. As we noted in chapter 8, stereotypes are cognitive processes that, although often negative in evaluative overtone, nevertheless are presumed to capture cultural or racial differences. Consistent with the United States' philosophy of assimilation and cultural homogeneity, psychologists have viewed stereotypes as inferior cognitive processes that are morally wrong (see chapter 8). They are "wrong" presumably because they reinforce cultural diversity and, as such, are contrary to the notion that immigrant and refugee contact with mainstream Americans should lead to assimilation and cultural homogeneity.

Direct tests of the inevitable assimilation of newcomers to the host society as a result of contact are difficult to design (see C. Hirschman, 1983). Where there is evidence contrary to assimilation, theorists can merely counter that the process is ongoing, but as yet incomplete. Anti-assimilationists argue, of course, that all that is required is one exception to the inevitable drift toward assimilation for the entire theory to be invalidated.

The Rise of Multiculturalism

While the United States was pursuing national unity through a social policy of assimilation, Canada and later Australia were committed to a policy of multiculturalism, designed to create "unity through diversity." The "melting-pot" image of the United States was countered by the "mosaic" concept in Canada.

More generally, however, the United States and Canada, and indeed virtually every immigrant-receiving nation in the world, were being besieged by an ethnic revolution. Key social scientists such as Glazer and Moynihan (1970), Greeley (1974), Novak (1972), and more recently Ferdman (1990, 1992) challenged the inevitability of assimilation, and the "revival of ethnicity" school was born (see C. Hirschman, 1983). Added to the theoretical vocabulary were constructs such as ethnic diversity, cultural pluralism, and multiculturalism, and the "mosaic" image was joined by similar popular images, including "tossed salad," "rainbow coalition," and "patchwork quilt."

What needs to be underscored, however, is that this ethnic revolution was not spearheaded by social policy or social theory. Rather, it was everyday people struggling with the concrete realities of "getting ahead" in society that made phrases such as "black power," "red power," "Hispanic," "Latino," "Québecois," and every conceivable ethnic label a part of North American vocabulary.

The desire of ethnic-group members to retain their heritage-culture and language would appear to be a North American–wide phenomenon. The widespread endorsement of heritage-culture maintenance by newly arrived groups may be dampened by experiences with discrimination. On the one hand, varieties of groups in North America, from Arab Americans to Mexican-Americans and Puerto Ricans strongly endorse multiculturalism (see Lambert & Taylor, 1990). On the other hand, visible minority immigrants seem to show psychological ambivalence toward heritage-culture retention (Moghaddam, 1992; Moghaddam & Taylor, 1987). Perhaps this is because culture and language retention makes minorities even more visible and thus a more likely target for hostility.

Multiculturalism, as a policy, was predicated on certain assumptions about the nature and result of contact between newcomers and the host society. The assumptions, captured in the form of a psychological need, were articulated directly in Canada's rationale for its official multiculturalism policy. Prime Minister Trudeau first proposed the idea in the House of Commons on October 8, 1971. The policy was one that encouraged ethnic groups to retain their language and culture, and this, it was felt, would lead to a sense of confidence and security, which in turn would be associated with positive and open attitudes toward other groups (Government of Canada, 1971). The premise, referred to as the "multiculturalism hypothesis" (Berry, Kalin, & Taylor, 1977; Berry, 1984), then, was that only when members of one group feel confident and secure in their own identity will they be open to, and accepting of, members of out-groups.

The multiculturalism hypothesis represents an important point of connection between social psychological research on intergroup relations, which tends to be laboratory oriented, and research on integration strategies among immigrants, which tends to be field oriented (Berry, 1984; Lambert & Taylor, 1990; Moghaddam, Taylor, & Lalonde, 1987, 1989). The common central issue is the relationship between in-group identity and the treatment of out-groups.

Both social identity theory (see chapter 4) and the multiculturalism hypothesis could be interpreted to imply that "positive" in-group identity will lead to more favorable orientations toward out-groups. Research arising from both social identity theory (Hogg & Sunderland, 1991) and multiculturalism (Berry et al., 1977; Lambert, Mermigis, & Taylor, 1986) provides some support for this proposition. However, both social identity theory and the multiculturalism hypothesis can be interpreted in a different manner. For example, social identity theory may lead to the prediction that a group can achieve "positive identity" by discriminating against another group. Acts of discrimination imply that one's own group is "superior" to the denigrated out-group. Moreover, the question of what exactly constitutes a "feeling of security" in multiculturalism is open to debate (Lambert et al., 1986). For example, if "security" means being well off economically, then only the more affluent groups will be tolerant of others. However, if security means "predictable," then even groups in a disadvantaged economic position may feel charitable toward other groups. Thus, further developments are required in order to achieve a fruitful connection between social identity theory and multiculturalism through the link of identity.

The issue of "distinctiveness" represents another point of connection between multiculturalism and social psychological theories. Multiculturalism entails the assumption that individuals will be motivated to be members of groups that retain their distinctive heritage cultures, rather than to "melt" into the mainstream. Just as social psychological models (Brewer, 1991; Tajfel and Turner, 1986) are wrestling with the challenge of "optimal distinctiveness," so too in multiculturalism policy the question "How distinctive should groups be?" is fundamental. More specifically, in multiculturalism, a question is, How distinctive can a group be in order that it maintain a separate identity yet still become completely integrated?

There is, then, a vigorous societal debate about whether the inevitable contact between newcomers and their hosts can be guided toward assimilation or heritage-culture maintenance, and the extent to which it is desirable for this to happen. Moreover, there are contrasting social psychological processes that lend some support for both sides of the debate. This social psychological evidence is, however, meager. To date, the research in support of assimilation or heritage-culture maintenance tends to be global and descriptive, limited to capturing the attitudes of group members at one particular point in time. Lacking is a better understanding of the motivation underlying the desire for assimilation or heritage-culture maintenance.

Progress has been made in terms of economic and political motives, but to date our understanding of fundamental psychological motives has not kept pace. In the domain of economic motivations, theory revolves around the oft-noted relationship between ethnicity and specific categories of occupation. Some theories, such as those of internal colonialism, reactive ethnicity (see Hechter, 1975, 1978), or Porter's (1965) vertical mosaic, emphasize how the host group pressures new arrivals into working in ethnic enclaves. This allows the host group to maintain economic control and dictate the form that intergroup contact will take. Alternatively, ethnic groups may choose to concentrate in a particular economic niche so that they can help one another and take some control over at least a segment of the economy.

Political theories also emphasize the double-edged nature of heritage-culture maintenance. On the one hand, "consociational democracies" (Lijphart, 1968) focus on situations where the ethnic composition of a governing body is explicitly designed to be proportional to the ethnic composition of the electorate. Thus, ethnic divisions are formally recognized, they have their own leadership, and the emphasis, in terms of intergroup contact, is on negotiation and accommodation, rather than conflict. The double-edged feature arises when heritage-culture maintenance is encouraged, not for the purposes of consociational democracy, but for purposes of political separation (Nagel, 1987). Genocide, ethnic cleansing, and apartheid are prototypic of political segregation. Policies of forced migration and relocation also fall into this category. The treatment of aboriginal peoples by the dominant group, involving land seizures and the creation of reservations, are prime examples of political segregation policies.

The interplay between economic and political factors in relations between ethnic groups has been analyzed by Esman (1987). He focuses on situations where a minority elite economically dominates the disadvantaged majority group. Relations between language groups in Quebec and between racial groups in South Africa are prototypic examples. Esman's (1987) thesis is that disadvantaged groups in these instances capitalize on their majority numerical status to gain political control. Then, by expropriation and nationalization, they set about to redress the disadvantaged economic status of the majority ethnic or racial group.

TOWARD "BALANCED MULTICULTURALISM"

Judging from media reports and discussions in professional politics, it would seem that multiculturalism is a new wave that is sweeping through many societies, not only in the developed, but also the developing, world. This would seem to suggest that multiculturalism is a well-defined and clearly understood concept. In reality, however, this is not the case.

The most formalized statements on multiculturalism are to be found in societies such as Canada and Australia, where the federal governments have adopted multiculturalism as an official policy. Indeed, there is now a Ministry of Multiculturalism in Canada. The Canadian policy seems bold and progressive and goes against an almost century-old social science tradition of conceiving ethnocentrism as universal and inevitable (Sumner, 1906). Because of the novelty and importance of Canadian multiculturalism policy, at least in a Western context, we pay particular attention to it in the conclusion of this chapter.

The Canadian model seems "unbalanced" in the sense that it lays stress on developing feelings of pride and security in the in-group, but pays insufficient attention to the nurturance of such feelings with respect to out-groups. The policy does call for a "sharing" of cultures, raising the expectation that such sharing will lead to a greater appreciation of out-group cultures and a more favorable orientation toward out-groups. However, a danger is that in its present "unbalanced" emphasis on retention of heritage cultures, the Canadian policy will encourage ethnocentrism.

With such critical issues in mind, a proposal has been made for a "balanced multiculturalism" policy (Moghaddam & Solliday, 1991). The objective of such a policy would be to maintain a balance between a group's pride in the in-group culture and its pride in being part of a culturally diverse society. Such a balance between in-group–based and out-group–based pride is already implied in slogans such as "celebration of diversity."

Finally, the question arises as to the social psychological requirements for achieving "balanced multiculturalism." There, one promising lead lies with Brewer's optimal distinctiveness theory (Brewer, 1991; Brewer, Manzi, & Shaw, 1993). She has conceptualized an optimal balance between the individual's needs for assimilation and differentiation. Presumably, in conditions when something close to such an optimal balance is achieved, individuals are more likely to be prepared to "celebrate diversity" and develop pride in out-groups, as well as in-groups.

NOTE

Portions of the section "Race Relations in the United States and Contact Between Language Groups in Canada" were excerpted from Taylor, D. M., Dubé, L., & Bellerose, J. (1986). Intergroup contact in Quebec: Myth or reality? In M. Hewstone and R. Brown (Eds.), *Contact and conflict in intergroup encounters* (pp. 107–118). New York: Blackwell. Used with permission.

SUGGESTED READINGS

Hewstone, M., & Brown, R. (Eds.). (1986). *Contact and conflict in intergroup encounters.* New York: Basil Blackwell.

LaFromboise, T., Coleman, H.L.K., & Gerton, J. (1993). Psychological impact of biculturalism: Evidence and theory. *Psychological Bulletin, 114*, 395–412.

10 ⸻⸻⸻⸻⸻⸻

Toward an Integrated Theory of Intergroup Relations

In this volume we have reviewed five major theoretical approaches to the social psychology of intergroup relations, analyzed Freud's contribution to the field, and discussed a series of important new social psychological concepts that are likely to play a significant role in any theory of intergroup relations. Having reviewed these theories in some detail, it is important that we highlight their similarities and differences, with a view to providing a constructive framework for future theory and research. As each theory was presented, similarities to and contrasts with the other theories were discussed. The purpose here is to highlight these in terms of all five theories so that an overall perspective can be achieved.

In order to provide a framework for our review, we focus on important themes that were raised in chapter 1 as recurrent issues or that emerged from our discussion of a particular theory. The major themes include level of analysis, time frame, "open" as opposed to "closed" groups, group structure, status relationship between groups, and social psychological processes.

We will discuss each of these themes in turn. Their status with respect to each of the five theories is presented in summary fashion in table 10.1. Although simplistic, the table has the advantage of allowing quick reference to the status of each theory with respect to all the different themes. We end the chapter with a brief discussion of two issues that arise from recent developments in the field. The first is the predominance of cognitive processes to the neglect of emotion, and the second is the growing importance of the self-concept.

Table 10.1
Status of Intergroup Theories in Terms of Major Themes

	REALISTIC CONFLICT THEORY	SOCIAL IDENTITY THEORY	EQUITY THEORY	RELATIVE DEPRIVATION THEORY	FIVE-STAGE MODEL
LEVEL OF ANALYSIS	group	individual and group	individual	individual	individual and group
TIME FRAME	long and short term	long and short term	short term	short term	long and short term
OPEN VS. CLOSED GROUPS	closed	open and closed	closed	closed	open and closed
GROUPS STRUCTURE	homogeneous	homogeneous	homogeneous	homogeneous	individual differences
STATUS OF GROUP FOCUSED UPON	equal status	disadvantaged	advantaged and disadvantaged	disadvantaged	disadvantaged
SOCIAL PSYCHOLOGICAL PROCESSES		categorization social identity psychological distinctiveness social comparison justice	justice social comparison dissonance	social comparison justice attribution	social comparison attribution justice

LEVEL OF ANALYSIS

A theme that has predominated our discussion of the different theories is reductionism. From our initial analysis of mainstream social psychology as an individual-oriented discipline, we have underscored the need for an approach to intergroup relations that includes a focus on group processes while retaining the integrity of the fundamental unit of psychological analysis, the individual. The need is for theories that discuss the psychological processes affecting the individual but that simultaneously take into account the role of group structure and the role that the dynamics of group relations play in the psychology of the individual.

The simple summary presented in table 10.1 indicates the dual nature of the challenge. For example, realistic conflict theory does address intergroup relations from a group perspective. However, it does not spell out the specific psychological processes that play a causal role in intergroup conflict. That is, the theory offers a macro analysis, with psychological processes being introduced only as an outcome of these broad social processes. Freud's theory of group processes, equity theory, and relative deprivation theory are depicted as reductionist, as being limited to an individual level of analysis. While generally true, this overview represents somewhat of an overgeneralization, since relative deprivation theorists (Crosby, 1982; Dion, 1986; Martin, 1980; Runciman, 1966) have addressed relative deprivation from a group perspective. We applaud this development and hope that this interest in collective processes will extend to such theories as equity, which has proved to have a wide application.

The two theories that do attempt an analysis at both the group and the individual level are social identity theory and the five-stage model of intergroup relations. Their attempts represent, we believe, the direction that future theories should take. This is not to suggest that the specific content and structure of these theories are more useful than those of the others, but only that in terms of unit of analysis, the social and individualistic dimensions should be integrated.

TIME FRAME

In the real world, relations between most groups have a history; they are often influenced by complex sociocultural factors that extend their influence over long periods of time. For example, to explain the present state of relations between blacks and whites in the United States, or the newly arrived immigrant groups and indigenous populations in Europe, or English and French Canadians, it is necessary to keep in mind the historical background to relations between each of these groups. The history of slavery in the United States is likely to be relevant to the present relations between blacks and whites in that country; the history of European colonialism is likely to be relevant to the present relations between newly arrived Third World immigrants and indigenous European populations; and the past history of English domination in Canada is likely to influence the present state of relations between English and French Canadians.

These historical examples suggest the presence of developmental processes in intergroup relations. Consequently, in order to explain the present state of relations between two social groups, it is useful to keep in mind the past history of their relations. However, not all theories that have been applied to intergroup relations explicitly attempt to incorporate such a developmental perspective.

The five-stage model is probably the one theory that explicitly and most directly incorporates a developmental perspective on intergroup relations. This theory adopts a cyclical view of the historical development of intergroup relations. Intergroup relations are assumed to pass through the same five developmental stages; the transition from one stage to another is assumed to take varying amounts of time, which can extend to several centuries. According to the five-stage model, in order to fully appreciate the state of relations between two groups, it is necessary to have information on the past history of the groups.

Realistic conflict theory has also, to some extent, given importance to the historical development of an intergroup relationship. This has evolved in both the theoretical writings of the researchers and the operationalization of concepts in research projects. For example, Sherif (1966) made a specific point of using real groups with a history in his research involving boys at summer camp. Moreover, he conceptualized a developmental process for intergroup relations. The most important stages of this process that were incorporated in his research were (1) spontaneous intergroup friendship choices, (2) group formation, (3) intergroup conflict, and (4) intergroup cooperation. The same concern for the development of intergroup relations over time was shown by Deutsch (1973, 1985) when he discussed the cycles of constructive and destructive conflict.

Social identity theory makes some attempt to incorporate longer-term developmental processes into its elaboration of intergroup relations. In particular, the importance that it gives to the development of cognitive alternatives and the perceived legitimacy-illegitimacy of the system leads to an emphasis on what generally tend to be long-term processes. Historically, the perception of cognitive alternatives to a system has tended to evolve over long time periods and has been influenced by large-scale structural changes. For example, the women's liberation movement has involved a radical change in perspectives, in that many women now conceive of a society where women enjoy parity with men. That is, most women have evolved cognitive alternatives to the traditional male-dominated society. However, the evolution of this cognitive alternative has been influenced by large-scale structural changes that have taken place over the last few centuries, such as those giving women a key role in the labor force and the economy.

Equity theory and relative deprivation theory have given little importance to the developmental aspects of intergroup relations and the long-term historical factors that might be involved. The main reason for this is probably that these are basically individualistic theories that have not yet been adequately extended to account for behavior at the intergroup level. However, such an extension should involve considerable attention to developmental processes in intergroup relations. Not only would this provide a broader understanding of intergroup relations, but it might also lead both equity theory and relative deprivation theory to become much better predictors of collective action. For example, justice is a central concept to both these theories, and the perception of justice by both minority and majority groups is likely to be influenced by the past history of each group and its relations with other groups.

OPEN AND CLOSED GROUPS

Just as a comprehensive theory of intergroup relations should include the complete range of power relations between groups, so must such a theory deal with both open and closed groups. There are two theories that deal with both types of groups: social identity theory and the five-stage model of intergroup relations. Both have the same implications: open groups are associated with individual action in the form of mobility between groups of different status; closed groups lend themselves to the instigation of collective action. The distinction between individual and collective action is so socially important that it must be taken into account by any theory of intergroup relations that seeks to be comprehensive.

The three theories that limit their attention to closed groups are realistic conflict theory, equity theory, and relative deprivation theory. Realistic conflict theory deals explicitly with the collective behavior associated with closed groups. Equity and relative deprivation theories deal with closed groups, but more by default than by design. Thus, it should be possible to extend both theories to incorporate the distinction without seriously altering their basic principles.

GROUP STRUCTURE

Freud's analysis of group processes (chapter 2) focused on two important categories of people within any group, the leader and followers. In this very fundamental way, Freud initiated a line of thought that we believe must be continued in order to achieve a broadly based theory of intergroup relations (see Kanungo, 1988). It is based on the assumption that a group should not be viewed as a homogeneous collection of individuals of equal role and status.

In his classic experiment in the context of realistic conflict theory, Sherif unfortunately did not capitalize on individual differences that he recognized within a group. For example, in the "group formation" stage of his field experiments, he noted how each group developed its own structure of roles and leadership. However, he did not pursue these individual differences in order to elaborate upon the extent to which they might play a particular role in the escalation of group conflict or its resolution.

Relative deprivation and equity theories focus little attention on groups generally and thus do not address the question of individual differences within groups. Social identity theory, despite explicitly dealing with groups, also makes no such distinction. Thus, individualistic and collective actions are hypothesized to arise among all or some members of a disadvantaged group under specified conditions.

By contrast, for the five-stage model, individual differences within a group are crucial. According to the theory, it is a special subgroup of individuals within the disadvantaged group who play an especially significant role in the instigation of action. It is the talented members of the disadvantaged group who instigate social mobility or collective action or engage in consciousness raising among other members.

The individual differences alluded to by the five-stage model are rudimentary at this stage. An integrated theory of intergroup relations will ultimately have to deal with the complexity of differences among individuals and subgroups who make up any particular group.

STATUS RELATIONSHIP BETWEEN GROUPS

Intergroup relations encompass different types of relationships between societal groups, especially in regard to the very important dimension of power. Consequently, relations between groups of equal power, and between disadvantaged and advantaged groups in an unequal relationship, must be addressed by any comprehensive theory. From table 10.1 it will be clear that this goal has not been met, which may well explain why the theories so often do not generate competing hypotheses, but hypotheses dealing with quite different intergroup situations.

Realistic conflict theory, perhaps the most influential theory to date, emphasizes equal status relations. However, in fairness we should note that certain key theorists in this tradition (such as Deutsch, 1973, 1985) do take into consideration differential power relations between the groups. Social identity theory, relative deprivation theory, and the five-stage model focus on the disadvantaged group, thus offering a somewhat limited perspective. Equity theory is listed in table 10.1 as being the only one to be equally concerned with both the advantaged and the disadvantaged group in a relationship. Equity theory certainly deals with both groups, but as Martin (1980) points out, it is ideologically biased in terms of the advantaged group.

Although we have criticized all five theories as being limited in their focus, it is clear that the various theories are broad enough to encompass the most important of the status relations that can exist between groups. That is, it would not be necessary for any of the theories reviewed in this volume to abandon their fundamental principles in order to achieve this aim. Rather, it would be necessary only to expand the range of principles offered so as to include the complete range of intergroup situations.

SOCIAL PSYCHOLOGICAL PROCESSES

An essential component of any social psychological theory of intergroup relations should be the fundamental psychological processes that are hypothesized to underlie relations between groups. The various theories addressed in this volume offer a range of important psychological processes that are broad enough to serve as building blocks for an integrated theory. Four psychological concepts form the basis of social identity theory: social categorization, social identity, social comparison, and psychological distinctiveness. Also, in terms of social identity theory, the norm of justice is central to the instigation of action. Equity theory, of course, focuses directly on the norms of justice and exchange, but includes the notions of social comparison and cognitive dissonance. Relative deprivation theory is fundamentally rooted in social comparison principles. However, the concepts of justice and attribution play a strong supporting role in relative deprivation theory. The five-stage model deals explicitly with the concepts of social comparison and social attribution, with the notion of justice implicitly involved at crucial periods in the process of maintaining a stage or moving from one stage to another.

The two concepts that arise most frequently are social comparison and justice. Does this mean that these are the most promising candidates for the focus of future theory and research on intergroup relations? Frequency may not be the only, or indeed the best, criterion for such a decision, but our critical review of the various theories discussed in this volume leads us to anticipate that justice and social comparison deserve more attention. The specific challenge will be to capitalize on the development of these concepts in mainstream social psychology, and to integrate this development with a truly intergroup perspective.

TWO EMERGING ISSUES: EMOTIONS AND THE SELF

Emotions: A Neglected Dimension of Intergroup Relations

In our review of research on the many theories and processes associated with intergroup relations, an important theme emerged that is partly methodological and partly conceptual. The issue is the extent to which research tends to neglect the powerful emotional experiences, and often apparently irrational behavior, that are such an essential aspect of intergroup conflict.

For example, consider the collective, shared emotions of group members involved in the Los Angeles riots of 1992, "ethnic cleansing" in the former Yugoslavia, or the Gulf War of 1992. These are obviously dramatic examples, and we are not implying that such cases involve "group minds." Rather, our proposal is that individual group members will, in the context of intergroup conflict, experience highly charged emotions that arise out of identification with their respective groups. To date, the major social psychological theories of intergroup relations have not paid sufficient attention to these emotions. Indeed, Freud (chapter 2) is the only major theorist to have considered the issue in depth.

There are at least two very good reasons for the lack of research involving emotionally laden situations. Aronson, Ellsworth, Carlsmith, and Gonzales (1990) blame the neglect of emotion on the predominant influence of "cognitive" social psychology. Increasingly, cognitive social psychologists are interested in how individuals process complex social information. As such, subjects in experiments become "observers" of social reality, and the experimenter is interested in how the individual intellectually deals with social stimuli. Thus, subjects are not involved in experiments, and they are not being asked to participate in situations, albeit in the laboratory, where powerful emotion-provoking stimuli are presented.

Ethics is a second important reason for the paucity of research that requires subjects to experience emotion-provoking stimuli. If the Milgram experiments are no longer ethically acceptable, it is difficult to imagine that researchers can justify exposing subjects to the equally provocative circumstances associated with intergroup conflict.

Neither of these are acceptable reasons for the lack of emotion in intergroup relations research. The cognitive "revolution" hardly captures the fear and horror that social psychologists interested in intergroup relations associate with revolution, although emotions can run high in psychology departments with active "cognitive science" groups. What is needed, clearly, is the development of intergroup theories that emphasize the emotional consequences associated with bitter conflict, and the apparent sheer irrationality of many current real-world intergroup conflicts.

The "ethics" of social psychological research need to be reconsidered. The social psychological interpretation of ethics, like many intergroup theories, has been individualistic in its perspective. As one of our black students pointed out, to our surprise, most people, particularly minority-group members, experience numerous events in their daily lives that are at least as stressful as, and often more stressful than, participation in a Milgram-type experiment. Her point was, first, that even Milgram-type laboratory experiments seem pale compared to the everyday real world in terms of the stress involved. She actually felt that participation in such experiments would prepare students for the realities of life. A second point was that psychologists show sensitivity to the treatment of individuals in laboratory settings, but that the ethics of professional research do not address the unethical treatment of groups. Thus, the predominance of cognitive social psychology, and ethical issues, are not barriers to research involving charged emotions. Once appropriate theory develops, researchers will always find a way to solve the methodological and ethical problems.

Self: A Recurrent Theme

The self-concept is one important construct that is not particularly salient in the five theories reviewed in this volume, but does emerge in many of the more recent topics that we have discussed. In particular, interest has centered on the role that social identity plays for the individual's definition of self (Breakwell, 1992). The one major theory that does focus on identity is, of course, social identity theory (chapter 4). Interestingly, the identity aspect has figured even more prominently in recent elaborations of the theory. It is the cornerstone of J. C. Turner's (Turner, 1985; Turner et al., 1987) self-categorization theory and Brewer's (1991) optimal distinctiveness theory.

The concept of self was also prominent in our discussion of the personal/group discrimination discrepancy and intergroup contact; in both cases the major theoretical challenge was to understand the relationship of the individual to his or her social identity. The very essence of the discrimination discrepancy is the apparent mismatch between the group and the individual as a member of the group. In terms of intergroup contact, we discussed a number of identity strategies that made it possible for individuals from conflicting groups to interact in harmony. Finally, in the case of multiculturalism, the issue was the relationship between the individual and his or her heritage-culture identity.

The construct of self emerged, albeit more indirectly, in our discussion of several other topics, including affirmative action, tokenism, and attributional ambiguities associated with discrimination. A central issue for all three topics is the extent to which the individual's personal identity is salient. Personal identity should be salient when the individual is operating within a meritocracy framework. However, the individual's social identity should be provoked in any context involving affirmative action, tokenism, or discrimination.

Missing in discussions of the self in an intergroup context are well-developed conceptualizations of how groups are incorporated within the self structure, although J. C. Turner (Turner et al., 1987) and others (see Breakwell, 1992) have at least raised some of the pertinent questions. For example, how do classic discussions of the self, such as the Jamesian "I/me" distinction, relate to the self as conceptualized in intergroup theories? Given that the self structure varies cross-culturally, what implications does this have for the self in intergroup contexts? These are basic questions that intergroup theories need to address.

INTERGROUP RELATIONS: A POSTSCRIPT

We began this volume by expressing optimism about the future development of intergroup relations as a major field of study. Having critically reviewed five major theoretical perspectives on intergroup relations, as well as describing typical examples of research studies stimulated by each theory, we are now in a better position to make a judgment on the future of this emerging field. The first point to emphasize is that social psychology *does* have an important and unique contribution to make to our understanding of intergroup relations. This contribution is already evident in the understanding provided by the major theories reviewed in this volume, as well as in the valuable insights provided by the research studies they have stimulated. While the structure of group relations and economic factors do have an important influence on behavior at the intergroup level, as suggested by realistic conflict theory, the central role of social psychological processes in determining the nature of such behavior has also become clear, as suggested by the theories and supporting evidence reviewed in this volume.

Two sets of factors are likely to increase the importance of intergroup relations as a field of study in the next few decades. First is the move toward a more "social" social psychology that is directly concerned with the relationship between human psychological behavior and macro-level social processes. It seems fair to claim that this movement has been spearheaded by European social psychology (see Abrams & Hogg, 1990; Tajfel, 1984). In discussing the development of European social psychology since the mid-1960s, Tajfel, Jaspers, and Fraser (1984) comment that "social psychology in Europe is today much more *social* than it was twenty years ago" (p. 1). The general perspective of this "new" European social psychology can be said to be "that social psychology can and must include in its theoretical and research preoccupations a direct concern with the relationship between human psychological functioning and the large-scale social processes and events which shape this functioning and are shaped by it" (Tajfel et al., 1984, p. 3). This move toward a more "social" social psychology inevitably involves a greater concern for processes at the intergroup level and a move away from reductionist explanations of intergroup behavior.

A second factor that is likely to increase the importance of intergroup relations as a field of study is the growing power of minorities in many societies, not only those in Europe and North America but those in the Third World as well. The women's liberation, gay rights, and black power movements probably represent the most visible examples of this phenomenon to date. However, ethnic minorities generally seem to be more vocal and increasingly concerned with improving their status. This trend appears to be reflected by the official acceptance of a multicultural policy in Canada and Australia, as well as by the "unofficial" prominence gained by minority cultures and languages in Europe and the United States. The cultural impact and growing political cohesion of South Asians in Britain, Algerians in France, Asian "guest workers" in West Germany, and the Hispanic minority in the United States bear witness to this trend. Finally, there are the ongoing struggles for freedom and distinctiveness that characterize Third World nations on the continents of Africa, Asia, and South America, as well as minorities within these nations. The influence of minorities seems to be gaining recognition, both in the larger society and in the more limited domain of social research (Doms, 1983; Mugny, 1984; Mugny & Pérez, 1991), and this in turn is leading to a greater concern with intergroup relations.

The increased possibility of conflict, whether between terrorists and authorities or between the superpowers, represents the more frightening aspects of intergroup life in the contemporary world. In the past, a great deal of theory and experimental research has been concerned with peace-making, although the approaches used by researchers have been seriously flawed—by reductionism, for example—and the practical importance of this work has been rather limited. The challenge that remains is to achieve a truly intergroup perspective on problems of intergroup conflict, and thus contribute effectively to efforts for achieving peace, cooperation, and *justice* between groups. An integral part of this challenge is a commitment to fully appreciating the social psychological processes that involve both minority and majority groups, and relations between them.

Bibliography

Abeles, R. P. (1976). Relative deprivation, rising expectations, and black militancy. *Journal of Social Issues*, *32*(2), 119–137.

Aboud, F. E., & Taylor, D. M. (1971). Ethnic and role stereotypes: Their relative importance in person perception. *Journal of Social Psychology*, *85*, 17–27.

Abrams, D. (1989). *How social is social identity?* Paper presented at the First European Congress of Psychology, Amsterdam, The Netherlands.

———. (1990). How do group members regulate their behaviour? An integration of social identity and self-awareness theories. In D. Abrams & M. A. Hogg (Eds.), *Social identity theory: Constructive and critical advances*. London: Harvester Wheatsheaf.

———. (1992). Processes of social identification. In G. M. Breakwell (Ed.), *Social psychology of identity and the self concept* (pp. 57–99). London: Academic/Surrey University Press.

Abrams, D., & Hogg, M. A. (1988). Comments on the motivational status of self-esteem in social identity and intergroup discrimination. *European Journal of Social Psychology*, *18*, 317–334.

———. (Eds.). (1990). *Social identity theory: Constructive and critical advances*. London: Harvester Wheatsheaf.

Adams, J. S. (1965). Inequity in social exchange. In L. Berkowitz (Ed.), *Advances in experimental social psychology* (Vol. 2, pp. 267–299). New York: Academic Press.

Adams, J. S., & Rosenbaum, W. B. (1962). The relationship of worker productivity to cognitive dissonance about wage inequities. *Journal of Applied Psychology*, *46*, 161–164.

Adorno, T. W., Frenkel-Brunswik, E., Levinson, D. J., & Sanford, R. W. (1950). *The authoritarian personality.* New York: Harper & Row.

Allen, V. L., & Wilder, D. A. (1975). Categorization, belief similarity, and group discrimination. *Journal of Personality and Social Psychology, 32,* 971–977.

Allport, G. W. (1954). *The nature of prejudice.* Cambridge, Mass.: Addison-Wesley.

———. (1968). The historical background of modern social psychology. In G. Lindzey & E. Aronson (Eds.), *The handbook of social psychology* (2nd ed.) (Vol. 1, pp. 1–80). Reading, Mass.: Addison-Wesley.

Altemeyer, B. (1981). *Right-wing authoritarianism.* Winnipeg, Manitoba, Canada: University of Manitoba Press.

———. (1988). *Enemies of freedom: Understanding right-wing authoritarianism.* San Francisco: Jossey-Bass.

Amir, Y. (1976). The role of intergroup contact in change of prejudice and ethnic relations. In P. A. Katz (Ed.), *Towards the Elimination of Racism* (pp. 245–308. Elmsford, N.Y.: Pergamon Press.

Aronson, E. (1984). *The social animal.* New York: W. H. Freeman.

Aronson, E., Ellsworth, P. C., Carlsmith, J. M., & Gonzales, M. H. (1990). *Methods of research in social psychology* (2nd ed.). New York: McGraw-Hill.

Aronson, E., Stephan, C., Sikes, J., Blaney, N., & Snapp, M. (1978). *The jigsaw classroom.* Beverly Hills, Calif.: Sage Publications.

Asch, S. E. (1956). Studies of independence and conformity: A minority of one against a unanimous majority. *Psychological Monographs, 70* (9, Whole No. 416).

Austin, W. G. (1979). Justice, freedom, and self-interest in intergroup conflict. In W. G. Austin & S. Worchell (Eds.), *The social psychology of intergroup relations* (pp. 121–143). Monterey, Calif.: Brooks/Cole.

Austin, W., & Walster, E. (1974). Reactions to confirmations and disconfirmations of expectations of equity and inequity. *Journal of Personality and Social Psychology, 30,* 208–216.

Austin, W. G., & Worchel, S. (Eds.). (1979). *The social psychology of intergroup relations.* Monterey, Calif.: Brooks/Cole.

Axelrod, R. (1984). *The evolution of cooperation.* New York: Basic Books.

Baron, R. A., & Byrne, D. (1977). *Social psychology: Understanding human interaction.* Boston: Allyn & Bacon.

Bellerose, J., & Taylor, D. M. (1984). *Interpersonal harmony in the context of intergroup conflict.* Paper presented at the Canadian Psychological Association meeting, Ottawa.

Bercovitch, J. (1984). *Social conflicts and third parties: Strategies of conflict resolution.* Boulder, Colo.: Westview.

Berkowitz, L. (1962). *Aggression: A social psychological analysis.* New York: McGraw-Hill.

Berlyne, D. E. (1968). American and European psychology. *American Psychologist, 23*, 447–452.

Bernard, J. (1950). Where is the modern sociology of conflict? *American Journal of Sociology, 56*, 11–16.

Bernstein, M., & Crosby, F. (1980). An empirical examination of relative deprivation theory. *Journal of Experimental Social Psychology, 16*, 442–456.

Berry, J. (1970). A functional approach to the relationship between stereotypes and familiarity. *Australian Journal of Psychology, 22*, 29–33.

Berry, J. W. (1984). Multicultural policy in Canada: A social psychological analysis. *Canadian Journal of Behavioural Science, 16*, 353–370.

Berry, J. W., Kalin, R., & Taylor, D. M. (1977). *Multiculturalism and ethnic attitudes in Canada*. Ottawa: Printing and Pub. Supply and Services Canada.

Berscheid, E., & Walster, E. (1967). When does a harmdoer compensate a victim? *Journal of Personality and Social Psychology, 6*, 435–441.

Bettelheim, B. (1943). Individual and mass behavior in extreme situations. *Journal of Abnormal and Social Psychology, 38*, 417–452.

———. (1943). Individual and mass behavior in extreme situations. In E. E. Maccoby, T. M. Newcomb, and E. L. Hartley, (Eds.), *Readings in social psychology* (pp. 300–310). New York: Holt.

Bielby, W. T., & Baron, J. N. (1984). A woman's place is with other women: Sex segregation within organizations. In B. F. Reskin (Ed.), *Sex segregation in the workplace: Trends, explanations, remedies* (pp. 27–55). Washington, D.C.: National Academy Press.

Billig, M. G. (1972). *Social categorization and intergroup relations*. Ph.D. diss., University of Bristol.

———. (1973). Normative communication in a minimal intergroup situation. *European Journal of Social Psychology, 3*, 339–343.

———. (1976). *Social psychology and intergroup relations*. London: Academic Press.

———. (1987). *Arguing and thinking: A rhetorical approach to social psychology*. Cambridge: Cambridge University Press.

———. (1991). *Ideology and opinions*. London: Sage.

———. (1992). *Talking of the royal family*. London: Routledge.

Billig, M. G., & Tajfel, H. (1973). Social categorization and similarity in intergroup behaviour. *European Journal of Social Psychology, 3*, 27–52.

Blake, R. R., & Mouton, J. S. (1962). The intergroup dynamics of win-loss conflict and problem-solving collaboration in union-management relations. In M. Sherif (Ed.), *Intergroup relations and leadership* (pp. 94–141). New York: John Wiley.

Blake, R. R., Shepard, H. A., & Mouton, J. S. (1964). *Managing intergroup conflict in industry*. Houston: Gulf.

Blanchard, F. A., & Crosby, F. J. (1989). *Affirmative action in perspective*. New York: Springer-Verlag.

Blau, P. M. (1964). *Exchange and power in social life*. New York: John Wiley.
Bourhis, R. Y. (1992). Power, gender, and intergroup discrimination: Some minimal group experiments. In M. Zanna & J. Olson (Eds.), *The psychology of prejudice: The Ontario Symposium on Personality and Social Psychology*. Hillsdale, N.J.: Erlbaum.
Bourhis, R. Y., Sachdev, I., & Gagnon, A. (1994). Intergroup research with the Tajfel matrices: Methodological notes. In M. P. Zanna & J. M. Olson (Eds.), *The psychology of prejudice: The Ontario symposium* (vol. 7, pp. 209–232). Hillsdale, N.J.: Lawrence Erlbaum Associates.
Bradley, G. W. (1978). Self-serving biases in the attribution process: A reexamination of the fact or fiction question. *Journal of Personality and Social Psychology, 36*, 56–71.
Brandt, L. W. (1970). American psychology. *American Psychologist, 25*, 1091–1093.
Breakwell, G. M. (1986). *Coping with threatened identities*. London: Methuen.
———. (Ed.). (1992). *Social psychology of identity and the self concept*. London: Academic/Surrey University Press.
Brewer, M. B. (1979). The role of ethnocentrism in intergroup conflict. In W. G. Austin & J. Worchel (Eds.), *The social psychology of intergroup relations*, pp. 71–84. Monterey, Calif.: Brooks/Cole.
———. (1991). The social self: On being the same and different at the same time. *Personality and Social Psychology Bulletin, 17*, 475–482.
Brewer, M. B., Manzi, J. M., & Shaw, J. S. (1993). In-group identification as a function of depersonalization, distinctiveness, and status. *Psychological Science, 4*(2), 88–92.
Brewer, M. B., & Miller, N. (1988). Contact and cooperation: When do they work? In P. A. Katz and D. A. Taylor (Eds.), *Eliminating racism: Profiles in controversy*. New York: Plenum Press.
Brigham, J. C. (1971). Ethnic stereotypes. *Psychological Bulletin, 76*, 15–38.
Brown, D. R., & Smith, J. E. Keith. (Eds.). (1991). *Frontiers of mathematical psychology: Essays in honor of Clyde Coombs*. New York: Springer-Verlag.
Brown, J. D., Collins, R. L., & Schmidt, G. W. (1988). Self-esteem and direct versus indirect forms of self-enhancement. *Journal of Personality and Social Psychology, 55*, 445–453.
Brown, R. J. (1984). The role of similarity in intergroup relations. In H. Tajfel (Ed.), *The social dimension* (Vol. 2, pp. 603–623). Cambridge: Cambridge University Press.
———. (1988). *Group processes: Dynamics within and between groups*. Oxford: Blackwell.
Brown, R. J., & Turner, J. C. (1981). Interpersonal and intergroup behaviour. In J. Turner & H. Giles (Eds.), *Intergroup behaviour*. Oxford: Basil Blackwell.
Brown, R. J., Wade, G., Mathews, A., Condor, S., & Williams, J. (1983). *Group identification and intergroup differentiation*. Paper presented at the an-

nual conference of the British Psychological Society (Social Psychology Section), Sheffield.

Brown, R. J., & Williams, J. A. (1983). *Group identification: The same thing to all people?* Unpublished manuscript, Social Psychology Research Unit, University of Kent.

Bruner, J. (1981). Forward. In H. Tajfel, *Human groups and social categories* (pp. xi–xiii). Cambridge: Cambridge University Press.

————. (1986). *Actual minds, possible worlds*. Cambridge, Mass.: Harvard University Press.

Bruner, J. S., Goodnow, J. J., & Austin, G. A. (1956). *A study of thinking*. New York: John Wiley.

Byrne, D. (1971). *The attraction paradigm*. New York: Academic Press.

Caddick, B. (1981). Equity theory, social identity, and intergroup relations. *Review of Personality and Social Psychology, 1*, 219–245.

Campbell, D. T. (1967). Stereotypes and the perception of group differences. *American Psychologist, 22*, 817–829.

Caplan, N., & Nelson, S. D. (1973). On being useful: The nature and consequences of psychological research on social problems. *American Psychologist, 28*, 199–211.

Cauthen, N. R., Robinson, I. E., & Krauss, H. H . (1971). Stereotypes: A review of the literature, 1926–1968. *Journal of Social Psychology, 84*, 103–126.

Chacko, T. T. (1982). Women and equal employment opportunity: Some unintended effects. *Journal of Applied Psychology, 67*, 119–123.

Chagnon, N. (1992). *Yanomamo* (4th ed.). New York: Harcourt Brace Jovanovich.

Christie, R., & Jahoda, M. (Eds.). (1954). *Studies in the scope and method of "The authoritarian personality."* New York: Free Press.

Clark, K. B., & Clark, M. P. (1947). Racial identification and preferences in Negro children. In T. M. Newcomb and E. L. Hartley (Eds.), *Readings in social psychology* (pp. 169–178). New York: Holt.

Cole, M. (1984). The world beyond our borders. *American Psychologist, 39*, 998–1005.

Commins, B., & Lockwood, J. (1979a). The effects of status differences, favoured treatment, and equity on intergroup comparisons. *European Journal of Social Psychology, 9*, 281–289.

————. (1979b). Social comparison and social inequality: An experimental investigation of intergroup behaviour. *British Journal of Social and Clinical Psychology, 18*, 285–289.

Connor, R. C., Smolker, R. A., & Richards, A. F. (1992). Two levels of alliance formation among male bottlenose dolphins. *Proceedings of the National Academy of Sciences, 89*, 987–990.

Cook, S. W. (1978). Interpersonal and attitudinal outcomes in cooperating interracial groups. *Journal of Research and Development in Education, 12*, 97–113.

———. (1979). Social science and school desegregation: "Did we mislead the Supreme Court?" *Personality and Social Psychology Bulletin, 5*, 420–437.

Cook, T. D., Crosby, F., & Hennigan, K. M. (1977). The construct validity of relative deprivation. In J. M. Suls & R. L. Miller (Eds.), *Social comparison processes: Theoretical and empirical perspectives* (pp. 307–333). Washington, D.C.: Hemisphere.

Cooley, C. H. (1956). *Human nature and the social order.* New York: Free Press.

Coser, L. (1956). *The functions of social conflict.* New York: Free Press.

Crocker, J., & Major, B. (1989). Social stigma and self-esteem: The self-protective properties of stigma. *Psychological Review, 96*, 608–630.

Crocker, J., Voelkl, K., Testa, M., & Major, B. (1991). Social stigma: The affective consequences of attributional ambiguity. *Journal of Personality and Social Psychology, 60*, 218–228.

Crosby, F. (1976). A model of egoistical relative deprivation. *Psychological Review, 83*, 85–113.

———. (1982). *Relative deprivation and working women.* New York: Oxford University Press.

———. (1984). The denial of personal discrimination. *American Behavioral Scientist, 27*, 371–386.

Crosby, F., & Bernstein, M. (1978). *Relative deprivation: Testing the models.* Paper presented at the meeting of the American Psychological Association, Toronto.

Crosby, F. J., & Blanchard, F. A. (1989). Introduction: Affirmative action and the question of standards. In F. A. Blanchard & F. J. Crosby (Eds.), *Affirmative action in perspective* (pp. 3–7). New York: Springer-Verlag.

Crosby, F. J., & Clayton, S. (1991). Affirmative action and the issue of expectancies. *Journal of Social Issues, 46*(2), 61–79.

Davis, J. (1959). A formal interpretation of the theory of relative deprivation. *Sociometry, 22*, 280–296.

Dawes, R. M. (1980). Social dilemmas. *Annual Review of Psychology, 31*, 169–193.

Deaux, K., & Wrightsman, L. S. (1984). *Social psychology in the 80s.* Monterey, Calif.: Brooks/Cole.

deCarufel, A., & Schopler J. (1979). Evaluation of outcome improvement resulting from threats and appeals. *Journal of Personality and Social Psychology, 37*, 662–673.

DeRidder, R., & Tripathi, R. C. (Eds.). (1992). *Norm violation and intergroup relations.* Oxford: Clarendon Press.

Deschamps, J. C., & Brown, R. J. (1983). Superordinate goals and intergroup conflict. *British Journal of Social Psychology, 22*, 189–195.

Deutsch, M. (1962). Psychological alternatives to war. *Journal of Social Issues, 18*(2), 97–119.

————. (1969a). Socially relevant science: Reflections on some studies of interpersonal conflict. *American Psychologist, 24,* 1076–1092.

————. (1969b). Conflicts productive and destructive. *Journal of Social Issues, 25,* 7–14.

————. (1973). *The resolution of conflict.* New Haven: Yale University Press.

————. (1975). Equity, equality, and need: What determines which value will be used as the basis of distributive justice? *Journal of Social Issues, 31*(3), 137–149.

————. (1985). *Distributive justice: A social-psychological perspective.* New Haven: Yale University Press.

Deutsch, M., & Krauss, R. M. (1960). The effect of threat on interpersonal bargaining. *Journal of Abnormal and Social Psychology, 61,* 181–189.

————. (1962). Studies of interpersonal bargaining. *Journal of Conflict Resolution, 6,* 52–76.

Diab, L. N. (1970). A study of intragroup and intergroup relations among experimentally produced groups. *Genetic Psychology Monographs, 82,* 49–82.

Dibble, U. (1981). Socially shared deprivation and the approval of violence: Another look at the experience of American blacks during the 1960's. *Ethnicity, 8,* 149–168.

Dion, K. L. (1975). Women's reactions to discrimination from members of the same or opposite sex. *Journal of Research in Personality, 9,* 294–306.

————. (1986). Responses to perceived discrimination and relative deprivation. In J. M. Olson, C. P. Herman, & M. P. Zanna (Eds.), *Relative deprivation and social comparison: The Ontario symposium* (Vol. 4, pp. 159–180). Hillsdale, N.J.: Erlbaum.

Dion, K. L., & Earn, B. M. (1975). The phenomenology of being a target of prejudice. *Journal of Personality and Social Psychology, 32,* 944–950.

Doise, W. (1978). *Groups and individuals: Explanations in social psychology.* Cambridge: Cambridge University Press.

Doise, W., Csepeli, G., Dann, H. D., Gouge, G. C., Larsen, K. & Ostell, A. (1972). An experimental investigation into the formation of intergroup representations. *European Journal of Social Psychology, 2,* 202–204.

Dollard, J., Doob, L., Miller, N., Mowrer, O., & Sears, R. (1939). *Frustration and aggression.* New Haven: Yale University Press.

Doms, M. (1983). The minority influence effect: An alternative approach. In W. Doise & S. Moscovici (Eds.), *Current issues in European social psychology* (vol. 1, pp. 1–32). Cambridge: Cambridge University Press.

Donnerstein, E., Donnerstein, M., Simon, S., & Ditrichs, R. (1972). Variables in interracial aggression: Anonymity, expected retaliation, and a riot. *Journal of Personality and Social Psychology, 22,* 236–245.

Dostoevsky, Feodor. (1972). Notes from the underground. In R. Fernandez (Ed.), *Social psychology through literature* (pp. 416–429). New York: John Wiley.

Douglas, A. (1957). The peaceful settlement of individual and intergroup disputes. *Journal of Conflict Resolution, 1*(1), 69–81.

Dovidio, J. F., & Gaertner, S. L. (1983). The effects of sex, status, and ability on helping behaviour. *Journal of Applied Social Psychology, 13*, 191–205.

Dovidio, J. F., Mann, J., & Gaertner, S. L . (1989). Resistance to affirmative action: The implications of aversive racism. In F. A. Blanchard & F. J. Crosby (Eds.), *Affirmative action in perspective* (pp. 83–102). New York: Springer-Verlag.

Durkheim, E. (1960). *The division of labor in society* (G. Simpson, Trans.) (4th ed.). Glencoe, Ill.: Free Press. (Original work published 1923.)

Eagly, A. H. (1987). *Sex differences in social behavior: A social-role interpretation.* Hillsdale, N.J.: Erlbaum.

Edwards, D. (1991). Categories are for talking: On the cognitive and discursive bases of categorization. *Theory and Psychology, 1*, 515–542.

Edwards, J. (1985). *Language, society, and identity.* Oxford: Blackwell.

——— . (1992). Language in group and individual identity. In G. M. Breakwell (Ed.), *Social psychology of identity and the self concept* (pp. 129–146). London: Academic/Surrey University Press.

Eiser, J. R., & Bhavnani, K. K. (1974). The effect of situational meaning on the behaviour of subjects in the Prisoner's Dilemma game. *European Journal of Social Psychology, 4*, 93–97.

Eiser, J. R., & Smith, A. J. (1972). Preference for accuracy and positivity in the description of oneself by another. *European Journal of Social Psychology, 2*, 199–201.

Ellemers, N., Wilke, H., & van Knippenberg, A. (1993). Effects of the legitimacy of low group or individual status on individual and collective status-enhancement strategies. *Journal of Personality and Social Psychology, 64*, 766–778.

Esman, M. J. (1987). Ethnic politics and economic power. *Comparative Politics, 19*, 395–417.

Ferdman, B. O. (1990). Literacy and cultural identity. *Harvard Educational Review, 60*(2), 181–204.

——— . (1992). The dynamics of ethnic diversity in organizations: Toward integrative models. In K. Kelley (Ed.), *Issues, theory, and research in industrial/organizational psychology* (pp. 339–384). Amsterdam: North-Holland.

Ferguson, C. K., & Kelley, H. H. (1964). Significant factors in overevaluation of one's own product. *Journal of Abnormal and Social Psychology, 69*, 223–228.

Festinger, L. (1954). A theory of social comparison processes. *Human Relations, 7*, 117–140.

——— . (1957). *A theory of cognitive dissonance.* Stanford, Calif.: Stanford University Press.

Fisher, R. J. (1983). Third party consultation as a method of intergroup conflict resolution. *Journal of Conflict Resolution, 27,* 301–334.

Fishman, J. A. (1956). An examination of the process and functioning of social stereotyping. *Journal of Social Psychology, 43,* 27–64.

Folger, R. (1986). A referent cognitions theory of relative deprivation. In J. M. Olson, C. P. Herman, & M. P. Zanna, (Eds.), *Relative Deprivation and Social Comparison: The Ontario Symposium,* Vol. 4. Hillsdale, N.J.: Erlbaum.

Forbes, H. D. (1985). *Nationalism, ethnocentrism, and personality.* Chicago: University of Chicago Press.

Frank. J. D. (1967). *Sanity and survival: Psychological aspects of war and peace.* London: Barrie & Rockliff.

Freud, S. (1953–1964). *The standard edition of the complete psychological works of Sigmund Freud* (J. Strachey, Ed. and Trans.). London: Hogarth Press.

———. (1915). *Thoughts for the times on war and death. Standard edition,* vol. 14.

———. (1920). *Beyond the pleasure principle. Standard edition,* vol. 18.

———. (1921). *Group psychology and the analysis of the ego. Standard edition,* vol. 18.

———. (1923). *The ego and the id. Standard edition,* vol. 19.

———. (1927). *The future of an illusion. Standard edition,* vol. 21.

———. (1930). *Civilization and its discontents. Standard edition,* vol. 21.

———. (1993). *Why war? Standard edition,* vol. 22.

Garcia, L. T., Erskine, N., Hawn, K., & Casmay, S. R. (1981). The effect of affirmative action on attributions about minority group members. *Journal of Personality, 49,* 427–437.

Gardner, R. C. (1973). Ethnic stereotypes: The traditional approach, a new look. *Canadian Psychologist, 14,* 133–148.

Gardner, R. C., & Kalin, R. (Eds.). (1981). *A Canadian social psychology of ethnic relations.* Toronto: Methuen.

Gardner, R. C., Kirby, D. M., & Finley, J. C. (1973). Ethnic stereotypes: The significance of consensus. *Canadian Journal of Behavioural Science, 5,* 4–12.

Gardner, R. C., Wonnacott, E. J., & Taylor, D. M. (1968). Ethnic stereotypes: A factor analytic investigation. *Canadian Journal of Psychology, 22,* 35–44.

Garland, H., & Price, K. H. (1977). Attributions toward women in management and attributions for their success and failure in managerial positions. *Journal of Applied Psychology, 62,* 29–33.

Gecas, V., & Schwalbe, M. L. (1983). Beyond the looking-glass self: Social structure and efficacy-based self-esteem. *Social Psychology Quarterly, 46,* 77–88.

Giles, H., Bourhis, R. Y., & Taylor, D. M. (1977). Toward a theory of language in ethnic relations. In H. Giles (Ed.), *Language, ethnicity, and intergroup relations* (pp. 307–348). London: Academic Press.

Giles, H., & Johnson, P. (1987). Ethnolinguistic identity theory: A social psychological approach to language maintenance. *International Journal of the Sociology of Language, 68,* 256–269.

Glazer, N. (1988). The future of preferential affirmative action. In P. A. Katz & D. A. Taylor (Eds.), *Eliminating racism: Profiles in controversy* (pp. 329–340). New York: Plenum Press.

Glazer, N., & Moynihan, D. P. (1970). *Beyond the melting pot* (2nd ed.). Cambridge, Mass.: MIT Press.

Goffman, E. (1963). *Stigma: Notes on the management of spoiled identity.* Englewood Cliffs, N.J.: Prentice-Hall.

Gordon, M. M. (1964). *Assimilation in American life.* New York: Oxford University Press.

———. (1981). Models of pluralism: The new American dilemma. In R. D. Lambert, A. W. Heston, & M. M. Gordon, (Eds.), *America as a multicultural society* (pp. 178–188). Philadelphia: American Academy of Political and Social Science.

Government of Canada. (1971). Statement by the Prime Minister (response to the report of the Royal Commission on Bilingualism and Biculturalism, Book 4, House of Commons), Ottawa, press release.

Greeley, A. M. (1974). *Ethnicity in the United States: A preliminary reconnaissance.* New York: John Wiley.

Guimond, S., & Dubé-Simard, L. (1983). Relative deprivation theory and the Quebec nationalist movement: The cognition-emotion distinction and the person-group deprivation issue. *Journal of Personality and Social Psychology, 44,* 526–535.

Gurr, T. R. (1970). *Why men rebel.* Princeton: Princeton University Press.

Hall, S. F., & Hall, D. T. (1976). Effects of job incumbents' race and sex on evaluation of managerial performance. *Academy of Management Journal, 19,* 476–481.

Hamilton, D. L. (1979). A cognitive-attributional analysis of stereotyping. In L. Berkowitz (Ed.), *Advances in experimental social psychology* (vol. 12, pp. 53–84). New York: Academic Press.

———. (Ed.). (1981). *Cognitive processes in stereotyping and intergroup behavior.* Hillsdale, N.J.: Erlbaum.

Hamilton, D. L., & Gifford, R. K. (1976). Illusory correlation in interpersonal perception: A cognitive basis of stereotypic judgments. *Journal of Experimental Social Psychology, 12,* 392–407.

Hardin, G. (1968). The tragedy of the commons. *Science, 162,* 1243–1248.

Harré, R. (1993). *Social being* (2nd ed.). Oxford: Blackwell.

Hechter, M. (1975). *Internal colonialism: The Celtic fringe in British national development, 1536–1964.* Berkeley: University of California Press.

————. (1978). Group formation and the cultural division of labor. *American Journal of Sociology*, *84*, 293–318.

Heider, F. (1946). Attitudes and cognitive organization. *Journal of Psychology*, *21*, 107–112.

————. (1958). *The psychology of interpersonal relations*. New York: John Wiley.

Heilman, M. E., Simon, M. C., & Repper, D. P. (1987). Intentionally favoured, unintentionally harmed? Impact of sex-based preferential selection on self-perception and self-evaluations. *Journal of Applied Psychology*, *72*, 62–68.

Hewstone, M. (1990). *Causal attribution: From cognitive processes to collective beliefs*. Oxford: Blackwell.

Hewstone, M., & Brown, R. (Eds.). (1986). *Contact and conflict in intergroup encounters*. New York: Basil Blackwell.

Hewstone, M., & Ward, C. (1985). Ethnocentrism and causal attribution in Southeast Asia. *Journal of Personality and Social Psychology*, *48*, 614–623.

Hirschman, A. O. (1970). *Exit, voice, and loyalty: Responses to decline in firms, organizations, and states*. Cambridge, Mass.: Harvard University Press.

————. (1974). Exit, voice, and loyalty. *Social Science Information*, *13*(1), 7–26.

Hirschman, C. (1983). America's melting pot reconsidered. *Annual Review of Sociology*, *9*, 393–423.

Hogg, M. A., & Abrams, D. (1988). *Social identifications: A social psychology of intergroup relations and group processes*. London: Routledge.

————. (1990). Social motivation, self-esteem, and social identity. In D. Abrams & M. A. Hogg (Eds.), *Social identity theory: Constructive and critical advances* (pp. 28–47). London: Harvester Wheatsheaf.

Hogg, M. A., & Sunderland, J. (1991). Self-esteem and intergroup discrimination in the minimal group paradigm. *British Journal of Social Psychology*, *30*, 51–62.

Hogg, M. A., Turner, J. C., & Davidson, B. (1990). Polarized norms and social frames of reference: A test of the self-categorization theory of group polarization. *Basic and Applied Social Psychology*, *11*, 77–100.

Homans, G. C. (1961). *Social behavior: Its elementary forms*. New York: Harcourt, Brace & World.

Homer-Dixon, T. F., Boutwell, J. H., & Rathjens, G. W. (1993). Environmental change and violent conflict. *Scientific American*, February, 38–45.

Horowitz, D. L. (1973). Direct, displaced, and cumulative ethnic aggression. *Comparative Politics*, *6*, 1–16.

Ittelson, W. H. (1973). *Environment and cognition*. New York: Seminar Press.

Ittelson, W. H., Proshansky, H. M., Rivlin, L. G., & Winkel, G. A. (1974). *An introduction to environmental psychology* (chap. 5, pp. 102–125). New York: Holt, Rinehart & Winston.

Jaspers, J. (1986). Forum and focus: A personal view of European social psychology. *European Journal of Social Psychology, 16*, 3–15.

Jones, A. J. (1991). *Affirmative talk, affirmative action: A comparative study of the politics of affirmative action.* New York: Praeger.

Jones, E. E., & Davis, K. E. (1965). From acts to dispositions: The attribution process in person perception. In L. Berkowitz (Ed.), *Advances in experimental social psychology* (vol. 2, pp. 220–256). New York: Academic Press.

Jost, J. T., & Azzi, A. (1992). *Normative effects of resource and recipient-level in the minimal group paradigm.* Paper presented at the annual meeting of the American Psychological Association, Washington, D.C.

Kandel, D. B. (1978). Similarity in real-life adolescent friendship pairs. *Journal of Personality and Social Psychology, 31*, 306–388.

Kanungo, R. (1988). *Charismatic leadership: The elusive factor in organizational effectiveness.* San Francisco: Jossey-Bass Publishers.

Kaplan, A. (1964). *The conduct of inquiry: Methodology for behavioral science.* San Francisco: Chandler.

Karlins, M., Coffman, T. L., & Walters, G. (1969). On the fading of social stereotypes: Studies in three generations of college students. *Journal of Personality and Social Psychology, 13*, 1–6.

Katz, D., & Braly, K. (1933). Racial stereotypes of one hundred college students. *Journal of Abnormal and Social Psychology, 28*, 280–290.

———. (1935). Racial prejudice and racial stereotypes. *Journal of Abnormal and Social Psychology, 30*, 175–193.

Kelley, H. H. (1973). The processes of causal attribution. *American Psychologist, 28*, 107–128.

Kelley, H. H., & Grzelak, J. (1972). Conflict between individual and common interest in an N-person relationship. *Journal of Personality and Social Psychology, 21*, 190–197.

Kennedy, S., Scheirer, J., & Rogers, A. (1984). The price of our success: Our monocultural science. *American Psychologist, 39*, 996–997.

Kidder, L. H., & Stewart, V. M. (1975). *The psychology of intergroup relations: Conflict and consciousness.* New York: McGraw-Hill.

Kramnick, I. (1972). Reflections on revolution: Definition and explanation in recent scholarship. *History and Theory, 11*, 26–63.

Kressel, K., & Pruitt, D. G. (Eds.). (1985). The mediation of social conflict. *Journal of Social Issues, 41*(2).

LaFromboise, T., Coleman, H.L.K., & Gerton, J. (1993). Psychological impact of biculturalism: Evidence and theory. *Psychological Bulletin, 114*, 395–412.

Lalonde, R. N. (1985). *Ethnic stereotype processing and organization as a function of group membership.* Ph.D. diss., University of Western Ontario.

Lalonde, R. N., & Silverman, R. A. (1994). Behavioral preferences in response to social injustice: The effects of group permeability and social identity salience. *Journal of Personality and Social Psychology, 66*, 78–85.

Lambert, W. E. (1969). A social psychology of bilingualism. *Journal of Social Issues, 23*(2), 91–109.

Lambert, W. E., Hodgson, R. C., Gardner, R. C., & Fillenbaum, S. (1960). Evaluational reactions to spoken language. *Journal of Abnormal and Social Psychology, 60*, 44–51.

Lambert, W. E., Mermigis, L., & Taylor, D. M. (1986). Greek Canadians' attitudes towards own group and other Canadian ethnic groups: A test of the multicultural hypothesis. *Canadian Journal of Behavioural Science, 18*, 35–51.

Lambert, W. E., & Taylor, D. M. (1986). *Cultural and racial diversity in the lives of urban Americans: The Hamtramck/Pontiac study.* Unpublished monograph, McGill University.

———. (1990). *Coping with cultural and racial diversity in urban America.* New York: Praeger.

Lasker, B. (1929). *Race attitudes in children.* New York: Holt.

Lawler, J. E. (1985). *Advances in group process,* vol. 2. Greenwich, Conn.: JAI Press.

Laws, J. L. (1975). The psychology of tokenism: An analysis. *Sex roles, 1*, 51–67.

Le Bon, G. (1897). *The crowd: A study of the popular mind.* London: T. Fisher Unwin.

Lemain, G., & Kastersztein, J. (1971–1972). Recherches sur l'originalité sociale et l'incomparabilité. *Bulletin de Psychologie, 25*, 673–693.

Lemyre, L., & Smith, P. M. (1985). Intergroup discrimination and self-esteem in the minimal group paradigm. *Journal of Personality and Social Psychology, 49*, 660–670.

Lerner, M. J. (1971). Justified self-interest and the responsibility for suffering: A replication and extension. *Journal of Human Relations, 19*, 550–559.

———. (1977). The justice motive: Some hypotheses as to its origins and forms. *Journal of Personality, 45*, 1–52.

Leventhal, G. S. (1979). Effects of external conflict on resource allocation and fairness within groups and organizations. In W. G. Austin & S. Worchel (Eds.), *The social psychology of intergroup relations* (pp. 237–252). Monterey, Calif.: Brooks/Cole.

Leventhal, G. S., & Lane, D. W. (1970). Sex, age, and equity behavior. *Journal of Personality and Social Psychology, 15*, 312–316.

LeVine, R. A., & Campbell, D. T. (1972). *Ethnocentrism: Theories of conflict, ethnic attitudes, and group behavior.* New York: John Wiley.

Lewicki, P. (1982). Social psychology as viewed by its practitioners: Survey of SESP members' opinions. *Personality and Social Psychology Bulletin, 8*, 409–416.

Liebrand, W.B.G. (1983). A classification of social dilemma games. *Simulation and Games, 14*, 123–138.

Lijphart, A. (1968). *The politics of accommodation: Pluralism and democracy in the Netherlands.* Berkeley: University of California Press.

Lord, C. G., & Saenz, D. S. (1985). Memory deficits and memory surfeits: Differential cognitive consequences of tokenism for tokens and observers. *Journal of Personality and Social Psychology, 49*, 918–926.

Lorenz, K. (1966). *On aggression* (M. Wilson, Trans.). New York: Harcourt, Brace & World.

Lott, A. J., & Lott, B. E. (1965). Group cohesiveness as interpersonal attraction: A review of relationships with antecedent and consequent variables. *Psychological Bulletin, 64*, 259–309.

Major, B. (1994). From social inequality to personal entitlement: The role of social comparisons, legitimacy appraisals, and group membership. In M. Zanna (Ed.), *Advances in experimental psychology* (Vol. 26, pp. 293–355). New York.

Major, B., & Crocker, J. (1993). Social stigma: The consequences of attributional ambiguity. In D. M. Mackie and D. L. Hamilton (Eds.), *Affect, cognition, and stereotyping: Interactive processes in group perception* (pp. 345–370). San Diego: Academic Press.

Manis, M. (1972). Social interaction and the self-concept. In D. R. Heise (Ed.), *Personality and socialization* (pp. 136–152). Chicago: Rand McNally.

Mansbridge, J. J. (Ed.). (1990). *Beyond self-interest.* Chicago: University of Chicago Press.

Manson, J. H., & Wrangham, R. W. (1991). Intergroup aggression in chimpanzees and humans. Current Anthropology, *32*, 369–390.

Maquet, J. J. (1961). *The premise of inequality in Ruanda: A study of political relations in a central African kingdom.* London: Oxford University Press.

Markus, H. R., & Kitayama, S. (1991). Culture and the self: Implications for cognition, emotion, and motivation. *Psychological Review, 98*, 224–253.

Martin, J. (1980). *Pay equality and the perception of injustice: A relative deprivation perspective* (Research Paper No. 553). Stanford, Calif.: Stanford University.

Martin, J., Brickman, P., & Murray, A. (1984). Moral outrage and pragmatism: Explanations for collective action. *Journal of Experimental Social Psychology, 20*, 484–496.

Martin, J., & Murray, A. (1983). Distributive injustice and unfair exchange. In D. M. Messick & K. S. Cook (Eds.), *Equity theory: Psychological and sociological perspectives* (pp. 169–202). New York: Praeger.

Martin, J., Price, R., Bies, R., & Powers, M. (1979). *Relative deprivation among secretaries: The effects of the token female executive.* Paper presented at American Psychological Association meeting, New York, September.

Matheson, K., Echenberg, A., Taylor, D. M., Rivers, D., & Chow, I. (1993). *Women's attitudes toward affirmative action: Putting actions in context.* Unpublished manuscript, Carleton University.

McCarthy, T. D., & Zald, M. N. (1977). Resource mobilization and social movements: A partial theory. *American Journal of Sociology, 82,* 1212–1241.

McDougall, W. (1920). *The group mind.* Cambridge: Cambridge University Press.

McPhail, C. (1980). Civil disorder participation: A critical examination of recent research. In M. D. Pugh (Ed.), *Collective behavior: A source book.* St. Paul, Minn.: West.

Merton, R. K. (1948). The self-fulfilling prophecy. *Antioch Review, 8 ,* 193–210.

Messick, D. M., & Cook, K. S. (Eds.). (1983). *Equity theory: Psychological and sociological perspectives.* New York: Praeger.

Messick, D. M., & Mackie, D. M. (1989). Intergroup relations. *Annual Review of Psychology, 40,* 45–81.

Middlebrook, P. N. (1974). *Social psychology and modern life.* New York: Alfred A. Knopf.

Middleton, J., & Tait, D. (1958). *Tribes without rulers: Studies in African segmentary systems.* London: Routledge & Kegan Paul.

Miller, A. G. (Ed.). (1972). *The social psychology of psychological research.* New York: Free Press.

——— . (1982). Historical and contemporary perspectives on stereotyping. In A. G. Miller (Ed.), *In the eye of the beholder: Contemporary issues in stereotyping* (pp. 1–40). New York: Praeger.

Miller, D. T. (1978). What constitutes a self-serving attributional bias? A reply to Bradley. *Journal of Personality and Social Psychology, 36,* 1221–1223.

Miller, D. T., & Ross, M. (1975). Self-serving biases in the attribution of causality: Fact or fiction? *Psychological Bulletin, 82,* 213–225.

Miller, R. L. (1977). Preferences for social vs. non-social comparison as a means of self-evaluation. *Journal of Personality, 45,* 458–468.

Milner, D. (1975). *Children and race.* Harmondsworth, England: Penguin Books.

Moghaddam, F. M. (1987). Psychology in the Three Worlds: As reflected by the crisis in social psychology and the move toward indigenous Third World psychology. *American Psychologist, 42,* 912–920.

——— . (1990). Modulative and generative orientations in psychology: Implications for psychology in the Three Worlds. *Journal of Social Issues, 46,* 21–41.

——— . (1992). Assimilation et multiculturalisme: Le cas des minorités au Québec. *Revue québécoise de psychologie, 13,* 140–157.

——— . (in press). Managing cultural diversity: North American experiences and suggestions from the German unification process. *International Journal of Psychology, 28.*

Moghaddam, F. M., & Harré, R. (1992). Rethinking the laboratory experiment. *American Behavioral Scientist, 36,* 22–38.

Moghaddam, F. M., & Hutchenson, L. (1993). *The generalized personal/group discrepancy: A test of the specificity of the personal/group discrimination discrepancy.* Unpublished manuscript, Georgetown University, Washington, D.C.

Moghaddam, F. M., & Perreault, S. (1992). Individual and collective mobility strategies among minority group members. *Journal of Social Psychology, 132,* 343–357.

Moghaddam, F. M., & Solliday, E. A. (1991). "Balanced multiculturalism" and the challenge of peaceful coexistence in pluralistic societies. *Psychology and Developing Societies, 3,* 51–72.

Moghaddam, F. M., & Stringer, P. (1986). "Trivial" and "important" criteria for social categorization in the minimal group paradigm. *Journal of Social Psychology, 126,* 345–354.

——— . (1988). Outgroup similarity and intergroup bias. *Journal of Social Psychology, 128,* 105–115.

Moghaddam, F. M., & Taylor, D. M. (1987). The meaning of multiculturalism for visible minority immigrant women. *Canadian Journal of Behavioural Science, 19,* 121–136.

Moghaddam, F. M., Taylor, D. M., & Lalonde, R. N. (1987). Individualistic and collective integration strategies among Iranians in Canada. *International Journal of Psychology, 22,* 301–313.

——— . (1989). Integration strategies and attitudes towards the built environment. *Canadian Journal of Behavioural Science, 21,* 160–173.

Moghaddam, F. M., Taylor, D. M., & Wright, S. C. (1993). *Social psychology in cross-cultural perspective.* New York: W. H. Freeman.

Moreland, J. K. (1965). Token desegregation and beyond. In A. M. Rose and C. B. Rose (Eds.), *Minority Problems.* New York: Harper & Row.

Morley, I. E., & Stephenson, G. M. (1969). Interpersonal and interparty exchange: A laboratory simulation of an industrial dispute at the plant level. *British Journal of Psychology, 60,* 543–545.

——— . (1970a). Strength of case, communication systems, and outcomes of simulated negotiations: Some social psychological aspects of bargaining. *Industrial Relations Journal, 1,* 19–29.

——— . (1970b). Formality in experimental negotiations: A validation study. *British Journal of Psychology, 61,* 383–384.

Mosca, G. (1939). *The ruling class.* New York: McGraw-Hill. (Translated from Italian edition of 1896.)

Moscovici, S. (1972). Society and theory in social psychology. In J. Israel & H. Tajfel (Eds.), *The context of social psychology* (pp. 17–68). London: Academic Press.

——— . (1976). *Social influence and social change.* London: Academic Press.

——— . (1980). Toward a theory of conversion behaviour. In L. Berkowitz (Ed.), *Advances in experimental social psychology* (Vol. 13, pp. 209–239). New York: Academic Press.

————. (1985). Social influence and conformity. In G. Lindzey & E. Aronson (Eds.), *The handbook of social psychology* (3rd ed.) (Vol. 2, pp. 347–412). New York: Random House.

Moscovici, S., Mugny, G., & Van Avermaet, E. (Eds.). (1985). *Perspectives on minority influence*. Cambridge: Cambridge University Press.

Mugny, G. (1984). The influence of minorities: Ten years after. In H. Tajfel (Ed.), *The social dimension* (Vol. 2, pp. 498–517). Cambridge: Cambridge University Press.

Mugny, G., & Pérez, J. A. (1991). *The social psychology of minority influence* (V. W. Lamongie, Trans.). Cambridge: Cambridge University Press.

Mulkay, M. J., & Turner, B. S. (1971). Over-production of personnel and innovation in three social settings. *Sociology, 5,* 47–61.

Mummendey, A., & Schreiber, H. J. (1983). Better or just different? Positive social identity by discrimination against, or by differentiation from outgroups. *European Journal of Social Psychology, 13,* 389–397.

Mummendey, A., & Simon, B. (1989). Better or just different? III: The impact of comparison dimension and relative ingroup size upon intergroup discrimination. *British Journal of Social Psychology, 28,* 1–16.

Nacoste, R. W. (1989). Affirmative action and self-evaluation. In F. A. Blanchard and F. J. Crosby (Eds.), *Affirmative action in perspective* (103–109). New York: Springer-Verlag.

Nagel, J. (1987). The ethnic revolution: Emergence of ethnic nationalism. In L. Driedger (Ed.), *Ethnic Canada: Identities and inequalities*. Toronto: Copp Clark Pitman.

Neisser, U. (1967). *Cognitive psychology*. New York: Appleton-Century-Crofts.

Nemeth, C. (1972). A critical analysis of research utilizing the Prisoner's Dilemma paradigm for the study of bargaining. In L. Berkowitz (Ed.), *Advances in experimental social psychology* (Vol. 6, pp. 203–234). New York: Academic Press.

Newcomb, T. M. (1961). *The acquaintance process*. New York: Holt, Rinehart & Winston.

Newell, D., McKillop, P., & Monroe, S. (1986). Arab-bashing in America. *Newsweek,* January 20, p. 21.

————. (1982). Power and intergroup discrimination. In H. Tajfel (Ed.), *Social identity and intergroup relations* (pp. 179–206). Cambridge: Cambridge University Press.

————. (1984). Social psychology and political economy. In H. Tajfel (Ed.), *The social dimension* (vol. 2, pp. 624–645). Cambridge: Cambridge University Press.

Ng, S. H. (1980). *The social psychology of power*. New York: Academic Press.

————. (1982). Power and intergroup discrimination. In J. Tajfel (Ed.), *Social identity and intergroup relations* (pp. 179–206). Cambridge: Cambridge University Press.

Novak, M. D. (1972). *The rise of the unmeltable ethnics.* New York: Macmillan.

Olson, J. M., Herman, C. P., & Zanna, M. P. (Eds.). (1986). *Relative deprivation and social comparison: The Ontario symposium* (Vol. 4). Hillsdale, N.J.: Erlbaum.

Pannen, D. E. (1976). *Anticipation of future interaction and the estimation of current rewards.* Ph.D. diss., University of Minnesota.

Papastamou, S. (1983). Strategies of minority and majority influence. In W. Doise & S. Moscovici (Eds.), *Current issues in European social psychology* (Vol. 1, pp. 33–83). Cambridge: Cambridge University Press.

Pareto, V. (1935). *The mind and society: A treatise on general sociology.* 4 vols. New York: Dover.

——— . (1971). *Manual of political economy.* New York: Augustus M. Kelley. (Translated from French edition of 1927.)

Park, B., & Rothbart, M. (1982). Perception of out-group homogeneity and levels of social categorization: Memory for the subordinate attributes of in-group and out-group members. *Journal of Personality and Social Psychology, 42,* 1051–1068.

Park, R. E. (1950). *Race and culture.* Glencoe, Ill.: Free Press.

Park, R. E., & Burgess, E. W. (1969). *Introduction to the science of sociology.* 3rd. ed. rev. Chicago: University of Chicago Press. (Original work published 1921.)

Perrott, S. B., & Taylor, D. M. (in press). Ethnocentrism and authoritarianism in the police: Challenging stereotypes and reconceptualizing ingroup identification. *Journal of Applied Social Psychology.*

Pettigrew, T. F. (1971). *Racially Separate or Together?* New York; McGraw-Hill.

——— . (1978). Three issues in ethnicity: Boundaries, deprivations, and perceptions. In J. M. Yinger & S. J. Cutler (Eds.), *Major social issues: A multidisciplinary view* (pp. 25–49). New York: Free Press.

——— . (1979). The ultimate attribution error: Extending Allport's cognitive analysis of prejudice. *Personality and Social Psychology Bulletin, 5,* 461–476.

Pettigrew, T. F. (1986). *Modern racism: American black-white relations since the 1960's.* Cambridge, Mass.: Harvard University Press.

——— . (1986). The intergroup contact hypothesis reconsidered. In M. Hewstone & R. Brown (Eds.), *Contact and conflict in intergroup encounters* (pp. 169–195). Oxford, England: Basil Blackwell.

Pettigrew, T. F., Allport, G. W., & Barnett, E. O. (1958). Binocular resolution and perception of race in South Africa. *British Journal of Psychology, 49,* 265–278.

Plon, M. (1974). On the meaning and notion of conflict and its study in social psychology. *European Journal of Social Psychology, 4,* 389–436.

Popper, K. R. (1959). *The logic of scientific discovery.* New York: Basic Books.

Porter, J. (1965). *The Vertical Mosaic.* Toronto: University of Toronto Press.

Porter, L. E., Taylor, D. M., & Koffman, M. A. (1993). *Women's endorsement of nondiscrimination and rejection of reverse discrimination.* Unpublished manuscript, McGill University.

Pruitt, D. G. (1971). Conclusions: Toward an understanding of choice shifts in group discussion. *Journal of Personality and Social Psychology, 20,* 495–510.

Pruitt, D. G., & Rubin, J. Z. (1986). *Social conflict: Escalation, stalemate, and settlement.* New York: Random House.

Rabbie, J. M., & Horwitz, M. (1969). Arousal of intergroup-outgroup bias by a chance win or loss. *Journal of Personality and Social Psychology, 13,* 269–277.

Rapoport, A., & Chammah, A. M. (1965). *Prisoner's dilemma: A study in conflict and cooperation.* Ann Arbor: University of Michigan Press.

Rappaport, J. (1977). *Community psychology.* New York: Holt, Rinehart & Winston.

Ray, J. J. (1985). Defective validity in the Altemeyer authoritarianism scale. *Journal of Social Psychology, 125,* 271–272.

Rokeach, M. (1960). *The open and closed mind.* New York: Basic Books.

Rosenberg, M. J., & Abelson, L. P. (1960). An analysis of cognitive balancing. In M. J. Rosenberg & C. I. Houland (Eds.), *Attitude organization and change* (pp. 112–163). New Haven: Yale University Press.

Ross, L. (1977). The intuitive psychologist and his shortcomings: Distortions in the attribution process. In L. Berkowitz (Ed.), *Advances in experimental social psychology* (Vol. 10, pp. 174–220). New York: Academic Press.

Rothbart, M., Dawes, R., & Park, B. (1984). Stereotyping and sampling biases in intergroup perception. In J. R. Eiser (Ed.), *Attitudinal judgment* (pp. 109–134). New York: Springer-Verlag.

Rubin, J. Z. (1981). *Dynamics of third party intervention: Kissinger in the Middle East.* New York: Praeger.

Ruggiero, K. M., & Taylor, D. M. (1993). *The social psychological consequences of being a victim of discrimination.* Unpublished manuscript, McGill University, Montreal, Quebec, Canada.

Runciman, W. G. (1966). *Relative deprivation and social justice: A study of attitudes to social inequality in twentieth-century England.* Berkeley: University of California Press.

Ryan, W. (1976). *Blaming the victim.* New York: Random House.

Sachdev, I., & Bourhis, R. Y. (1984). Minimal majorities and minorities. *European Journal of Social Psychology, 14,* 35–52.

———. (1985). Social categorization and power differentials in group relations. *European Journal of Social Psychology, 15,* 415–434.

———. (1987). Status differentials and intergroup behavior. *European Journal of Social Psychology, 17,* 277–293.

———. (1990). Language and social identification. In D. Abrams & M. Hogg (Eds.), *Social identity theory: Constructive and critical advances* (pp. 211–229). New York: Harvester Wheatsheaf.

———. (1991). Power and status differentials in minority and majority group relations. *European Journal of Social Psychology, 21*, 1–24.

———. (in press). Ethnolinguistic vitality: Some motivational and cognitive considerations. In M. Hogg & D. Abrams (Eds.), *Group motivation: Social psychological perspectives.* London: Harvester Wheatsheaf.

Saenz, D. S., & Lord, C. G. (1989). Reversing roles: A cognitive strategy for undoing memory deficits associated with token status. *Journal of Personality and Social Psychology, 56*, 698–708.

Sampson, E. E. (1975). On justice as equality. *Journal of Social Issues, 31*, 45–63.

———. (1976). *Social psychology and contemporary society.* 2nd ed. New York: John Wiley.

———. (1977). Psychology and the American ideal. *Journal of Personality and Social Psychology, 35*, 767–782.

———. (1981). Cognitive psychology as ideology. *American Psychologist, 36*(7), 730–743.

Schelling, T. C. (1957). Bargaining, communication, and limited war. *Journal of Conflict Resolution, 1*(1), 19–36.

Schiffman, R., & Wicklund, R. A. (1992). The minimal group paradigm and its minimal group psychology: On equating social identity with arbitrary group membership. *Theory and Psychology, 2*(1), 29–50.

Schmitt, D. R., & Marwell, G. 1972. Withdrawal and reward allocation as responses to inequity. *Journal of Experimental Social Psychology, 8*, 207–221.

Schofield, J. W. (1986). Black-white contact in desegregated schools. In M. Hewstone and R. Brown (Eds.), *Contact and conflict in intergroup encounters.* New York: Basil Blackwell.

Schofield, J. W., & Sagar, H. A. (1977). Peer interaction patterns in an integrated middle school. *Sociometry, 40*(2), 130–138.

Sexton, V. S., & Misiak, H. (1984). American psychology and psychology abroad. *American Psychologist, 39*, 1026–1031.

Shaw, M. E. (1976). *Group dynamics: The psychology of small group behaviour* (2nd ed.). New York: McGraw-Hill.

Shaw, M. E., & Costanzo, P. R. (1982). *Theories of social psychology.* 2nd ed. New York: McGraw-Hill.

Sherif, M. (1951). A preliminary experimental study of inter-group relations. In J. H. Rohrer & M. Sherif (Eds.), *Social psychology at the crossroads* (pp. 388–424). New York: Harper.

———. (1966). *Group conflict and co-operation: Their social psychology.* London: Routledge & Kegan Paul.

Sherif, M., Harvey, O. J., White, B. J., Hood, W. R., & Sherif, C. W. (1961). *Intergroup conflict and cooperation: The Robber's Cave experiment.* Norman: University of Oklahoma Book Exchange.

Sherif, M., & Sherif, C. W. (1953). *Groups in harmony and tension.* New York: Harper.

———. (1969). *Social psychology.* New York: Harper & Row.

Sherif, M., White, B. J., & Harvey, O. J. (1955). Status in experimentally produced groups. *American Journal of Sociology, 60,* 370–379.

Sighele, S. (1981). *La coppia criminale.* Turin: Bocca.

Simard, L. M. (1981). Cross-cultural interaction: Potential invisible barriers. *Journal of Social Psychology, 113,* 171–192.

Skevington, S. (1980). Intergroup relations and social change within a nursing context. *British Journal of Social and Clinical Psychology, 19,* 201–213.

Skevington, S., & Baker, D. (Eds.). (1989). *The social identity of women.* London: Sage.

Smith, P. (1985). *Language, the sexes, and society.* Oxford: Basil Blackwell.

Steiner, I. D. (1974). Whatever happened to the group in social psychology? *Journal of Experimental Social Psychology, 10,* 94–108.

Stephen, W. G. (1985). Intergroup relations. In G. Lindzey & E. Aronson (Eds.), *The handbook of social psychology* (3rd ed.) (Vol. 2, pp. 599–658). New York: Random House.

Stephenson, G. M., & Brotherton, C. J. (1975). Social progression and polarization: A study of discussion and negotiation in groups of mining supervisors. *British Journal of Social and Clinical Psychology, 14,* 241–252.

Stephenson, G. M., & Kniveton, B. H. (1978). Interpersonal and interparty exchange: An experimental study of the effect of seating position on the outcome of negotiations between teams representing parties in dispute. *Human Relations, 31,* 555–565.

Stouffer, S. A., Suchman, E. A., DeVinney, L. C., Star, S. A., & Williams, R. M. (1949). *The American soldier: Adjustment during army life* (Vol. 1). Princeton: Princeton University Press.

Suls, J. M., & Miller, R. L. (Eds.). (1977). *Social comparison processes: Theoretical and empirical perspectives.* Washington, D.C.: Hemisphere.

Sumner, W. G. (1906). *Folkways.* Boston: Ginn.

Tajfel, H. (1957). Value and the perceptual judgement of magnitude. *Psychological Review, 64,* 192–204.

———. (1959). Quantitative judgement in social perception. *British Journal of Psychology, 50,* 16–29.

———. (1969). Cognitive aspects of prejudice. *Journal of Social Issues, 25,* 79–97.

———. (1970). Experiments in intergroup discrimination. *Scientific American, 223*(5), 96–102.

————. (1972a). Introduction. In J. Israel & H. Tajfel (Eds.), *The context of social psychology* (pp. 1–13). London: Academic Press.

————. (1972b). Experiments in a vacuum. In J. Israel & H. Tajfel (Eds.), *The context of social psychology* (pp. 69–119). London: Academic Press.

————. (1974a). Social identity and intergroup behaviour. *Social Science Information, 13*(2), 65–93.

————. (1974b). *Intergroup behaviour, social comparison, and social change.* Unpublished manuscript, Katz-Newcomb lectures, University of Michigan at Ann Arbor.

————. (1978a). Social categorization, social identity, and social comparison. In H. Tajfel (Ed.), *Differentiation between social groups* (pp. 61–76). London and New York: Academic Press.

————. (1978b). *Differentiation between social groups: Studies in the social psychology of intergroup relations.* London and New York: Academic Press.

————. (1978c). The achievement of group differentiation. In H. Tajfel (Ed.), *Differentiation between social groups* (pp. 77–98). London and New York: Academic Press.

————. (1978d). Intergroup behaviour: II. Group perspectives. In H. Tajfel & C. Fraser (Eds.), *Introducing social psychology* (pp. 423–441). Harmondsworth, England: Penguin Books.

————. (1979). Individuals and groups in social psychology: A reply to Taylor and Brown. *British Journal of Social and Clinical Psychology, 18*, 183–190.

————. (1982a). Social psychology of intergroup relations. *Annual Review of Psychology, 33*, 1–39.

————. (Ed.). (1982b). *Social identity and intergroup relations.* Cambridge: Cambridge University Press.

————. (Ed.). (1984). *The social dimension.* 2 vols. Cambridge: Cambridge University Press.

Tajfel, H., Flament, C., Billig, M. G., & Bundy, R. F. (1971). Social categorization and intergroup behaviour. *European Journal of Social Psychology, 1*, 149–177.

Tajfel, H., Jaspers, J. M., & Fraser, C. (1984). The social dimensions in European social psychology. In H. Tajfel (Ed.), *The social dimension* (Vol. 1, pp. 1–8). Cambridge: Cambridge University Press.

Tajfel, H., & Turner, J. C. (1979). An integrative theory of intergroup conflict. In W. G. Austin & S. Worchel (Eds.), *The social psychology of intergroup relations* (pp. 33–47). Monterey, Calif.: Brooks/Cole.

————. (1986). The social identity theory of intergroup behavior. In S. Worchel & G. Austin (Eds.), *Psychology of intergroup relations* (pp. 7–24). Chicago: Nelson-Hall.

Tajfel, H., & Wilkes, A. L. (1963). Classification and quantitative judgement. *British Journal of Psychology, 54*, 101–113.

Taylor, D. M. (1981). Stereotypes and intergroup relations. In R. C. Gardner & R. Kalin (Eds.), *A Canadian social psychology of ethnic relations* (pp. 151–171). Toronto: Methuen.

Taylor, D. M., & Brown, R. J. (1979). Towards a more social social psychology? *British Journal of Social and Clinical Psychology, 18*, 173–180.

Taylor, D. M., & Doria, J. R. (1981). Self-serving and group-serving bias in attribution. *Journal of Social Psychology, 113*, 202–211.

Taylor, D. M., Doria, J. R., & Tyler, K. (1983). Group performance and cohesiveness: An attribution analysis. *Journal of Social Psychology, 119*, 187–198.

Taylor, D. M., & Dubé, L. (1986). Two faces of identity: The "I" and the "we." *Journal of Social Issues, 42*(2), 81–98.

Taylor, D. M., Dubé, L., & Bellerose, J. (1986). Intergroup contact in Quebec: Myth or reality? In M. Hewstone and R. Brown (Eds.), *Contact and conflict in intergroup encounters* (pp. 107–118). New York: Basil Blackwell.

Taylor, D. M., & Jaggi, V. (1974). Ethnocentrism in a south Indian context. *Journal of Cross-Cultural Psychology, 5*, 162–172.

Taylor, D. M., & Lalonde, R. N. (1987). Ethnic stereotypes: A psychological analysis. In L. Driedger (Ed.), *Ethnic Canada: Identities and inequalities.* Toronto: Copp, Clarke, Pitman.

Taylor, D. M., & Lambert, W. E. (1985). *Social significance of bilingualism for minorities in North America.* Paper presented at the American Psychological Association meetings, Los Angeles.

Taylor, D. M., & McKirnan, D. J. (1984). A five-stage model of intergroup relations. *British Journal of Social Psychology, 23*, 291–300.

Taylor, D. M., & Moghaddam, F. M. (1988). Review of "Nationalism, ethnocentrism, and personality." *Canadian Journal of Political Science, 11*, 385–387.

Taylor, D. M., Moghaddam, F. M., & Bellerose, J. (1989). Social comparison in an intergroup context. *Journal of Social Psychology, 129*, 499–515.

Taylor, D. M., Moghaddam, F. M., Gamble, I., & Zellerer, E. (1987). Disadvantaged group responses to perceived inequality: From passive acceptance to collective action. *Journal of Social Psychology, 127*(3), 259–272.

Taylor, D. M., & Simard, L. M. (1979). Ethnic identity and intergroup relations. In D. J. Lee (Ed.), *Emerging ethnic boundaries* (pp. 155–171). Ottawa: University of Ottawa Press.

Taylor, D. M., Wong-Rieger, D., McKirnan, D. J., & Bercusson, J. (1982). Interpreting and coping with threat in the context of intergroup relations. *Journal of Social Psychology, 117*, 257–269.

Taylor, D. M., Wright, S. C., Moghaddam, F. M., & Lalonde, R. N. (1990). The personal/group discrimination discrepancy: Perceiving my group, but not myself, to be a target for discrimination. *Personality and Social Psychology Bulletin, 16*, 254–262.

Taylor, D. M., Wright, S. C., & Porter, L. E. (1993). Dimensions of perceived discrimination: The personal/group discrimination discrepancy. In M. P. Zanna and J. Olson (Eds.), *The psychology of prejudice: The Ontario symposium* (Vol. 7, pp. 233–255). Hillsdale, N.J.: Erlbaum.

Thibaut, J. W., & Kelley, H. H. (1959). *The social psychology of groups.* New York: John Wiley.

Tougas, F., & Veilleux, F. (1988). The influence of identification, collective relative deprivation, and procedure of implementation on women's responses to affirmative action: A causal modelling approach. *Canadian Journal of Behavioural Science, 20,* 15–28.

Triandis, H. C. (1971). *Attitude and attitude change.* New York: John Wiley.

———. (1979). Commentary. In W. G. Austin & S. Worchel (Eds.), *The social psychology of intergroup relations* (pp. 321–334). Monterey, Calif.: Brooks/Cole.

Triandis, HJ. C., & Vassiliou, V. (1967). Frequency of contact and stereotyping. *Journal of Personality and Social Psychology, 7,* 316–328.

Tripathi, R. C., & Srivastava, R. (1981). Relative deprivation and intergroup attitudes. *European Journal of Social Psychology, 11,* 313–318.

Turner, F. J. (1920). *The frontier in American history.* New York: Holt.

Turner, J. C. (1975). Social comparison and social identity: Some prospects for intergroup behaviour. *European Journal of Social Psychology, 5,* 5–34.

———. (1978a). Social categorization and social discrimination in the minimal group paradigm. In H. Tajfel (Ed.), *Differentiation between social groups* (pp. 101–140). London and New York: Academic Press.

———. (1981). The experimental social psychology of intergroup behaviour. In J. C. Turner & H. Giles (Eds.), *Intergroup Behaviour* (pp. 66–101). Oxford: Basil Blackwell.

———. (1985). Social categorization and the self concept: A social cognitive theory of group behaviour. In E. J. Lawler (Ed.), *Advances in group processes* (Vol. 2, pp. 77–122). Greenwich, Conn.: JAI Press.

———. (1990). Forward. In M. A. Hogg & D. Abrams, *Social identifications: A social psychology of intergroup relations and group processes* (pp. x–xii). London: Routledge.

Turner, J. C., & Brown, R. J. (1978). Social status, cognitive alternatives, and intergroup relations. In H. Tajfel (Ed.), *Differentiation between social groups* (pp. 201–234). London and New York: Academic Press.

———. (1981). Interpersonal and intergroup behaviour. In J. C. Turner & H. Giles (Eds.), *Intergroup behaviour* (pp. 33–65). Oxford: Basil Blackwell.

Turner, J. C., Brown, R. J., & Tajfel, H. (1979). Social comparison and group interest in ingroup favouritism. *European Journal of Social Psychology, 9,* 187–204.

Turner, J. C., & Giles, H. (Eds.). *Intergroup behaviour.* Oxford: Basil Blackwell.

Turner, J. C., Hogg, M. A., Oakes, P. J., Reicher, S. D., & Wetherell, M. S. (1987). *Rediscovering the social group: A self-categorization theory.* Oxford: Blackwell.

Valenzi, E. R., & Andrews, I. R. (1971). Effect of hourly overpay inequity when tested with a new induction procedure. *Journal of Applied Psychology, 55,* 22–27.

Van den Berghe, P. L. (1967). Race and racism in South Africa. In P. L. Van den Berghe (Ed.), *Race and racism: A comparative perspective* (pp. 96–111). New York: John Wiley.

Vanneman, R. D., & Pettigrew, T. F. (1972). Race and relative deprivation in the United States. *Race, 13,* 461–486.

Vaughan, G. M. (1972). Ethnic awareness and attitudes in New Zealand children. In G. M. Vaughan, *Racial issues in New Zealand: Problems and insights.* Auckland: Akarana Press.

Veilleux, F., & Tougas, F. (1989). Male acceptance of affirmative action programs for women: The results of altruistic or egoistical motives? *International Journal of Psychology, 24,* 485–496.

Walker, I., & Pettigrew, T. F. (1984). Relative deprivation theory: An overview and conceptual critique. *British Journal of Social Psychology, 23,* 301–310.

Walster, E., Berscheid, E., & Walster, G. W. (1973). New directions in equity research. *Journal of Personality and Social Psychology, 25,* 151–176.

Walster, E., Walster, G. W., & Berscheid, E. (1978). *Equity: Theory and research.* Boston: Allyn & Bacon.

Watson, G. (1985). *Social factors in justice evaluation.* Ph.D. diss., Oxford University.

Weary, G. (1979). Self-serving attributional biases: Perceptual or response distortions? *Journal of Personality and Social Psychology, 37,* 1418–1420.

Weiner, B., Frieze, I., Kukla, A., Reed, L., Rest, S., & Rosenbaum, R. M. (1972). Perceiving the cause of success and failure. In E. E. Jones, D. E. Kanouse, H. H. Kelley, R. E. Nisbett, S. Valins, & B. Weiner (Eds.), *Attribution: Perceiving the causes of behavior* (pp. 95–120). Morristown, N.J.: General Learning Press.

Wetherell, M. (1982). Cross-cultural studies of minimal groups: Implications for the social identity theory of intergroup relations. In H. Tajfel (Ed.), *Social identity and intergroup relations.* Cambridge: Cambridge University Press.

Wicker, A. W. (1969). Attitudes versus actions: The relationship of verbal and overt behavioral responses to attitude objects. *Journal of Social Issues, 25*(4), 41–78.

Widdicomb, S., & Wooffitt, R. (1990). "Being" versus "doing" punk: On achieving authenticity as a member. *Journal of Language and Social Psychology, 9,* 257–277.

Wilder, D. A. (1984). Prediction of belief homogeneity and similarity following social categorization. *British Journal of Social Psychology, 23,* 323–333.

Williams, J. A. (1984). Gender and intergroup behaviour: Towards an integration. *British Journal of Social Psychology, 23,* 311–316.

Williams, J. A., & Giles, H. (1978). The changing status of women in society: An intergroup perspective. In H. Tajfel (Ed.), *Differentiation between social groups* (pp. 431–469). London and New York: Academic Press.

Williams, R. M. (1947). *The Reduction of intergroup tensions.* New York: Social Science Research Council.

Wilson, A. (1970). *War Gaming.* Harmondsworth, England: Penguin Books.

Wilson, W., & Kayatani, M. (1968). Intergroup attitudes and strategies in games between opponents of the same or a different race. *Journal of Personality and Social Psychology, 9,* 24–30.

Wilson, W., & Wong, J. (1968). Intergroup attitudes towards cooperative vs. competitive opponents in a modified prisoner's dilemma game. *Perceptual and Motor Skills, 27,* 1059–1066.

Wood, J. V. (1989). Theory and research concerning social comparisons of personal attributes. *Psychological Bulletin, 106,* 231–248.

Worchel, S., Andreoli, V. A., & Folger, R. (1977). Intergroup cooperation and intergroup attraction: The effect of previous interaction and outcome of combined effort. *Journal of Experimental Social Psychology, 13,* 131–140.

Worchel, S., & Austin, W. G. (Eds.). (1986). *The social psychology of intergroup relations* (2nd ed.). Monterey, Calif.: Brooks/Cole.

Worchel, S., & Norvell, N. (1980). Effect of perceived environmental conditions during cooperation on intergroup interaction. *Journal of Personality and Social Psychology, 38,* 764–772.

Wright, S. C., & Taylor, D. M. (1992). *Success under tokenism: Tokens as barriers to or agents of social change.* Paper presented at American Psychological Association meetings, San Diego.

————. (1993). *Tokenism: The responses of victims.* Unpublished manuscript, University of California at Santa Cruz.

Wright, S. C., Taylor, D. M., & Moghaddam, F. M. (1990a). The relationship of perceptions and emotions to behaviour in the face of collective inequality. *Social Justice Research, 4*(3), 229–250.

————. (1990b). Responding to membership in a disadvantaged group: From acceptance to collective protest. *Journal of Personality and Social Psychology, 58,* 994–1003.

Young, R. (1986). Affirmative action and the problem of substantive racism. In M. W. Combs & J. Gruhl (Eds.), *Affirmative action: Theory, analysis, and prospects* (pp. 9–19). Jefferson, N.C.: McFarland.

Zanna, M. P. (1994). On the nature of prejudice. *Canadian Psychology, 35,* 11–23.

Zanna, M. P., & Olson, J. (Eds.). (1993). *The psychology of prejudice: The Ontario symposium* (Vol. 7). Hillsdale, N.J.: Erlbaum.

Zartman, I. W., & Berman, M. R. (1982). *The practical negotiator.* New Haven: Yale University Press.

Zartman, I. W., & Touval, S. (1985). International mediation: Conflict and power politics. *Journal of Social Issues, 41*(2), 27–45.

Ziller, R. C. (1965). Toward a theory of open and closed groups. *Psychological Bulletin, 64*, 164–182.

Subject Index

Author Index

About the Authors

DONALD M. TAYLOR is Professor of Psychology at McGill University, Montreal, Canada. Professor Taylor's research interest is in intergroup relations, including such topics as prejudice, discrimination, and social justice. His research has been conducted in diverse regions of the world, including the United States, Canada, Britain, South and Southeast Asia, and native communities in Canada. Professor Taylor has published prolifically in Canadian, American, European, and Asian journals. He is coauthor of *Coping with Cultural and Racial Diversity in Urban America* (with W. E. Lambert), and *Social Psychology in Cross-Cultural Perspective* (with F. M. Moghaddam and S. C. Wright).

FATHALI M. MOGHADDAM is a social psychologist on the faculty of Georgetown University, Washington, D.C. He has previously taught at McGill University and Tehran University and has also worked for the United Nations Development Program. Professor Moghaddam's primary research interests are intergroup relations, with particular focus on minority-group perspectives, and indigenous psychology for the Third World. His concern for achieving an international perspective in psychology is reflected in his contributions to international, American, and European journals. Professor Moghaddam has coauthored a recent book entitled *Social Psychology in Cross-Cultural Perspective* (with D. M. Taylor and S. C. Wright).